RESCUE!

God's Promise To Save

Peter Lewis
Roy Clements
Greg Haslam

Christian Focus Publications

ISBN 1-85792-147-X

Published in 1995 by
Christian Focus Publications Ltd.
Geanies House, Fearn, Ross-shire,
IV20 1TW, Scotland, Great Britain.

Previously published as
Chosen For Good
by Kingsway Publications

Cover design by Donna Macleod

Printed and bound in Great Britain by
Cox & Wyman Ltd, Reading, Berkshire.

Contents

Foreword

'That is what I call a rescue,' said the man just saved from drowning in the river. And the theme of this book is: 'This is what God calls a rescue'.

The genius of these five chapters is that, like the Bible but unlike much contemporary Christian teaching, they are all God-centred. They are all about God and us, but first about God and then about us. They open up five basic truths as God sees them. This makes these chapters singularly refreshing and stimulating. The book is neither a 'how to' manual nor a series of therapeutic recipes. It gives God's angle on us – our past, present and future.

The opening chapter looks at the fundamental predicament in which we men and women find ourselves before God. It probes deep, getting beneath the 'my life's in a mess and where's the feel-good factor?' to uncover the ultimate problem: where we all stand before God and, as answerable to him, what does he think of us?

Chapter two establishes God as alone having absolute free will and then looks at the nature of his unprecedented love. The way we conduct our lives and keep God out deserves his displeasure: his love is neither axiomatic nor automatically ours as of right. The chapter relates God's love to his wrath and shows why and how God gives his grace.

Next, by opening up the agony of sin to a moral

God, the book displays the centrality of the cross of Christ – why it was necessary, what it cost, how it rescues, where we would be without it, what it achieved and who may enjoy its benefits.

Those benefits, as chapter four explains, come by the grace of God. Christianity is not a matter of doing God a favour by our actions or devotion, but of finding God's favour. The power and wonder of his grace are unique.

And then the final questions: How will it end? Will we make it through? What if we should stumble or doubt or deny? What about final perseverance?

In addition to being God-centred, these chapters are honest in facing alternative ideas and all conclude by tackling some hard questions. The authors' test of all views is not whether they are congenial, but whether they are true to the Bible.

Many of us long to get beyond the superficial and the trite and into some depth and richness in our relationship with God. This book will help us towards that. It is the authors' prayer that readers will find themselves drawn to God as the centre and source of their life and salvation. For from him and to him and through him are all things (Romans 11:36).

Robert M Horn
May 1995

1

Walking Tall, Fallen Short

Peter Lewis

A few years ago I was speaking at a series of 'convention meetings' in the historic town of Chester. One afternoon I visited one of its fine museums. I shall never forget being confronted with two exhibits, which then stood side by side. In a glass case there lay the complete skeleton of a Roman slave, whose body had been thrown down a deep well; it had been covered with the rubble of a fire, which had destroyed the 3rd-century hostelry where he had presumably worked for high-positioned Romans. As a slave his body had been possessed as a mere implement and in death it had been tossed aside as refuse. Next to this exhibit stood a Roman altar, dedicated to 'the divine emperor Augustus'! The contrast between the two was total: in the one man was degraded; in the other he was deified. Each extreme was an appalling evil in the world which God had made 'good' and for his glory. Each showed a total loss of understanding about man: who he was and what he was for.

The Christian understanding of man is redeemed from this grim confusion by God's revelation in holy Scripture. For Scripture is given to tell us not only about God, but also about men. Wherever the testimony of Scripture has been unknown or neglected or repudiated, man has lost not only the true knowledge of God but also the true knowledge of himself, his fellow men, his world and his society. The Bible's doctrine of man is crucial because it is true to *life* – and not just to appearances. It stresses both the dignity of man and the sinfulness of man; it guides us away from the callous abuse of man at the one extreme and from a naive trust in man's 'better nature' at the other. We are to understand men and women so as to respect and pity them, love and withstand them, expose and entreat them. And we are to go to the Bible for this understanding.

If someone came up to you and said, 'Tell me, what is the Bible all about?', what would be your reply? I think a good many Christians might give the short answer: 'Well, the Bible is about God; it is God's word about himself.' Now no doubt that would be right as a short answer, but it would be wrong as a long one! The Bible is, to be sure, a profoundly God-centred book, but though it places God at the centre, it does not dismiss man to the periphery. It does not put God everywhere and man nowhere. Man, too, is the focus of attention. From Genesis to Revelation the Bible is a book which tells us quite as much about man as it does about God. It speaks of God over man and man before God; God and man estranged and at enmity with each other; and God in Christ reconciling the fallen world of man to himself.

Nothing is allowed to obscure this twofold focus. The Bible does not tell us about other worlds (except heaven), because it is concerned with this world. It does not tell us much about angels, because it is more concerned about men and women.

It does not even tell us a great deal about God in a way which abstracts him from human life and from his concern with us. Only in a certain way are we to 'forget about ourselves and concentrate on him'. We must never imagine that the Bible is a kind of 'tourists' guide to God'. It is, throughout, the story of God's mighty acts in redeeming and saving a lost race, recovering in man the full beauty of the image of God in which he was made.

Yet the biblical view of man is not unopposed in the world – even in our modern world. Our societies do not hire slaves and they do not worship emperors, but they do manipulate masses and exploit individuals. They do teach man to worship himself, to pay homage to his proud self-image, to serve his lusts and his ambitions, to rely upon himself, his own understanding and his own potential – as if there were no God above him to adore, or alongside him to thank, or before him to meet. Let us look more closely at some of these alternative views of man.

'Get God out of the picture' –
the Marxist view of man

The Marxist position is one which we might label 'optimistic atheism'. The Marxist, of whatever shade, is absolutely certain that man can do without God. In fact, for him there is no god anyway, so man had better get on without him! He is so convinced about this that he says, first of all, that man has it within himself to make it on his own; and secondly, that he will *not* make it on his own if he has religion, because religion acts like an opiate and dulls his senses. Marx held that, if people's lives were always orientated around a non-existent God and a non-existent after-life, they would never get where they ought to get. Religion, he said, simply diverts attention from the matters in this world (the only world there is for man) that need to be put right. For man to achieve his destiny, he must orientate himself around himself. He must get God out of the picture entirely, become utterly absorbed with himself and explain this world purely in terms of man.

Marxism is man-centred, and makes everything rely on man. This 'optimistic atheism', moreover, is sure that man *will* make it on his own; not, however, by gradual evolution, but by revolution. If man can change his society, change the class system, change the politics, change the economics, change the ownership of wealth, change the circumstances, then he can flower in his being and make his own Garden of Eden without the inconvenience of God. Change these outward factors and you change man.

'The universe is absurd' – the existentialist view of man

A second view of man has an unfamiliar name (existentialist), but a very familiar appearance. It is still frequently to be seen on our television screens. Some will remember the weekly *Wednesday Play* on the BBC in Britain in the 1960s; it was often a typical example of existential philosophy. Even today many novels and TV plays, in their sophisticated ways, are saturated with the mentality of the existentialist. This view is basically that the universe is, quite simply, absurd. It is there by chance, it has no meaning, you have no reason to think that it actually exists in any meaningful way. The world makes no sense, life has no point at all. You cannot relate to it, you cannot be sure of anyone or anything around you or above you. You cannot try to define your society, as the old philosophers used to do. You cannot think about truth in traditional ways because absolute truth does not exist outside yourself. Truth exists only in a person's existential relationship, their subjectivity, their passionate commitment to an activity. Apart from this life is just a mirage, unreal. You cannot verify it.

The only thing you can do is to accept that life is pointless and meaningless and then heroically assert yourself by living authentically in the freedom of your own choices and allowing others to do so. This is the sum and substance of your worth. You are going to die like everybody else, your life is not going to have any objective value, but at least you will have been heroic and authentic in your loneliness. You will have cried out against the pointlessness of it all.

That was the philosophy behind many of the old kitchen sink TV dramas. They were a comment on the emptiness and boredom of life (and were they boring!); they had not plot or purpose, no beginning, no middle, no end. That was their whole view on life. Many, moreover, had a pessimistic and dismal ending. Whereas the Marxist is an optimistic atheist, the existentialist, like Jean-Paul Sartre for instance, is a pessimistic atheist: there's no point in anything. It is perhaps a small sign that this outlook does not ring true, that every now and again sentimental plays or films appear, where they all do 'live happily ever after'. But, without God, sentimentalism is as baseless as existentialism.

'Man's reason is the key' – the humanist view of man

This leaves God out as decidedly as the other two views. Unlike Marxism, however, it does not explain man in terms of class and economics, nor does it prescribe revolution as the answer. Unlike existentialism it is not pessimistic, but believes that man's reason can produce meaning and values and progress. Humanism is not new. It was in the ascendancy in Victorian days among poets and politicians and scientists too. Poets like Alfred Lord Tennyson dreamed of the future 'Parliament of Man' and moralized on our latent power to climb 'on the stepping stones of our dead selves' to higher things. Men applied Darwin's theory of biological evolution to social progress and looked forward to man's continued progress and self-refinement, as he journeyed from the primaeval slime to the stars! All the talk here was of man's nobility, power and possibilities for good.

This did not leave God out as the other views did, but it did leave behind the true biblical doctrine of the Fall. Even many of the Victorian preachers erred here in the general euphoria, promising that the imminent 20th century would see the most wonderful flowering of all man's latent goodness. Man was turning the corner and everything seemed to prove it: Victorian expansionism, British colonialism, America conquering its west, the flowering of the arts, the advance of science, the banishment of superstition, the success of politics in peace and prosperity. In all this it was man's reason which was stressed as the key to the future – reason as the way forward, discussion as the solution to conflict, science as the path to fulfilment, education as the route to a better world. Man, Victorian man, would turn the key of reason and open the golden gate of the 20th-century paradise.

But the gateway was not golden and the paradise proved to be a wasteland of war and blighted hopes. The First World War, which devastated civilization, ended that whole humanist era of optimism. The shallow, romantic hopes of two generations lay dismembered among the corpses which littered the battlefields of Europe. Humanism was dead – or it would have been, if it had not been for the incorrigible pride of man and his determination to trust to his own resources and to organize his society without God. So it survives still, in forms both secular and religious, always known by the first article of its creed: 'I believe in man'.

'Man stands before God' – the Christian view of man

The Christian understanding of man is radically different from all these opposing positions. That is because it is entirely controlled by the crucial consideration of man's relation to God. We say that the only way for man to understand himself is by understanding his God. The great 16th-century Reformer, John Calvin, who is very significant in regard to the church's recovery of the biblical doctrine of man, put it like this: 'Man never achieves a clear knowledge of himself until he has first looked upon God's face and then descends from contemplating him to scrutinise himself' (*Institutes of the Christian Religion* Vol. I, chapter 1:2; Westminster Press, 1977 edition).

We must start with God if we want to make sense of anything, including (and especially!) ourselves. That is why Christians listen to God to learn about themselves, their world and their society. And we can acquire God's wisdom in these matters, for we have a speaking God, personal and concerned, holy and loving, all-knowing and utterly trustworthy. His explanation of man's failure and his uncovering of man's sin are painful and embarrassing, yet they are also hopeful and purposeful, for they are part of the means by which he leads us to his glorious revelation: salvation by Jesus Christ his Son our Lord, in whom we have redemption, the forgiveness of our sins.

The Bible sets out to explain man at the very beginning. The early chapters of Genesis are still the best explanation of the human race and of man in the 1990s. Man began as a unique being and not merely a member of the animal kingdom evolving by chance. The Bible tells us that from the start man had a unique purpose under the heavens. He was given tremendous dignity, being made in the image of God: 'Let us make man in our image, in our likeness' (Genesis 1:26). Man is still in the image of God; that has not ceased to exist in him. But it is fearfully marred and seriously distorted; sin has added to it, as well as subtracted from it; sometimes it is hardly recognizable. 'Yet,' said Calvin, 'some rays of God's glory are to be found in man.' Even fallen man is still in God's image (Genesis 6:5; 9:6; 1 Corinthians 11:7; James 3:9) and therefore has immense value, dignity and significance.

It is out of this conviction that Christians have effectively transformed life for women in challenging their subject status and abuse in the ancient world; for the weak and the ill in pioneering asylums and hospitals; for the aged and for the outcasts in society. Christianity, with its doctrine of man in the image of God, could never have condoned a caste system, a slave trade or a doctrine of racial inferiority. And while Christians too have often been children of their times and short-sighted and wrong-minded because of sin, yet it remains a towering fact of human history that Christianity has done more than its opponents (who are in some respects its products!) will ever give it credit for.

Man in sin is like an ancient temple which has fallen into decay and ruin. Even in the ruins there is a certain grandeur that wins respect. 'If it is like this now,' we think, 'what must it have been like in its original glory?' Fallen man is a majestic ruin. Or he might be compared to a crippled athlete. 'I remember him,' we say, 'when he was so strong and straight-backed, a fine figure with great strength and reserve, so fast. Now look at him, twisted, broken, bent, racked with a cough, eaten away by disease, incapable even of walking.' That is Christianity's diagnosis of man in himself, a very serious diagnosis; one which is urgently necessary for a man to know about. The Bible X-rays man and holds his trouble up to the light. His great trouble is his sin, and the true nature and character of sin is only seen when man in sin is shown in his relation to God. It is then, and only then, that we see sin as it really is – not as immaturity, not as social maladjustment, not even as selfishness or self-centredness merely – but as *rebellion* against God.

What man is like now
What is man's present state, especially in relation to God?

He is hostile
What does Scripture say about man as he is now, by nature, in relation to God? It says first and foremost that he is deeply *hostile* to God. Paul says that 'the sinful mind is hostile to God. It does not submit to God's law, nor can it do so. Those controlled by the sinful nature cannot please God' (Romans 8:7-8). We have here a very strong expression in the Greek which does not simply say man is 'hostile', but that he is 'hostility' against God. There is in man now, and that at the centre of his being, a real and thoroughgoing, even violent, enmity towards God. Nothing challenges him, nothing threatens him, nothing provokes a hostile reaction in him, like God in his holy demands and his unbearable approach!

Of course, man is a religious, worshipping being. Yet the devastating indictment of Romans 1 is that man is as much a rebel in his religion as he is in any other part of his life. Even there he sins, suppressing unpalatable truth about God, bringing God down in his imagination to the level of the rest of fallen creation and exchanging the truth of God for a lie (Romans 1:18, 23, 25). Thus he tries to 'tame' God and appease his own conscience. But where the real God is concerned, as distinct from his convenient idol or his toy god, his opposition is radical, his rebellion is exposed. When the true God is preached, he reacts in fury or contempt. When the holy God approaches, he runs away in horror. 'God-haters' is Paul's summary description of mankind in this regard (Romans 1:30). Statements do not come stronger than that!

In his first letter to the Corinthians the apostle writes in a searching exposure of man's bankruptcy in spiritual matters: 'The man without the Spirit does not accept the things that come from the Spirit of God, for they are foolishness to him and he cannot understand them, because they are spiritually discerned' (1 Corinthians 2:14). Elsewhere he locates the reasons for this and traces them to a twofold source: the hardening of the sinner's heart from within (Ephesians 4:18) and the blinding of the sinner's eye by Satan at work in 'his' society (2 Corinthians 4:4). The effect is as profound as anything can be, for as a consequence: 'The mind of sinful man is death, but the mind controlled by the Spirit is life and peace' (Romans 8:6). Any life not 'controlled by the Spirit' – and consequently the life of every non-Christian – comes into the category of 'death'. Even in his virtue, even in his

worship, even in the highest reaches of his understanding and the greatest achievement of his moral
character, he is – 'death'!

He is condemned in that hostility

Although it is beyond the scope of this chapter to
go into detail about the doctrine of wrath in God
against sin, we need to know not only that man is
hostile to God, but also that he is guilty and condemned in that hostility. His condemnation is not
simply the inevitable outworking of some imper-
sonal law, but the effect of a personal reaction in
God: the wrath of God. God's wrath is a corollary
of his holiness as much as his love. When confronted with purity, righteousness and obedience,
God's character expresses itself in blessing; when
confronted with impurity, rebellion or sin in any
of its forms, it expresses itself in wrath. All Scripture unites in this testimony, without which we
cannot have a proper understanding of God. The
Old Testament idea of wrath is not in fact crude,
as is so often supposed, but rather is refined and
sensitive, aware of the holiness of God and its im-
plications. All told, there are more than twenty
words in the Hebrew Old Testament to express
God's wrath and over 580 references to it.

The recognition of God's personal and outgoing wrath against sin, and so against man in sin
(for sin does not exist apart from moral agents), is
just as clear in the New Testament in the teaching

of Jesus and of Paul. The apostle makes it clear that because of sin, not only is man hostile to God, but God is hostile to man: 'The wrath of God is being revealed from heaven against all the godlessness and wickedness of men who suppress the truth by their wickedness' (Romans 1:18). The picture that follows is of wrath, not only as an attitude in God, not even as a strong revulsion in the heart of God, but as a movement from God. A revulsion expressing itself, a wrath which is, in the words of John Murray, 'dynamically, effectively operative in the world of men... proceeding from heaven, the throne of God' (*Epistle to the Romans*, Marshall Morgan and Scott, 1967). The wrath of God is operative in human history now and not just reserved for the endtime of present history, and its greatest penalty, short of death and immediate damnation, is the repudiation of men and women 'giving them up' to greater sin and greater condemnation (Romans 1:24, 26, 28).

That condemnation is clearly and finally exposed in the third chapter of Paul's letter to the Romans, where he shows with unsparing insight the depravity that characterizes all men, so that 'Jews and Gentiles alike are all under sin' (Romans 3:9-18) and concludes: 'Now we know that whatever the law says, it says to those who are under the law, so that every mouth may be silenced and the whole world held accountable to God' (Romans 3:19). Man in sin, man fallen, rebellious and depraved, is beyond self-redemption. He cannot rise to God's demands, he cannot atone for his past sins, he cannot justify himself (Romans 3:20).

He is hopeless in 'good' works, dead in sin
Every attempt to 'buy off' God's wrath and to earn his forgiveness is doomed to failure – and indeed to further condemnation. Natural religion can go a long way, especially since God is at work in *common grace* in every man, restraining sin and encouraging goodness. But this, as we shall see, is abused by man. He sees his human 'righteousness' not as unworthy before God, not even (inasmuch as it is really present), as something achieved in him by God. He sees it as something with which to placate God, something which will one day be an effective protest against his final condemnation, something which can even indebt God to him. So fallen man turns religious – for a shorter or longer period of time – and tries to put himself right with God.

Jesus was faced with one of the most 'cleaned-up' men of his generation: religious, sincere and self-controlled Nicodemus. Jesus for ever spells the doom of all natural religion, the religion of unconverted man, when he says: 'I tell you the truth, unless a man is born of water and the Spirit, he cannot enter the kingdom of God. Flesh gives birth to flesh, but the Spirit gives birth to spirit' (John 3:5-6). 'Flesh' here means the nature of fallen man, the unconverted heart. Jesus is saying that such a man, however motivated or self-changed, can only produce a religion that is fleshly, unconverted, polluted and corrupt. Fallen man is beyond self-help, he needs help from the outside. He needs precisely the thing he most dreads: the approach and the entry into his inner being of the holy God. He needs to be born 'from above' (a better translation than born 'again'), for only what God does will be sufficient for God and only what God gives will be acceptable to God.

When God comes, however, he will devastate man's self-confidence, rip up man's self-image, exposing his sin and his helplessness in sin. The man controlled by the Spirit admits this, indeed he insists on declaring it, that God might have all the glory of his salvation. 'Apart from me,' Jesus says, 'you can do nothing' (John 15:5). 'I know,' responds Paul, 'that nothing good lives in me, that is, in my sinful nature' or 'flesh' (Romans 7:18). Already we can perhaps see the folly of supposing a kind of moral neutrality to man in his better moments. He never rises above himself. And where is he in himself in spiritual terms? The starkest answer to that is given in the second chapter of Paul's letter to the Ephesians. Yet grim as the picture painted is, it is precisely in locating the hope of man *outside* himself that the apostle reveals the good news of the grace of God:

As for you, you were dead in your transgressions and sins, in which you used to live when you followed the ways of this world and of the ruler of the kingdom of the air, the spirit who is now at work in those who are disobedient. All of us also lived among them at one time, gratifying the cravings of our sinful nature and following its desires and thoughts. Like the rest, we were by nature objects of wrath. But because of his great love for us, God, who is rich in mercy, made us alive with Christ even when we were dead in transgressions – it is by grace you have been saved (Ephesians 2:1-5).

The picture of man – as not simply straying, not merely sick, but actually dead – could not be more extreme. Yet it precisely reflects his plight in sin. Moreover, the further image of a resurrection for man in the powerful grace of God is just as precisely suited to his need, for it is not enough to bring the gospel to man, man must be brought to the gospel, his heart must be changed to welcome 'the light of the knowledge of the glory of God in the face of Christ' (2 Corinthians 4:6). That is no easy matter, as we shall now see.

How man responds when faced with the gospel
Man's profound antipathy towards God nowhere comes out more clearly than in his attitude to the truth of the gospel, when faced with its claims. As we saw earlier, fallen man is a great suppressor of

the truth. In order that he might pacify his conscience and allay his fears, he does two things. First, he suppresses 'what may be known' about the true God (Romans 1:19) and then he replaces it with a religion of his own, one which may be more easily lived with. In Paul's words, 'They exchanged the truth of God for a lie' (Romans 1:25). Consequently, when we come to the sinner with a gospel truth, he measures it *against his lie*. And the lie wins for him every time, because if he is wrong in his religion, he is wrong everywhere – and that he will not admit! In Jesus' words: 'If then the light within you is darkness, how great is that darkness!' (Matthew 6:23).

Man's religion is the greatest enemy of God's truth, for man's religion is his self-righteousness, his one way of escape from the desert of his sins. Tell a man he is a sinner in his beer and he will probably agree with you; tell him he is a sinner in his religion and he may well strike you! Paul continually found, when witnessing to his fellow Jews, that it was not their impiety which kept them from God, but their religion; not their sins, but their righteousness. Hence he writes sorrowfully: 'Since they did not know the righteousness that comes from God and sought to establish their own, they did not submit to God's righteousness' (Romans 10:3). God had found a way to justify them, by giving his Son to live the perfect life that they could never live, and to die the atoning death for their sins. God's own righteousness in Jesus Christ was offered to them in the gospel, but they would not have it at any cost. They were so pleased with their own law-keeping that they rejected the righteousness of God for the righteousness of man. The bankrupt is offered £1,000,000, but will not admit he is bankrupt! He forfeits the wealth he so desperately needs, in order to keep up the appearance of solvency and hide the truth. So man, when faced with the gospel, continues to suppress and reject the truth.

Paul was writing about his generation, but might well have been writing about ours. He said to the Corinthian Christians that the message of the cross was 'foolishness' to their contemporaries – not something complicated, but something contemptible:

> The message of the cross is foolishness to those who are perishing, but to us who are being saved it is the power of God. For since in the wisdom of God the world through its wisdom did not know him, God was pleased through the foolishness of what was preached to save those who believe (1 Corinthians 1:18, 21).

And what was it that was preached against all rival systems? One thing and one thing only: 'Jews demand miraculous signs and Greeks look for wisdom, but we preach Christ crucified: a stumbling block to Jews [for the cross was a place of cursing] and foolishness to Gentiles [for how could a crucified man be a Saviour?].' It was contemptible to them all, 'but to those whom God has called, both Jews and Greeks, Christ the power of God and the wisdom of God' (1 Corinthians 1:22-24).

We today are ourselves faced with precisely the same kind of response. Our neighbours say: 'Well, if there are miracles, why don't you do a few?' Or: 'If God's there, why doesn't he appear and do something to convince me?' Or, if they are more intellectual: 'What's all this talk about blood? It's immoral to condemn somebody else for another person's sins. Anyway, there can't be any connection between an execution 2,000 years ago, and my marriage breaking up or my drink problem. It doesn't make sense.'

Under his protests, however, and under his reasoning, are the deeper reasons, as we have seen. Man is not kept from God by his intellectual integrity, but by his sin, his rebellious heart. We hear the modern 'Greek', the 'wise men' of the age who often say: 'If I become a Christian, I'll be committing intellectual suicide.' But underneath their abstract reasons are the actual reasons – pride, guilt, fear and a profound dislike for God. The reasons why men are not Christians are fundamentally always the same. It does not matter whether someone is illiterate or whether he has five doctorates.

Man's need when faced with the gospel

Some people appear to have no problem here. Some people believe that man's only need is to hear the gospel. They say: 'Oh, if we can only get the gospel out to people, everything else will follow; people only need to know.' Just as if it were only necessary for God to do his part and then leave the rest to man. But we can surely see the shallowness of such an attitude and its superficial understanding of man in sin, man in rebellion. God's work is far from done when he has brought the word of truth to man. The great work then is to get it past his prejudices and into his mind, to take it through his resistance and into his heart. God does not wait upon man for such a work or he would wait for ever. Here, if anywhere, grace needs to work *in its own power*.

For man in sin, when faced with the gospel, is unable to understand it. He fails to see his need of such provision or indeed the relevance of the provision of the death and resurrection of Christ. These things, says Paul, are 'foolishness to him'. He 'cannot understand them, because they are spiritually discerned' (1 Corinthians 2:14) and he by nature is destitute of the Spirit of God at this level. Moreover, he is the possession of 'the god of this age' who 'has blinded the minds of unbelievers, so that they cannot see the light of the gospel' (2 Corinthians 4:4). Sin within, society around and Satan over all – these are the factors which strive furiously to keep the gospel out of the heart and mind of the natural man.

The idea that man is morally neutral in some way is completely contrary to the word God has given us about man in sin. That word does not allow that, given an influence contrary to the world's influence, given an alternative to his present life in darkness by the approach of light, he will surely receive the light and embrace the new influence. 'The light shines in the darkness,' writes John, 'but the darkness has not understood it' (John 1:5). Men are not morally neutral, says Jesus, they are in bondage to sin and need to be set free: 'Then you will know the truth, and the truth will set you free .... I tell you the truth, everyone who sins is a slave to sin' (John 8:32, 34). The truth itself, that is, the power of God working with and in and by the truth, is alone able to deliver men. Grace works in its own power.

The most explicit statements of Jesus to this effect are found in John 6 and they deserve our particular attention, as they show Jesus' own understanding of his opponents and his inevitable rejection by a God-hating world. There, faced with the profound distrust of his critics, he clearly articulates the doctrine of man's moral or spiritual inability: '"Stop grumbling among yourselves," Jesus answered. "No-one can come to me unless the Father who sent me draws him"' (John 6:43-44).

Earlier he had spoken of this 'drawing', not as a general calling or an indiscriminate grace which always accompanied the preaching of the gospel, but as an effective power and a particular act of God confined to a particular class of persons: 'All that the Father gives me will come to me, and whoever comes to me I will never drive away' (John 6:37).

Later, upon finding many of his disciples about to desert him, and knowing their hearts and the utter insufficiency of mere moral influences, he repeated his earlier words: 'This is why I told you that no-one can come to me unless the Father has enabled him' (John 6:65).

Such teaching, repeatedly given in Scripture, has given rise in Protestant theology to the doctrine of man's inability to respond to the gospel as he should. *The Confession of Faith* of the 17th-century Westminster Divines defines the doctrine of man's inability and his need for God's grace to work sovereignly and in its own power thus:

> Man, by his fall into a state of sin, hath wholly lost all ability of will to any spiritual good accompanying salvation; so as a natural man, being altogether averse from that good, and dead in sin, is not able, by his own strength, to convert himself, or to prepare himself thereunto (Chapter 9, *Of Free Will*).

Now it is very important for us to stress the *moral* nature of this inability. It is not the inability of the wheelchair, but the inability of the will. A man confined to a wheelchair by a physical disability is helpless in a different way and is not responsible for his inability to walk or run. But this is a very particular inability and one which leaves a man wilful and responsible in that inability. It is a bondage of the will which is also a wilful bondage. This is clear from Scripture, however difficult it may be in logic. Paul, writing to the Ephesian Christians of the Gentiles who lived 'in the futility of their thinking', said that they were 'darkened in their understanding and separated from the life of God because of the ignorance that is in *them due to the hardening of their hearts*' (Ephesians 4:17-18, italics mine). Jesus spoke of it when he said to the Pharisees: 'You *refuse* to come to me to have life' (John 5:40, italics mine). He also spoke of it when he wept over Jerusalem: 'How often I have longed to gather your children together ... but *you were not willing*' (Matthew 23:37, italics mine). The great 19th-century preacher, C H Spurgeon, used to say: 'All their cannots are will nots.' That is what leaves men guilty as well as helpless.

The question of free will

It is here that we meet head-on the controversial question of free will. It is controversial partly because justice must be done to both sides of the matter. C H Spurgeon had a delightful way (and a considerable gift) of reducing difficult things to simple and memorable explanation. He says:

> It is a difficult task to show the meeting-place of the purpose of God and the free agency of man. One thing is quite clear, we ought not to deny either of them, for they are both facts. It is a fact that God has purposed all things both great and little; neither will anything happen but according to his eternal purpose and decree. It is also a sure and certain fact that often times events hang upon the choice of men. Now how these two things can both be true I cannot tell you; neither probably after long debate could the wisest men in heaven tell you, not even with the consistence of cherubim and seraphim .... They are two facts that run side by side, like parallel lines .... Can you not believe them both? And is not the space between them a very convenient place to kneel in, adoring and worshipping him whom you cannot understand? (Metropolitan Tabernacle, Vol. 39, p 169).

Much unnecessary dispute would be avoided if we carefully defined the term 'free will' against the background of the clear New Testament teaching about man's bondage in sin. The true and proper doctrine of human freedom is that man is free to choose what he pleases – that is, he is free to do according to his *real* desire. In his *Systematic Theology* (Banner of Truth) Louis Berkhof puts it thus:

There is a certain liberty that is the inalienable possession of the free agent, namely, the liberty to choose as he pleases, in full accord with the prevailing dispositions and tendencies of his soul (Part 2, p 248).

The importance of this definition is that the will is not abstracted from the rest of a man's nature as if it were an independent and sovereign faculty. Man's will is determined by his whole character, it is rooted in the heart. Hence the unregenerate man's will can never be neutral when his mind is 'hostile to God' (Romans 8:7) and his heart 'desperately wicked' (Jeremiah 17:9).

A fine illustration of this is given in an article, 'Man's Will - Free yet Bound' by W J Chantry. He writes:

In modern times we observe rockets fired so that they escape from earth's gravity. To accomplish this there is a great complex of electrical wires, all woven into one control centre, called in the US, 'Mission Control'. According to the Bible, the heart is the Mission Control of a man's life. The heart is the motivational complex of a man, the basic disposition, the entire bent of character, the moral inclination. The mind, emotions, desires and will are all wires which we observe; none is independent, but all are welded into a common circuit. If mission control is wired for evil, the will cannot make the rockets of life travel on the

34

path of righteousness .... 'Will' may be the button which launches the spacecraft. But the launching button does not determine the direction.

He concludes:

> [the will] cannot choose without consulting your intelligence, reflecting your feelings and taking account of your desires. You are free to be yourself. *The will cannot transform you into someone else* .... Here is the tragic truth about man's will. While free from outward coercion, it is in a state of bondage (Article in *Banner of Truth* magazine).

Hence: 'Men are not sinners because they choose to sin; they choose to sin because they are sinners!'

The answer of free grace

Everything we have seen so far ought to lead us to the conclusion that man's only hope is God, that in himself fallen man has no hope. His dignity is not his hope, for he is a ruined temple. His morality is not his hope, for even his righteous acts are like filthy rags (Isaiah 64:6). His will is not his hope, for while free from outward compulsion, he is in a state of bondage within, self-made bondage, self-determined bondage, self-sustained bondage. The prison is his own nature, not God's decree. Now only God's initiative, power and provision in Christ

Jesus can rescue man and raise him. And that initiative, which sent the Son into an unwelcoming world, has to bring the provision of his atonement and resurrection into an unwelcoming heart by the power of an irresistible grace. *That* is the extent of man's need and that is the extent of God's mercy. Hence Paul's devastating picture of man 'dead in transgressions and sin', in the second chapter of his letter to the Ephesians, changes dramatically as the light of the grace of God breaks into the scene:

> You were dead in your transgressions and sins ... but because of his great love for us, God, who is rich in mercy, made us alive with Christ even when we were dead .... For it is by grace you have been saved, through faith – and this not from yourselves, it is the gift of God – not by works, so that no-one can boast (Ephesians 2:1, 4-5, 8-9).

It is something of a red herring to protest that 'the gift of God', which is said to be not 'from yourselves', may in the Greek (as in the English!) refer not to 'faith' but 'salvation', for it should surely be clear from our study that we cannot look for saving faith from the unregenerate sinner. Faith – that is, true and saving faith – implies a cleared understanding (however small) of the things that come from God, a true desire for God in his holy love and lordship, and a heart which is out of love with sin, sorrowing for a godless life. Man by

nature is now incapable of such a self-transforma-
tion. He cannot rise above himself.

Paul's whole point in these verses is, therefore,
to show that God has done for the believer what
the believer could not do for himself. Our first
thoughts of him were from him before they were
of him. The first gleams of understanding of the
gospel were the advance guard of his invading
Light. Our dawning faith and earliest repentance
were his gifts of love before they were our responses of love:

> For who makes you different from anyone else?
> What do you have that you did not receive? And
> if you did receive it, why do you boast as though
> you did not? (1 Corinthians 4:7).

Paul's death and resurrection metaphor in the
Ephesians passage is as final as anything can be:
the dead have no initiating or co-operating part in
their own resurrection. They move because they
have been moved; they live because they have been
given life; they are free because they have been
released from an extreme bondage. Man can affirm his 'freedom' until he is blue in the face and
cold in the grave, but what he needs is resurrection. And that is precisely what God brings to men
and women in the effective working of the gospel.

This is why the historic Reformed creeds and
canons have defended so strongly what are often

called the doctrines of grace. It is not so much a case of defending party dogmas as defending and asserting the true nature of grace and the unassailable place it has in the theology of our redemption. God is rebuilding the ruined temple, God is restoring the crippled athlete, God is raising up from a graveyard world a living church, a Bride who will live for ever with the Husband who chose her, for: 'Where sin increased, grace increased all the more' (Romans 5:20).

Some questions about human nature before God

Q: You referred to 'common' grace. What is this?

A: The old Reformed theologians, wishing to do justice to all God's acts and operations of goodness and mercy in the world and in the lives of fallen men and women, distinguished two kinds of grace in God's government of the world: his common grace and his saving grace.

Saving grace is the undeserved favour of God drawing the soul to himself. It is an effective work of his love, in which the Holy Spirit moves in the depths of the sinner's being, enlightening his mind, turning his will and changing his heart. It is a work which issues in the new birth. As its name implies it really is saving and as such it is confined to God's elect.

Common grace is the more general, indeed

universal, work of God in this fallen world and in the minds, wills and hearts of sinful men and women, restraining sin, exciting 'goodness' (at a human level) and reaching men and women with the familiar blessings of daily and seasonal life. It is the outflow of God's decision to love his enemies, even the non-elect, and to send rain and sun 'on the righteous and the unrighteous' (Matthew 5:45). Even Reformed theologians have differed on details here, however, and I refer you for more prolonged treatments (though at a quite popular level) to the theologies of W G T Shedd and Louis Berkhof. Shedd I find quite outstandingly helpful and enjoyable.

Q: How is God revealing his wrath today? Is God's wrath a withdrawal of common grace or an actual pouring out of wrath?

A: It can be both. Many people are so conceited about their achievements and their morality ('I've never done this or that ...') and then later they run off with their secretary or fiddle the accounts. God may indeed withdraw common grace as a penalty for sin and this abandons the sinner to new levels of transgression and condemnation. This is the picture in Romans 1, of course, and you have perhaps a similar instance of it in the hardening of Pharaoh's heart in chapter 9. God's wrath, however, is shown in many other ways – including violence, injustice, disaster, tragedy, sickness and death – in fact all the penalties of the Fall. These are still real enough in the world, *even as penalties*. It is not only Adam who was punished! Even the believers are afflicted to a degree (Psalm 90:7-10, 15), though in their case the sting of wrath and the curse are taken away (1 Corinthians 15:56-57).

Q: How much should we make of common grace?

A: In understanding man and in understanding the ways of God, I think we should make much of it. If we do not we shall, for instance, be unable to explain the goodness that there clearly is in fallen men and women – and that will make us much less convincing in the sight of people with whom we try to reason and talk. We should show them that they are all debtors at every level to the God they deny or neglect. Moreover, if we do not understand the reality and place of common grace, we may well find ourselves handing the case over to the Catholics and Liberals, who have an inadequate (but more palatable and popular!) view of the Fall.

This doctrine helps us also to recognise God's complete freedom from blame when men reject the gospel. In correspondence with his desire for the salvation of all men, God gives them his common grace; that alone would be sufficient to incline and enable them to respond to his offers of salvation, *if it were not resisted*. The depth of man's antipathy for God, however, means that it always is resisted (Acts 7:51-52). Common grace *in itself* is sufficient, but because of the hostility of man it is not now and in fact sufficient. Grace is given and only sin makes inadequate. W G T Shedd goes so far as to say: 'If common grace should prevail over the sinner's resistance, it would be saving grace.' But God, as we shall see in the next chapter, is not obliged upon the refusal of the first grace to come again with the second. That he does so in the case of the elect is *his* freedom and *his* right!

2

Loved with Everlasting Love

Peter Lewis

If ever a subject could make us bristle, this one could: the Bible's teaching on election! The very mention of it is enough to raise defences, prejudices and wagging fingers, as Christians argue their different positions. So why study it at all? I could suggest many reasons, but I mention only two. My first would be this, without apology: it is *a doctrine of Scripture*. It is in the whole of Scripture, not just in one or two obscure and odd verses. It is written large in our Old and New Testaments. It was given to ancient Israelites as it is to modern Christians. Moses, David and Isaiah taught it; our Lord Jesus himself taught it; so did Paul and John and Peter. There is no dissenting voice on this in the whole of Scripture. If we are Bible believers, we neglect what the Bible says to our loss, especially on a subject which is so deep and which is such a high privilege to enter.

A doctrine of love
A second reason is this: it is first and foremost *a doctrine of love*. We are all concerned with the love of God; its height and length, its depth and breadth. Here we will find riches of God's love that will astonish us, thrill us and move us to heights of praise and thanksgiving, gratitude and love. Some folk misconceive election and think it must be anti-love. The exact opposite is the case. Election is very much a doctrine of God's love to you and me. It tells us that he has loved us, that he

loved us before we loved him, that we love him because he first loved us. It tells us that God knew us before we were born, that he cared for us, that we had significance with him from all eternity, that we were never lost in the crowd. This is vital for the Christian's self-understanding, to know his God and know what place he has in the heart of his God.

A doctrine of freedom

Further, and most important of all, it is *a doctrine of the freedom of God*. Dr Carl Henry states: 'At the heart of the election doctrine throbs God's freedom.' With typical shrewdness and insight the great Reformed preacher, C H Spurgeon, said long ago:

> It is said by someone that men give free will to everyone but God, and speak as if God must be the slave of men. Aye, we believe that God has given to man a free will – *that* we do not deny; but we will have it that God has a free will also – and that, moreover, he has a right to exercise it and does exercise it. You do not believe that God can justly give to some men more grace than to others. Very well. Let us kneel down and pray together .... You cry (concerning relatives and friends): 'Lord draw them, Lord break their hearts, renew their spirits.' Now I very heartily use this prayer, but how can you do it, if you think it unrighteous in the Lord to endow this people with more grace than he does the rest of the human race?

46

These alone are sufficient reasons for looking at this truth.

The next question is: how are we to approach such a profound subject? How do we swim in such deep waters? I suggest three answers.

Approach with humility

The first is: *with humility*. We should listen to the voice of God about this, not man. It is helpful to remember that when we were governed by non-Christian or worldly thinking, we stumbled at every Bible doctrine. They all appeared as offensive as this one may still appear to some. We once were offended at the doctrine that we were sinners, lost and damned, that our righteousness was as filthy rags, that there was a hell before us and a Judge above us. There was a time when we were offended at the gospel of blood and sacrifice and cross and suffering. We objected to being told that we could not save ourselves and had to be saved by another and on his terms. But we learned, by the Holy Spirit's work, humbly to listen to what God had to say about our sin and need, and his way of redemption. In this matter of election therefore we need simply to recapture that early humility and be willing to sit at the feet of God.

Approach with caution

My second answer as to how we should handle these truths is: *with caution*. We must stick to the plain statements of Scripture and avoid any logical flights into the doctrine of predestination that take it further than the natural sense of Scripture. We must believe *all* that Scripture tells us, but not *more* than Scripture tells us. For instance, Scripture commits us to the doctrine of unconditional predestination to eternal life, but not to that of unconditional predestination unto eternal damnation. I do not believe Scripture shows a double predestination of this kind, in which the two things are equal – as though God simply decided that he would create some for heaven and some for hell. That is more than Scripture tells us, and is, in my opinion, a quite monstrous idea. It is true that sometimes great theologians have attempted to press logic too far in safeguarding what they thought were the rights and glory of God. But we need caution, lest we go beyond Scripture into philosophy, into insoluble problems (like the origins of evil), into doctrines that are extravagant and repugnant, even if apparently logical.

If a man is saved it is because he has been elected in the love of God to this salvation, and if a man is lost it is not because God has predestined him to be lost, but because he has rejected the offered love and salvation of God in Jesus Christ. God is the cause of faith; man is the cause of unbelief. God does not work in the unbeliever 'to will and to do' what is sinful as he works in the believer 'to will and to do' his good pleasure

(Philippians 2:13). In a manner quite inscrutable to us, his sovereignty is as complete over the one as it is over the other; yet it operates so differently that God is never the author of sin and never the cause of man's perdition. Salvation is all of God, damnation is all of man.[1]

Dr J I Packer writes in his book, *Evangelism and the Sovereignty of God*:

---

1. Reformed theology has consistently defined God's *rejection* in terms of his *reaction*. That is, God does not decree to reject anyone, except on the ground of their sin. Only on this basis are some 'prepared for destruction' (Romans 9:22). Hence the Westminster Confession of Faith defines predestination to eternal life as 'out of his [God's] mere free grace and love, without any foresight of faith or good works ... or any other thing in the creature as conditions, or causes moving him thereunto' (Chapter 111, para 5). But it is careful to avoid an *equal ultimacy* in the decrees of election and rejection, as if *both* proceed alike from God 'without any foresight ... or any other thing in the creature ... moving him thereunto'. 'Election to life' proceeds purely from God 'to the praise of his glorious grace'. However, in regard to the decree of reprobation, we read in the *Confession*: 'The rest of mankind, God was pleased, according to the unsearchable counsel of his own will... to pass by and to ordain them to dishonour and wrath *for their sin*, to the praise of his glorious justice.' The phrase 'for their sin' is crucial. The 'passing by' is the rejection of *fallen* beings, men and women considered (albeit long before the event) as having rejected God. They are rebels before they are rejected.

> God's sovereignty and man's responsibility are taught side by side in the same Bible .... It follows that they must be held together and not played off against each other. Man is a responsible moral agent, while he is divinely controlled; man is divinely controlled, while he is also a responsible moral agent (pages 22-23).[2]

These things seem to contradict one another, but both are taught in Scripture and must be kept together. They do not contradict each other in God's wisdom, only in our limited minds. We ought not to be surprised when we find such mysteries in God's word, for the Creator is incomprehensible to his creatures. C H Spurgeon was once asked if he could reconcile these two truths to each other. 'I wouldn't try,' he replied. 'I never reconcile friends who haven't fallen out!'

Approach with gratitude
The third answer to the way in which we should tackle election is: *with gratitude*. We are looking

---

2. This is expressed in the famous words of the *Westminster Confession of Faith* in the chapter, 'Of God's eternal decrees': God from all eternity did, by the most wise and holy counsel of his own will, freely and unchangeably ordain whatsoever comes to pass: yet so as thereby neither is God the author of sin, nor is violence offered to the will of the creatures, nor is the liberty or contingency of second causes taken away, but rather established (Chapter 111, para 1).

at the most exalted gifts of the supreme majesty and mercy of God to the most unlikely and undeserving. To think that he should set his love on us! The Christian is bowled over by that, lost in wonder, love and praise. Listen again to C H Spurgeon, whose preaching, like his life, was fuller of the joy of salvation than most. Here is an extract from a sermon entitled, 'David dancing before the ark because of his election' (on 2 Samuel 6:20-22):

> Dear brethren, there is great power in the truth of election when a man can grasp it, when he knows for himself, truthfully, and by indisputable evidence, that the Lord has chosen him, then he breaks forth in songs of divine adoration and praise: then is his heart lifted up, and he pays homage to God which others would not think of paying. Personally, I have overflowing joy in the doctrines of eternal, unchanging love. It is bliss to know that the Lord has chosen me .... Election sets the soul on fire with enthusiastic delight in God. Certain doctrines would not make a mouse move one of its ears; but the grand old doctrines of grace stir our blood, quicken our pulse and fill our whole being with enthusiasm (*Metropolitan Tabernacle Pulpit*, Vol. 34).

With such feeling and doxology does Paul open his letter to the church at Ephesus: 'Praise be to the God and Father of our Lord Jesus Christ ... for he chose us' (Ephesians 1:3-4). Gratitude!

Among the various historic definitions of this doctrine of election the one put forward by the Synod of Dort in the early 17th century is one of the best and is worthy of concentrated attention:

Election is the unchangeable purpose of God, whereby, before the foundations of the world were laid, he elected from the whole human race that had fallen from its primaeval integrity into sin and destruction by its own fault, according to the most free good pleasure of his will, out of pure grace, a fixed number of men neither better nor worthier than others, but prostrate with the others in common wretchedness, to salvation in Christ, whom he appointed mediator right from eternity and the head of all the elect and the foundation of salvation; and resolved to give him to save them and to call and bring them effectually into his own communion through his own word and Spirit .... He decreed to present them with true faith in himself, to justify and sanctify them, and at last, being powerfully protected in the communion of his Son, to glorify them, for a proof of his mercy and for the praise of his glorious grace.

Strictly speaking, election refers to the people and predestination to the destiny he maps out for them, but we shall use the various terms (including foreknowledge, choice, decree, etc.) as virtual synonyms for the same base concept. Let us look now at Scripture, not merely from the standpoint of man and his opportunities, but from the standpoint of God and his *plan of salvation.*

Predestination and Christ

Jesus Christ himself was predestined to come to this world, as the Old Testament predictions showed – the types, the prophecies, the sacrificial system and those remarkable and astonishing passages in Isaiah 53 and Psalm 22. Those Old Testament features leave no doubt that it was planned and ordained that Christ should come into the world to live and die as he did.

Yet Peter tells us that the predestination of Christ goes back even beyond Old Testament days: 'He was chosen before the creation of the world, but was revealed in these last times for your sake' (1 Peter 1:20). Peter is referring to Christ in his capacity and office as mediator. He is referring to the plan that he should become the God-man, to live and die and rise again for us, to accomplish the work of our salvation and redemption. That, he says, was ordained. Christ was chosen before the creation of the world. P T Forsyth once put it in a startling phrase in his book *The Person and Place of Jesus Christ*: 'There was a Calvary above, the mother of it all!'

Christ's own consciousness

That Christ was predestined is also clear in Jesus' own self-awareness. His consciousness that these things were planned and ordained for him comes over again and again:

> He then began to teach them that the Son of Man must suffer many things and be rejected by the elders, chief priests and teachers of the law, and that he must be killed and after three days rise again (Mark 8:31).

He lived his whole life under the 'must' of prophecy. He knew that 'it is written that the Son of Man must suffer much and be rejected' (Mark 9:12). In the Garden of Gethsemane he said:

> Do you think I cannot call on my Father, and he will at once put at my disposal more than twelve legions of angels? But how then would the Scriptures be fulfilled that say it must happen in this way? (Matthew 26:53-54).

Or again:

> It is written: 'And he was numbered with the transgressors' [Isaiah 53]; and I tell you that this must be fulfilled in me. Yes, what is written about me is reaching its fulfilment (Luke 22:37).

As he predicted his death, he said: 'Now my heart is troubled, and what shall I say? "Father, save me from this hour"? No, it was for this very reason I came to this hour' (John 12:27). After his resurrection he said the same:

He said to them, 'This is what I told you while I was still with you: Everything must be fulfilled that is written about me in the Law of Moses, the Prophets and the Psalms' (Luke 24:44).

The purpose and the motive

This indeed was the purpose and motive of the incarnation (Hebrews 2:14-15): Bethlehem was in order to Calvary, the child was born to die, the Son was decreed to come for that great purpose. Nothing could be plainer. His whole life was a pre-destined and conscious pilgrimage to the cross. Christ was predestined to come, and – deeper mystery still – predestined to die. Now, if this were the only fact we knew about this doctrine, it would still be fundamental for us all. It is a difficult doctrine, we may find it a riddle of a doctrine, and yet it is the key to so many other riddles. It shows us the greatest, freest person in the world being predestined to do his work.

To those who say that predestination makes men robots, we respond by asking: 'Was Jesus a robot?' Nobody was more ordained than he. He said that he could do nothing by himself, but only what he saw his Father doing (John 5:19). His whole life was a looking to the Father for his will. Nobody was more predetermined than Jesus in every word he spoke and every deed he did, but nobody was freer or more responsible, more decisive or more in command.

Yet his predestination clearly extended to the darkest event in his life, to the most terrible deed ever done, to the greatest enormity sinful man could commit, to the foulest, most vicious, most horrific, most tragic and most perplexing act in the world – Calvary! That was ordained and Christ was predestined to it.

No accident, no mere murder
The Bible forbids us ever to imagine that the cross was just an accident, any more than it was merely a murder. It was a purposed sacrifice. It is not as though God somehow rescued something in the end out of what was never meant to be; it was always meant to be. In the first Christian sermon, one Jew said to his fellow countrymen:

> Men of Israel, listen to this: Jesus of Nazareth was a man accredited by God to you by miracles, wonders and signs, which God did among you through him, as you yourselves know. This man was handed over to you by God's set purpose and foreknowledge; and you, with the help of wicked men, put him to death by nailing him to the cross. But God raised him ... (Acts 2:22-24).

'Handed over by God's set purpose and foreknowledge'! Peter uses three terms: handed over by God, God's set purpose, and God's foreknowledge. That foreknowledge is not God looking down a telescope to see what will happen and then trying to juggle events around it to make it all come right in the end. God knows what is going to happen, because he has decreed *either* to do it *or* to permit it to be done. He is never the author of sin, yet he is in control of all things – including the fall, the corruption, the chaos *and* the cross.

The Bible never has God on the sidelines, looking to see what will happen outside himself; that is no Christian doctrine. This comes out vividly in a prayer meeting – not a theological dissertation, but a prayer and praise meeting for ordinary believers in the early church. Peter and John had been threatened by Jewish authorities for preaching Christ, but then, with reluctance, were freed. All the believers responded to the news of their release with great joy. They raised their voices to their 'sovereign Lord' in prayer and praise, and in their prayer we hear them give utterance to this conviction:

> Indeed Herod and Pontius Pilate met together with the Gentiles and the people of Israel in this city to conspire against your holy servant Jesus, whom you anointed. They did what your power and will had decided beforehand should happen (Acts 4:27-28).

Can we see the point? They (out of malice) did what his power and will had decided before (out of sacrificial love) should happen. God is never taken by surprise. Calvary, though the most terrible thing that God ever did, was in his mind from the start.

Astonishing love
This makes his love astonishing; that he should create a world to be the scene of this terrible agony; that at the beginning of time he should contour a hill which would become Golgotha; that when he first said, 'Let there be light,' he should start a series of events that would lead to the darkness in which his Son cried out: 'My God, my God, why have you forsaken me?' (Matthew 27:46). It adds a breathtaking dimension to the love of God, that he was so determined to give us life eternal that, knowing the cost of it, nothing could stop him doing it. You may protest: 'But if it was so decreed, how could Judas or anyone be blamed for it?' Again we are given only two answers to that: God's sovereignty and man's responsibility, without further resolution. Jesus, who was privy to the most secret counsels of his Father, even when in the flesh, simply says: 'The Son of Man will go as it has been decreed, but woe to that man who betrays him' (Luke 22:22).

God acted for reasons unutterably good; Caiaphas, Pilate, Judas and the crowd acted for reasons despicably bad. God 'so loved the world that he gave [even up to the cross] his only Son' (John 3:16). He 'gave him up for us all' (Romans

8:32). He 'presented him as a sacrifice of atonement' (Romans 3:25). *He did it,* says Paul repeatedly, in those passages, with the full co-operation
and will of the Son. God – 'who works out everything in conformity with the purpose of his will'
(Ephesians 1:11) – fathered the greatest act of self-
sacrifice that ever was or will be. God sovereignly
overruled the malice of men.

Not merely made available

But, and this too is a recurring refrain, God did
not send his Son to perform an empty gesture or
merely to make salvation available to all. Jesus'
preaching brings out again and again that there
were people whom the Father had given him from
all eternity, who would – unfailingly and without
exception – be drawn to him. His death would most
certainly be effective for them because of his deliberate, predestined and infallible intention to save
them. This is no human theory, but the statement
of Jesus in John 6:37 (starting from verse 35 to get
the sense):

> Then Jesus declared, 'I am the bread of life. He
> who comes to me will never go hungry, and he
> who believes in me will never be thirsty. But as I
> told you, you have seen me and still you do not
> believe. All that the Father gives me will come to
> me, and whoever comes to me I will never drive
> away. For I have come down from heaven not to

do my will but to do the will of him who sent me. And this is the will of him who sent me, that I shall lose none of all that he has given me, but raise them up at the last day. For my Father's will is that everyone who looks to the Son and believes in him shall have eternal life, and I will raise him up at the last day' (John 6:35-40).

All the elements are there. Jesus is freely available ('he who comes ...'). Men are responsible ('still you do not believe ...'). God is sovereign ('All that the Father gives ...'). Christ is central ('I will raise him up ...'). Predestination is a glorious fact ('I shall lose none of all that he has given me').

If we want to see how this operates in the consciousness of Jesus, we have but to turn to John 17. Jesus is about to die a death which will infallibly secure the redemption of his church. 'I have revealed you to those whom you gave me out of the world. They were yours; you gave them to me and they have obeyed your word' (John 17:6). Again: 'I pray for them. I am not praying for the world, but for those you have given me, for they are yours' (John 17:9). 'The world' there means the unbelieving, hostile world. Or yet again the same themes recur:

> Father, I want those you have given me to be with me where I am, and to see my glory, the glory you have given me because you loved me before the creation of the world (John 17:24).

Jesus tells us that he was not predestined to bring us merely to a temporary decision, that may or may not last for the rest of our life, but right through to glory – nothing less. And to do this for all his people in the ongoing work of the gospel in all the succeeding centuries – for those who will believe in the future (John 17:20).

The covenant of redemption

In these passages Jesus refers to a pact, or covenant, in eternity between the Father and himself, an agreement in which all the elect were given to him to be his eternal possession. This has been called in Protestant theology the covenant of redemption (the *pactum salutis*). It is not to be confused with the covenant of grace. The covenant of grace was made with men, in time; the covenant of redemption was made between the Father, Son and Holy Spirit in eternity.

This piece of teaching is no mere abstract or irrelevant speculation. It roots the church's election in the *Trinitarian* love of God. (The reason the Holy Spirit is not explicitly referred to is simply to focus attention on the Son's capacity as mediator.)

It rests the doctrine of election on the unshakeable faithfulness of God, who is committed *within himself* to the final salvation of all the elect.

The 'pact' itself does not so much indicate a 'moment' of decision in God (for we are loved

61

from eternity in Christ), as a *plane* of decision, a level of commitment and a unity of purpose within the Godhead. It is surely the ultimate antidote to dark and fearful feelings about this subject of election in the minds of Christians. You and I were the subjects of a loving and eager agreement between the Persons of the Godhead in eternity:

> Grace first inscribed my name
> In God's eternal book;
> 'Twas grace that gave me to the Lamb,
> Who all my sorrows took.
>
> *Philip Doddridge*

Predestination relates to Christ; it also relates to the believer.

Predestination and the believer

Old Testament believers knew a good deal about this doctrine, for they had been told, and not just once: 'For you are a people holy to the Lord your God'. Holy means special, cut off, set apart for God. 'The LORD your God has chosen you out of all the peoples on the face of the earth to be his people, his treasured possessions' (Deuteronomy 7:6). God did not choose Egypt, Assyria or Greece, but he did choose Israel (Isaiah 43:3-4). For thousands of years they were the only people in the world who had the saving light of the gospel in its Old Testament form.

In the Old Testament, however, election was not

just for the nation. By obvious implication and also by clear examples and explicit statements, it was for individuals also. As the Puritan, Thomas Goodwin, points out in his massive exposition of Ephesians (1:1-2:11), expounding the words 'the great love wherewith he loved us':

> God in his love pitcheth upon persons. God doth not pitch upon propositions only; as to say, 'I will love him who believeth and save him' as those of the Arminian opinion hold. No, he pitcheth upon persons. And Christ died not for propositions only but for persons .... He loved us nakedly; he loved *us* not *ours*. It was not for our faith, nor for anything in us, 'not of works' saith the Apostle; no, nor of faith neither. No, he pitcheth upon naked persons; he loves you, not yours (*Works*, Vol. 2, p 151; Nicholl, 1861).

God's choice of persons is as clear in both Old and New Testaments as his choice of a nation. Abraham, the father of all the believers, was sovereignly chosen, selected and called out from Ur of the Chaldeans (Genesis 12:1). His line of believing descent started with Isaac and Jacob and ran right on into the new era of Christ. Paul makes it clear that this involved individuals from the start, that Jacob was chosen before he was born:

> Rebecca's children had one and the same father, our father Isaac. Yet, before the twins were born or had done anything good or bad – in order that

God's purpose in election might stand: not by works but by him who calls – she was told 'The older will serve the younger'. Just as it is written: 'Jacob I loved, but Esau I hated' (Romans 9:10-13).

Selected or passed over

This election involves an element of *selection*. That is how Jacob was chosen and Esau was rejected. Now there is nothing unjust in that, any more than there was injustice in God rejecting Pharaoh and using him, even 'hardening his heart', to further the divine purposes. Both Esau and Pharaoh were clay in the hands of the Potter, as Paul says (Romans 9:21). But the human clay which God shaped and directed, passing over and ordaining to destruction (Romans 9:22), was *fallen* humanity; human nature in its sinful state; people whom God bore with great patience, despite their impenitence (Romans 9:22). Even Esau in the womb (like Jacob for that matter) is part of a fallen race, a sinful totality (see Psalm 51:5).

When we grasp that important theological truth, we can perhaps understand C H Spurgeon's swift reply to someone who objected to the statement: 'Jacob have I loved but Esau I hated'. Spurgeon retorted: 'Yes, I too have difficulty with that text: but it is not quite your difficulty. My difficulty is not why God should hate Esau, but why he should love Jacob!' That is a good example of wisdom and *humility* before holy Scripture.

You will find, moreover, that not only are Abraham, Isaac and Jacob spoken of in this way, but other individuals also. Take Jeremiah:

> The word of the LORD came to me, saying, 'Before I formed you in the womb I knew you, before you were born I set you apart; I appointed you as prophet to the nations' (Jeremiah 1:4-5).

Paul explains his own ministry in the echo of these words and in the same way: 'God, who set me apart from birth and called me by his grace, was pleased to reveal his Son in me so that I might preach him among the Gentiles' (Galatians 1:15-16).

The great and the ordinary
No one, however, should think that only the leading figures in the church of God are singled out like this with special love and purpose. The great passages on the doctrine of election in the New Testament are written to entire churches of believers (young and old, weak and strong), who can all draw confidence from the *doctrine and their part in it* (for example, Romans 8:28-30; Ephesians 1:3-14; 2 Thessalonians 2:13-15; 1 Peter 1:1-5, 2:9). We shall have space to examine more closely only the first of these. It would be enough, even if there were no other! In the eighth chapter of his letter to the Romans Paul writes (to a church he had never met, but a church of believers who were, like him, 'loved by God and called to be saints'):

And we know that in all things God works for the good of those who love him, who have been called according to his purpose. For those whom God foreknew he also predestined to be conformed to the likeness of his Son, that he might be the firstborn among many brothers. And those he predestined, he also called; those he called, he also justified; those he justified, he also glorified (Romans 8:28-30).

The golden chain

This has been called the golden chain of salvation, and it is a pity that some are embarrassed or unwilling to wear it! Notice that its first link and its last are in eternity. It speaks of a love for each Christian man, woman and child which reaches from eternity past to eternity future. Notice too that it speaks of *individuals* throughout ('those') and the *same* individuals throughout. Notice above all that it ascribes their eternal salvation to God and to God alone. It is God who works for their good, it is his 'purpose' which ensures their effective calling; it is God who 'foreknew' them and it is he who predestines them, he who calls them, he who justifies them and he who glorifies them. Nothing is clearer or more clearly emphasized throughout the passage than the primary truth that God initiates, sustains and carries through to a triumphant completion the saving work of his grace. The fact that Paul employs throughout verse 30 a tense which is used to point to a past accomplished event (the Greek aorist tense), is meant to point out with dramatic force this glorious truth: that the future of believers is as certain as their present and that nothing in all creation will be able to separate them from the love of God that is in Christ Jesus their Lord.

No attempt should be made to reduce the force of this passage. People have tried to do this in various ways. It has been said that the word 'foreknow' – 'those God foreknew he also predestined' – refers to foreseen faith and repentance; and that God's election is not unconditional, but based on his foreknowledge of our faith. This is refutable from several points. First, the passage says nothing of the sort. God does, of course, know who will turn and believe, but only because he has purposed to give to them the grace of faith and repentance. As the previous chapter has shown, man by nature consistently rejects all God's calls to faith and repentance. Listen to C H Spurgeon again:

> It is further asserted that the Lord foreknew who would exercise repentance, who would believe in Jesus and who would persevere in a consistent life to the end. This readily granted, but a reader must have pretty powerful magnifying spectacles before he will discover that sense in the text. Upon looking carefully at my Bible again I do not perceive such a statement. Where are those words which you have added, 'Whom he did foreknow to repent, to believe, and to persevere in grace'?

.... As I do not find those words there, begging your pardon, I do not believe in them *(Metropolitan Tabernacle Pulpit*, Vol. 18, p 182, 1872).

What does foreknowledge mean?
Furthermore, this word 'foreknowledge' is not at all meant to lead us to imagine God looking on or looking forward, passively, to see what men will do. Such a picture would be in total contradiction to the whole thrust of the passage which, as we have seen, speaks repeatedly of *God's* activity. The term 'foreknowledge' is, in fact, full of positive content, just like the other terms that follow it. It has a twofold significance: foreordination and distinguishing love. God foreknows because he plans, he decrees, he determines. In the light of Acts 2:23 and 4:27-28 *foreknowledge is clearly on the basis of foreordination*. God knows believers because he plans them and their lives (Psalms 139:15-16). But he plans them not merely out of his power but also out of love. As Professor John Murray states in his commentary on Romans:

Many times in Scripture 'know' has a pregnant meaning beyond that of mere recognition. It is used in a sense practically synonymously with 'love', to set regard upon, to know with peculiar interest, delight, affection and action (see Genesis 18:19; Psalm 1:6; Amos 3:2; Matthew 7:23; 1 John 3:1, etc.). 'Whom he foreknew' means 'whom he set regard upon' or 'whom he knew from eternity with distinguishing affection and delight' and is virtually equivalent to 'whom he foreloved' (*op cit*, page 317).

It is of great importance to get this right in our minds if we are fully to appreciate the love of God. He has not loved us so incomparably and so effectively because of something he foresaw in us, but because of something free and wholly undeserved in him. As far as mere foresight was concerned, all he could see in us was rebellion, sin and stubborn unbelief. Hence, says Professor Murray of the Romans passage:

It is not foresight of difference but the foreknowledge that makes the difference to exist, not a foresight that recognizes existence but the foreknowledge that determines existence. It is sovereign distinguishing love (*ibid,* page 318).

No wonder then, that Dr Martyn Lloyd-Jones, in expounding this passage in his great 'Romans' series, says that this term 'foreknowledge' is 'the most important term of the five' that occur in verses 28-30 (*The Final Perseverance of the Saints*, page 22, Banner of Truth). 'Indeed,' he says later, 'there is very little difference between foreknowledge and predestination.' The particular force of the term, however, reminds us that it was 'in love' that he 'predestined us to be adopted as his sons through Jesus Christ' (Ephesians 1:4-5) (*ibid* page 239).

A further serious warning against misusing this word 'foreknowledge' is given by Professor Donald MacLeod:

> The very meaning of election to salvation is that our obedience is the result (and therefore cannot be the cause) of the divine choice. Our first movements towards God are due to his grace: 'Except a man be born again he cannot see the kingdom of heaven' ... 'unto you it is given to believe on him' .... Election based on faith and repentance is nothing other than love earned by faith and repentance. And then grace is no more grace (*Banner of Truth* magazine, April 1969).

The 'golden chain' is golden in its every link, from foreknowledge in eternity past to glorification in eternity to come. Let those who are in Christ Jesus wear it with joy, knowing that their names were written in heaven (Luke 10:20) before the foundation of the world (Ephesians 1:4; Revelation 17:8).

A doctrine of comfort for the believer

We should recognise already that this is not a doctrine to avoid, but rather to glory in. It is not given to frighten us or to make us feel insecure in our salvation, but rather the opposite. We need not doubt our election if we have believed on the Lord Jesus Christ, for (as John Calvin emphatically and repeatedly taught): 'Christ is the mirror of our election'. In him as our Saviour and Lord we see the irrefutable evidence of our election by God. No one who has trusted Jesus Christ as their Saviour and given themselves up to him to be their Lord should have their confidence eroded by this doctrine – but rather established. It is the supreme comfort and strength of any Christian who is tempted to fear that he or she might not endure to the end or might not hold out against so many doubts and pressures and failures.

Paul's entire use and application of this doctrine answers this anxiety, allays such fears and establishes more firmly than ever the confidence of the believer. 'What, then, shall we say in response to this?' he asks at the end of the Romans passage. 'If God is for us, who can be [effectively] against us?' (Romans 8:31). The majestic assurance of the ensuing verses to the end of the chapter, are the outflow of this doctrine. They lead to the climactic cry of verse 38, that nothing in all creation 'will be able to separate us from the love of God that is in Christ Jesus our Lord'. Indeed, it has been said that the entire section which follows (Romans 9-11) is an exposition of that very statement given in the face of apparent denials and discouragements.

Similarly, Paul opens his letter to the Ephesian Christians, young and old, unstable and mature, with the same doctrine as a universal ground of confidence and rejoicing. Everyone, he says, who is in Christ, every believer, has in Christ Jesus blessings from eternity to eternity. All the blessings of a full salvation have been purposed for us in the Father's decree, purchased for us in the Son's redemption, and decisively and definitively applied to us in the Spirit's ministry:

> Praise be to the God and Father of our Lord Jesus Christ, who has blessed us in the heavenly realms with every spiritual blessing in Christ. For he chose us in him before the creation of the world to be holy and blameless in his sight. In love he predestined us to be adopted as his sons through Jesus Christ, in accordance with his pleasure and will .... In him we were also chosen, having been predestined according to the plan of him who works out everything in conformity with the purpose of his will .... And you also were included in Christ when you heard the word of truth, the gospel of your salvation. Having believed, you were marked in him with a seal, the promised Holy Spirit, who is a deposit guaranteeing our inheritance until the redemption of those who are God's possession – to the praise of his glory (Ephesians 1:3-5, 11, 13-14).

It is very interesting to notice that John Calvin kept within this perspective very firmly when expounding this great doctrine. He did not attempt to construct a system around election or the decrees of God. Indeed he did not *start* with this doctrine at all. Some have done exactly that. They have begun their thinking with the divine decrees and have worked logically from that. And they have, variously, produced iron-clad systems which failed to do justice to *all* Scripture. Calvin was too firm and fair a biblicist to do that. In his great work, *Institutes of the Christian Religion*, he proceeds like this. *Book One* is on the knowledge of God the Creator; *Book Two* is on the knowledge of God the Redeemer; *Book Three* is on how we receive the grace that Christ has won for us. It is only in *Book Three*, and towards the end of that book, that Calvin begins to expound this ancient doctrine of election – as a word of pastoral comfort! If we kept that perspective in mind we should be less likely to wrangle on so glorious a subject.

A doctrine of direction for the believer
We are elected, not only to be happy in heaven but also to be holy on earth. Again and again this is brought out in the apostolic writings. God is not merely concerned that we should be happy; he has ordained that we shall be holy, a holy people in the holy Son, a holy people for a holy God:

> For those God foreknew he also predestined to be conformed to the likeness of his Son (Romans 8:29).

> ... from the beginning God chose you to be saved through the sanctifying work of the Spirit (2 Thessalonians 2:13).

... who have been chosen according to the foreknowledge of God the Father, by the sanctifying
work of the Spirit, for obedience to Jesus Christ
... (1 Peter 1:2).

His divine power has given us everything we need
for life and godliness (2 Peter 1:3).

All these statements, like many others, tell us that
God has elected us both to the goal and also to the
way to that goal. Election is meant to strengthen
us for service, not relax us for idleness. Knowing
our sure and certain destiny, we 'press on towards
the goal to win the prize for which God has called'
us (Philippians 3:14), making our 'calling and election sure' (2 Peter 1:10) by remembering who we
are (2 Peter 1:9) and developing the new life of
the Spirit which is in us (2 Peter 1:5-8).

We may never abuse this doctrine of election
by saying or thinking: 'Well, I'm chosen to eternal life, therefore I can now live in sin with impu-
nity.' The new man or woman in Christ cannot take
up such an attitude. Indeed, such is our change of
heart toward God that we long to be nearer and
more like our Father. If we were to be offered a
choice between, on the one hand, heaven with a
life in sin and, on the other, heaven with a life of
righteousness, we would not hesitate to choose the
second every time.

Only the carnal heart regrets its farewell to sin,
only an unregenerate person wants salvation *and*

sin. For all our failures and trespasses, we are at war with all ungodliness and long for the day of our perfection. There is not a true Christian alive who prizes the doctrine of election as if it allowed him to live in squalor and look forward to heaven.

C H Spurgeon must have felt his blood stir when he addressed himself to this point in one sermon:

It is whispered by some that election is a licentious doctrine. Say it out loud and I will answer you .... The men who have believed this doctrine have been the wide world over the most zealous, most earnest, most holy men .... Never were men more heavenly-minded than the Puritans .... When a man believes that he is chosen to be a king, therefore would it be a legitimate inference to draw from it – 'I am chosen to be a king, therefore I will be a beggar; I am chosen to sit upon a throne, therefore I will wear rags' .... No! The man, knowing that a peculiar dignity has been put upon him by God, feels working in his bosom, a desire to live up to his dignity. 'God has loved me more than others,' says he, 'then will I love him more than others. He has put me above the rest of mankind by his sovereign grace; let me live above them: let me be more holy: let me be more eminent in grace than any of them' .... I heard a man say once, 'Sir, if I believed that doctrine, I should live in sin.' My reply to him was this, 'I dare say *you* would! I dare say *you* would' .... To a man that is renewed by grace, there is no doctrine that could make him love sin .... Here is a lion roaring for its prey. I will change him into a lamb; and I defy you to make that lamb, by any doctrine, go and redden its lips with blood. It cannot do it – its nature is changed (*New Park Street Pulpit*, Vol. 6, p 136, 1860).

A doctrine of mighty encouragement in evangelism and life

The doctrine of election is as far removed as possible from being a hindrance to our evangelism. It is, rather, an effective spur to it. That is implicit in what Jesus said in his great shepherd and sheep discourse: 'I have other sheep that are not of this sheep pen. I must bring them also' (John 10:16). It is all planned. Nothing can prevent it. And we are chosen to bring it to pass! This truth gave Paul heart in Corinth, the Soho of the ancient world. He was feeling challenged by the darkness, so overburdened by it that he did not know whether he should stay there. But:

One night the Lord spoke to Paul in a vision: 'Do not be afraid; keep on speaking, do not be silent. For I am with you, and no-one is going to attack and harm you, because I have many people in this city' (Acts 18:9-10).

They were not the Lord's people yet; they were still out in the world, maybe murderers, perjurers or sexual perverts, in a terrible state.

Paul later said of the church he founded at Corinth: 'And that is what some of you were, but you were washed, you were sanctified' (1 Corinthians 6:11). At the time of his vision they were certainly not washed or sanctified. They were lost, right out of the world! But God said: 'Many of these are mine, my elect, though as yet uncalled. I know where they are, in the back streets of this city, in the sewers of this Soho, but I'm going to draw them. They will be trophies of my grace. So Paul, you stay on and don't be afraid, for I'll protect you.' We know what a harvest Paul reaped there. They may have been a problem church, but they were also a glorious church, the crown of rejoicing for him in the last day.

The same truth appears in Acts 13:48: 'When the Gentiles heard this, they were glad and honoured the word of the Lord; and all who were appointed for eternal life believed.' This is an encouragement to our evangelism. To imagine that everything depends on us or on the other person would drive us frantic. If it were up to us to grab enough people and shake them and cajole them; if it depended on the fervency of our prayers or the cogency of our arguments or the consistency of our love ... who would be saved? We would be in a panic. But New Testament evangelism is not panic! If we follow the apostolic way, we will listen to the Spirit and we will get up in the morning and say: 'Lord, who today? Where today? How today?'

True, we will evangelize indiscriminately. We will not be trying to pry into God's secret plans, for only 'The Lord knows those who are his' (2 Timothy 2:19). But we will always be listening in case God has further guidance, further direction. We will know that, if our hearts and lives are right, we need not be frantic; the Lord will fulfil his will through us.

This is a doctrine of encouragement in our whole lives, as well as our work and witness. The doctrine of God's decrees, his predestination of events and places, people and things, time and circumstance may terrify the non-Christian who is at war with God, but it should not terrify us. Where else would we like our life to be, but in the hands of our Father? Is there anyone else whom we would prefer to have sovereignty over every part of our life? Would *you* like to have sovereignty over your own life? I would not over mine. Horatius Bonar wrote in one of his fine hymns:

> I dare not choose my way,
> I would not if I might;
> Choose thou for me my God,
> So shall I choose aright.

Even the non-Calvinistic Christian is constrained to say that. As Joseph Parker's hymn puts it:

> God holds the key to all unknown,
> And I am glad;

If other hands should hold the key,
Or if he trusted it to me,
I might be sad.

What if tomorrow's cares were here
Without its rest,
I'd rather he unlocked the day
And as the hours swing open, say,
'*My will is best.*'

Predestination and the churches

The doctrine of election is no sectarian or 'party'
doctrine. It has been the age-old teaching of the
Christian church and an awe-inspiring line of her
greatest theologians have stood forth to teach and
to defend it. Sometimes they have had to defend it
from attack and dilution within the church itself.

The mighty Augustine expounded it against the
humanism of Pelagius. Anselm and Aquinas wrote
in its defence. Martin Luther wrote of it in his book
The Bondage of the Will, against the humanism of
Erasmus. The 16th and 17th century Calvinists,
the Reformers and the Puritans, preached it against
the Arminians. George Whitefield, the revival
leader in England, and Jonathan Edwards, the great
theologian in New England, defended it against
the attack of the Wesley brothers. It is largely to
John Wesley, great man of God though he was,
that we must attribute much of the disfavour into
which the old 'doctrines of grace' fell among evangelicals of the past 200 years. Yet in the 19th cen-

tury, notwithstanding, William Carey and the Baptist Missionary Society, the Church Missionary Society and its earliest promoters, C H Spurgeon and his outstanding preaching ministry, were all products of (call it what you will) the old Augustinian, Reformed, Calvinistic theology of grace. Now, in the second half of the 20th century, we are seeing a recovery of the old apostolic doctrines of grace. In Britain this has been fostered through the pulpit ministry of the late Dr Martyn Lloyd-Jones and the work of the Banner of Truth Trust. A new generation of evangelicals have rediscovered their roots and uncovered the foundations of their apostolic faith.

There has been a widespread unanimity about it in the great *Confessions of Faith* of the historic denominations. The *Thirty-nine Articles* of the Church of England say:

> Predestination to life is the everlasting purpose of God whereby before the foundations of the world were laid, he has constantly decreed, by his counsel, secret to us, to deliver from curse and damnation those whom he has chosen in Christ out of mankind and to bring them by Christ to everlasting salvation (Article 17).

In the Puritan *Westminster Confession of Faith* of the Presbyterian churches the introduction on 'God's eternal decree' reads:

God from all eternity did, by the most wise and holy counsel of his own will, freely and unchangeably ordain whatsoever comes to pass, yet so as thereby neither is God the author of sin nor is violence offered to the will of the creatures, nor is the liberty or contingency of second causes taken away, but rather established; ... those of mankind that are predestined unto life God, before the foundation of the world was laid, according to his eternal and immutable purpose, and the secret counsel and good pleasure of his will, hath chosen in Christ, unto everlasting glory out of his mere free grace and love, without any foresight of faith or good works or perseverance in either of them or any other thing in the creature as conditions or causes moving him thereunto, and all to the praise of his glorious grace.

The *1689 Baptist Confession of Faith* says:

By the decree of God for the manifestation of his glory, some men and angels are predestined or foreordained to eternal life through Jesus Christ, others being left to act in their sin to their just condemnation.

There is a great unity in the historic Confessions and we may feel ourselves to be part of that unity. Our generation is very arrogant intellectually. People seem to think that other ages, former generations, knew nothing. That conceit sometimes can spill over into the church. Christians today can fall into the trap of believing that now they alone have got it together. We must sit, rather, at the feet of age-old teachers, not only the Calvins, the Luthers and the Augustines, but the Pauls and Johns and the Peters, the Isaiahs and Jeremiahs. Through and with them, we must sit at the feet of the One who said: 'I have loved you with an everlasting love; I have drawn you with lovingkindness' (Jeremiah 31:3):

> Loved with everlasting love,
> Led by grace that love to know,
> Spirit, breathing from above,
> *Thou hast taught me, it is so.*

Some questions about election

Q: Do you need to know the exact moment when you became a Christian in order to know that you are elect?

A: No. One person, who did not know the day on which she was saved, had often worried about it. Then she came to see these truths and said: 'Now that I know that I was chosen before the foundation of the world, the exact moment of conscious experience does not seem so important.'

Our present trust in Christ's finished work testifies daily to our election. We do not need to remember the day we were born to know that we are alive.

Q: 'I will have mercy on whom I have mercy' (Romans 9:15) seems to conflict with what Scripture says elsewhere about God's free offers of grace. Who has the ultimate choice?

A: God does and his choice is this: he has chosen not to take 'No' for an answer from his people who are among a race who all said 'No', and whom he knew would keep on saying 'No' until they were in hell. In that sense, he alone makes the ultimate decision.

Q: What does it mean when it speaks of God hardening Pharaoh's heart (Romans 9:19)?

A: It means what it says. It is clear, first of all, that we are not looking at a neutral Pharaoh, any more than we are dealing with a neutral human race. When God is said to 'harden' (either here, or in Isaiah 6, or elsewhere), he envisages man as rebellious, his human heart as *already* hard. And he is judicially 'giving him up', withdrawing his 'common grace' and leaving the sinner unrestrained in sin as in Romans 1. His hardening is not arbitrary, but judicial: a judge's response to a hardness already there. The sinner in question has abandoned his rights and has made himself liable to all sorts of penalty.

So Paul's answer is his abrupt: 'Who are you

to reply against God?' If God does it, it must be right. And God does it in the context of enduring wrong, of being patient with the men ('the just and the unjust') on whom he sends his good gifts of the rain and the sun. All these explanations put the responsibility and the fault of damnation firmly on the shoulders of the sinner, not on the shoulders of God.

Q: Is it a waste of time to pray for people who are not elect?

A: We do not know who the elect are, so we have to go by what God tells us to do. He says: 'Pray.' That is how he gets things done on earth, through his people praying and speaking. I can, therefore, pray with complete confidence that this is what God wants me to do. I do not need to know if the people are elect. I know, on the basis of what God has said, that the chosen method by which he brings people in is by prayer and preaching. Often, when he lays in our paths people who seem interested, it is part of his sovereign working to lead us to pray and so to bring them in. The Lord has destined not only those who will be saved, but also the *means* by which they will be saved. If the Lord lays someone on your heart, that means God may be working in them – and you can pray with even greater expectancy for them.

Q: How does this truth of election relate to our praying for non-Christians?

A: We are commanded to pray for all kinds of men, and can pray for everybody we have ever met or shall meet. Prayer is never wasted, even if the answer is 'No'. First of all, the good of it comes back to us. Secondly, God himself, as old Thomas Goodwin the Puritan, put it, 'keeps it on a file' and may answer it years later. The Puritans who were ejected in 1662 prayed (Oh, those 2,000, how they could pray!) and prayed and prayed for twenty or thirty years, and then died in obscurity. But those prayers were not lost; the great revival under John Wesley and George Whitefield was the result of those prayers. That great outpouring was, in a sense, the outpouring of those great Puritan prayers.

When we come to praying for the unbeliever, we should indeed pray indiscriminately, but also we should learn to pray with a listening ear. Being 'burdened', being moved or guided in prayer is not to be treated lightly. If anything is 'laid on your heart', then you should follow it through. And if, when you are praying, you get a sense of victory in that prayer, then you are understanding the old saying: 'Prayer is the footfall of the divine decree'. The first hint you have of God's secret plan is there in that quiet assurance: 'It is going to happen! I'm sure it's going to happen!' Prayer is an adventure and it is exciting – never wasted, always purposeful. So we should seek guidance in our prayers, to be in line with the will of God.

A woman came to the church I serve whose parents had been godly people. They had prayed for her all her life until they died. Then, fourteen years later, she was converted. God had stored up those prayers in his heart and then poured out his answer 'in the day of his power'.

Q: Can somebody who is not among the elect be saved?

A: The previous chapter contains the answer to that. God knows that apart from election no one will ever receive his offer of life. That is because of the strength of man's opposition to God. The unconverted man is at enmity with God and those who are in the flesh cannot please God (Romans 8:7-8). The natural man cannot understand spiritual things because they are spiritually discerned; they make no sense to him (1 Corinthians 2:14). The god of this world has blinded their minds (2 Corinthians 4:4). They are darkened in their understanding, due to their hardness of heart (2 Timothy 4:17-18). Always the element of responsibility is emphasized. But the inevitability of their negative reaction is obvious; there is no way in which salvation is welcomed, despite all the overtures and encouragements of God.

That was the state of the Jerusalem over which Jesus wept: 'I have longed ... but you were not willing!' (Luke 13:34). Yet John 10:16 perhaps allows us to add as his thought: 'I knew you wouldn't, so now I've chosen sheep from all over the world, to bring them to myself.' This is God refusing to be defeated by the depravity of man. When the real gospel is presented to a person, he is outraged by it, he rejects it: it is 'a stumbling block to Jews and foolishness to Gentiles' (1 Corinthians 1:23). God's response in the case of the non-elect is to leave them (reluctantly and sadly) to their will in the matter. They do, as we saw in the previous chapter, receive grace, but they resist it effectively. That indeed is true of the elect also. But in their case God chose to 'come again', as it were, with the special power of an irresistible grace, which would not take 'No' for an answer. (That will be the subject of chapter four.)

Q: I have heard that since God is in eternity and not time, past, present and future have no meaning with him and that therefore this whole matter is irrelevant and all controversy needless. How would you reply to this?

A: The attempts to oppose time and eternity in this way have been pretty well critiqued by some contemporary theological scholarship. Oscar Cullman wrote a celebrated book *Christ and*

3

A Death to Abolish Death

Roy Clements

Moses died at the age of 120 and the Bible tells us that when he died he was as strong as ever. Buddha died at the age of eighty in peaceful serenity. Right to the end he had been surrounded by a great host of devotees who had been won over to his philosophy. Confucius died at the age of seventy-two. He had had setbacks in his early life, but at the end returned to his home town of Lu and had a great company of noble disciples there to continue his work. Muhammad died at the age of sixty-two, having thoroughly enjoyed the last years of his life as the political ruler of a united Arabia. He passed away, so we are told, in his harem at Mecca in the arms of his favourite wife.

You will sometimes hear people say that the origin of all religions is basically the same. They are all the creation of men of great intellect and spirituality. As the result of their reflection, they each discover some universal religious truth and then spend their lives teaching that truth to others. Eventually they succeed in producing an entire culture round that new insight. As far as Judaism, Buddhism, Confucianism or Islam are concerned, there is obviously a good element of truth in that opinion. All those religions were founded by people who died in ripe old age, having spent their lives teaching what they held. They died amid vast popular acclaim, with the future of their movements guaranteed.

In the whole spectrum of world religions only

one is radically different: Christianity. Jesus died at the age of thirty-three, after a teaching ministry of three years at the most. He was ostracized by his own society, betrayed and denied by his own small circle of supporters, mocked by his opponents, forsaken – even by God himself.

He suffered one of the most ignominious and agonizing forms of public execution ever devised by human imagination. The founder of Christianity did not die in ripe old age, after a lifetime of teaching amid wide popular acclaim. His death was premature, tragic, lonely, on a cross, despised and rejected by man – a man of sorrows and familiar with suffering.

How on earth?

The big puzzle is this: how on earth did a man, who ended his life amid such shame and ridicule, become the founder of the most influential world religion of all? The wonder of this is obscured for us, because we come 2,000 years after; we are used to thinking of the cross as a specifically religious symbol with a certain amount of holiness surrounding it. It has even become an item of jewellery to wear around our necks or an emblem to adorn our church buildings.

In Jesus' own day it was anything but religious or beautiful. It was repulsive, ignominious and offensive. The great Roman orator, Cicero, said that the very name of the cross should never come near the body of a Roman citizen: it should not even enter his thoughts, his sight or his hearing. Yet the early Christians not only admitted that their founder had died in this contemptible manner, they boasted about it. 'May I never boast except in the cross of our Lord Jesus Christ,' said the apostle Paul (Galatians 6:14). 'We preach Christ crucified,' said the early church, though it is 'a stumbling block to Jews and foolishness to Gentiles.' To them it was 'the power of God and the wisdom of God' (1 Corinthians 1:23-24).

What possible significance, then, could that bizarre and shocking death have assumed for them, that turned it from being an unmentionable infamy to a badge of honour? How did the symbol of criminal execution come to adorn Christian buildings and even Christian people? And why? Why did Jesus die? No single question is more important than that. The third chapter of Paul's letter to the Romans gets us off to a good start in answering that question by showing us that it had to do with sin, with human moral failure, and with total depravity. In that chapter he says: 'For all have sinned and fall short of the glory of God, and are justified freely by his grace through the redemption that came by Christ Jesus' (verses 23-24).

'Of course he'll pardon me!'

Many people make a great mistake at this point – people who know a little bit about Christianity,

93

but not enough. They think that it is easy for God to forgive sins: 'Of course he'll pardon me, that's his business.'

But it is not as straightforward as that and it is crucial to see why it isn't. The explanation is all tied up with a phrase that comes several times in Romans 3, but particularly in verse 21: 'a right-eousness from God'. Now *we* can forgive with no difficulty at all, because we are guilty. If we did not forgive people who sinned against us, it would be terrible hypocrisy.

For God it is quite different. First of all, he is morally perfect; that means that sin is a thousand times more offensive to him than it is to us. He is much more sensitive to it. Secondly, and even more importantly, God is the ground of all moral values in this universe. None of us is that, but he is. Take love, for instance.

Everybody agrees that love is better than ha-tred, but why do we believe that? Where does that moral value come from? What gives it substance? Is it just our emotional preference? Is it just a so-cial convention that we have all accepted? Is it an instinct bred into us by our evolutionary origins? No. According to the Bible, love is better than ha-tred because God is love. That is the root of it. It is God's moral character that guarantees moral val-ues and makes them absolutes – things that are true for all of us, whether we agree with them or not.

We can overlook evil and it does not matter too much, but God is not like us. If God overlooks evil, it is as good as saying that evil does not matter – does not matter anywhere, does not matter in the universe at all.

That is an accusation which God cannot allow to pass unchallenged. Put in a single sentence, God's difficulty with forgiveness is this: how do you distinguish forgiveness from moral indifference?

If morality is to be preserved in the universe, it is absolutely necessary that God's righteousness should not only be done, but be seen to be done. In Paul's word, it needs to be 'demonstrated' (Romans 3:25-26). God must in some way dissociate himself personally from evil in the world. He must make a clear stand against it. If he does not, then all morality, standards and values are themselves undermined.

In the role of judge

How can God do that? One very obvious way in which he can do that is to assume the role of judge. He can promulgate a law, defining the moral standards for which he stands. He can translate his own moral character into the imperative, into commands for us. He can then exact penalties from anyone who breaks those laws. That, according to the Bible, is precisely what God does. Under the terms of the old covenant, in the Old Testament, that is what he was doing in what we call the Ten Commandments. He was expressing his moral character in laws and saying that if people do not keep them, they will be punished.

The trouble with that particular demonstration of God's righteousness is that it results in the universal condemnation of the world. As Paul says: 'There is no-one righteous ... every mouth may be silenced and the whole world held accountable to God' as a result of this law (Romans 3:10, 19). As God casts his eyes around the universe, his verdict is: 'There is no-one righteous, not even one.' His demonstrated righteousness becomes his manifested wrath.

That is the central theme of the first three chapters of Romans. It is the difficulty, if we may put it this way, that God is under in seeking and planning to save the world. This sin problem is so deeply embedded in everybody, and the law cannot help.

Any alternative?

Is there an alternative? Is it possible for God's moral character still to be asserted, his righteousness still to be demonstrated, but in some other way? Is it possible that instead of condemning human beings, his justice could actually acquit human beings? That seems impossible because we are guilty. How could God ever treat us as anything other than what we are? Yet Paul's astonishing news is that such an alternative is actually available. 'But now,' he says (notice these words in verse 21: they mark a line that separates history into two great epochs), 'but now' something dramatic has happened, as a result of which it is possible for God still to be fully righteous, and yet at the same time to declare human beings who are sinners righteous. He can be just *and* 'the one who justifies the man who has faith in Jesus' (3:26). 'There is,' he says, 'a righteousness from God apart from law.'

'Apart from law' does not mean that we can learn about it anywhere else except in the Bible. It means that the Bible does not contain this demonstration of God's justice in the same way that it contains the Ten Commandments.

It is not a matter of law. It is not a matter of God standing as judge against sinners. God adopts a different role in this demonstration of his justice.

The focus of this new demonstration of God's righteousness is Jesus. 'This righteousness from God,' he says, 'comes through faith in Jesus Christ to all who believe' (3:22).

This is the central answer we are looking for to the question: why is the death of Jesus so important?

Christians sometimes talk in a rather gory manner about the blood of Christ. And if we have had any knowledge at all of the Christian gospel, we know that blood has something to do with forgiveness, as it says in the children's hymn:

> He died that we might be forgiven,
> He died to make us good;
> That we might go at last to heaven,
> Saved by his precious blood.

Many people have some vague idea of that kind, but the vast majority even of Christian people, have little understanding of precisely how that death of Jesus is connected to forgiveness.

A moral influence?

Many people try to interpret the death of Jesus as if it were just some kind of moral influence on us. That kind of interpretation of the death of Jesus goes back a long way in history, to a man called Peter Abelard. In the Middle Ages he was a considerable theologian. He said that the purpose of Jesus' death on the cross is to move us to love God. That is the way he saves us from our sins. He dies on the cross, he makes a great demonstration of God's love on the cross, and that moves us so much, emotionally, that we want to love God.

A man who came later had a similar theory. Socinius, the founder of the Unitarians, said that the death of Jesus was a moral example. It was the completion of Jesus' perfect obedience to the will of God. According to him, Christ saves us by revealing to us the way we ought to live; the cross, he said, is the final focus of that.

Whether people follow the line of moral influence with Abelard or of moral example with Socinius, they are saying something like this: that as we look at the cross, we feel conscience-stricken about our sin, we realize where we have been going wrong, and we determine to put our lives in order as a result. That is their theory of how the cross works. Christ's death becomes a kind of model of self-sacrificial love, that moves us to be better people or sets a great example to us.

There is a strong element of truth in the view that Christ's death has the power to move our emotions and to be a supreme example to us. Many people have been challenged by its dramatic power, by its exemplary power. There's no doubt about that. But such a view of the death of Jesus is open to major objections.

Moral blackmail

First of all, take the moral influence theory of Peter Abelard. That savours of a particularly vicious form of moral blackmail. Do we really believe that God, faced with a morally rebellious world, would try to manipulate us with emotional levers?

To say that Jesus' death is a moral influence on us reduces his cross to the level of a political prisoner's hunger strike. A hunger strike embarrasses the people who have to watch so much that they are manipulated into doing something – at least, that's the theory. It does not actually achieve anything: it is a gesture, some might even say a rather infantile gesture, certainly a purely histrionic gesture. It does not actually do anything, except to manipulate emotionally those who allow it to happen. It is a kind of moral blackmail. Can we seriously accept that that is what God was doing in Jesus?

Totally irrational

Or take Socinius's view, that the death of Christ is a moral example. That is open to the charge of being totally irrational. Think of it this way. Imagine a boy and a girl, walking along a river bank, in love. The boy says to the girl: 'I love you and to show how much I love you, I'm going to jump into this river and drown.' The girl might be a little perplexed by that. I think the logic would not be transparent to her: 'All right, he loves me and he dies for me, but – well I don't quite see the connection. It doesn't make sense, it's irrational.'

In order to prove love, the loved one must benefit from the dying in some genuine way. It is no good anyone saying, 'I'm setting you an example of my love,' unless some benefit accrues to the loved one as a result of the dying.

If, however, the girl were in the water, drowning, and the boy said, 'I love her. I will dive in and rescue her,' that would make sense. Then we could see the connection between his risking his life and his love for her. Unless there is some clear benefit of that kind coming to the girl as a result of his dying, it is nonsense to talk about an example of love being there in the death.

It is the same with Jesus. Many people cannot understand the cross because in the terms of this illustration, they imagine Jesus walking along hand in hand with them on the river bank. 'Everything's nice in the world because God loves me and isn't it wonderful?' The Bible says the true picture is that we are in the water, perishing, and we need to be rescued. It is only because Christ came to achieve that rescue that we can speak of his death being 'loving'.

Totally subjective

The problem with these views of moral influence or moral example is that they both touch only our feelings. They are totally subjective. They suggest that the purpose of the cross is to change our inward attitude to our sins, and so to move us to some kind of self-reform.

Now, whatever grain of truth about the cross there may be in that, what Paul is talking about in Romans 3 is totally opposite. He is saying there that the cross makes a difference – not to how *we* feel about our sin, but to how *God* feels about our sin.

The cross is not a means of influencing us subjectively or of setting us an example; it is an objective vindication of God's righteousness. He did it, he says, to demonstrate his justice. That is what was going on on the cross. God was demonstrating his justice, in a parallel way to how he demonstrates his justice when he punishes sinners in hell.

His moral indignation against sin *has* to be expressed somehow or else God would leave himself open to the charge of moral indifference. On the cross, instead of asserting his horror at sin by judging *us*, according to his law, God displays that same horror at sin by punishing Jesus in our place. That is what it is all about.

Substitutionary sacrifice

It is this vital truth which Christian theologians have sought to preserve when they speak of the death of Christ as a 'substitutionary sacrifice'. It is not a totally adequate phrase. The cross of Christ has more to it than that; but if we do not grasp the meaning in that phrase, we have not even got to first base in understanding what the cross is about.

Ransoming or redeeming

Three important word groups in the New Testament's teaching about the cross have this idea of substitutionary sacrifice in them. Paul uses two of them in Romans 3. The first word group is 'ransom' or 'redemption'. It occurs in verse 24: 'The redemption that came by Christ Jesus.' The background of that word group is the slave market. It describes a slave, who is released on payment of a price. The money paid for him is, as it were, a substitute for the slave. The man does not have a slave any longer, but he has money instead. So a cost is involved in finding a substitute to release that slave.

Mark 10:45 is an important verse in this connection, coming from the mouth of Jesus himself. It shows that Paul was not proposing his personal speculations in this area, but was taking his lead from Jesus's own understanding of his death. Jesus said: 'Whoever wants to be first must be slave of all. For even the Son of Man did not come to be served, but to serve [to be a slave], and to give his life as a ransom for [literally, *instead of*] many'. A ransom, a redemption-price, instead of many. That is the substitutionary idea. Here is a person who is enslaved; Christ comes as a suffering servant and gives his life instead of that person, so that he or she may go free. That is the meaning of redemption or ransom.

Appeasing anger

Paul uses a second word group: 'propitiation' or 'sacrifice of atonement' (Romans 3:25). The idea is this: if somebody is angry and you appease their anger or avert it, you are said to have propitiated them. You have turned their anger away, so that you no longer feel the heat of it.

That is the force behind the word here. Paul says that God presented Jesus as a propitiation, someone who averts the wrath of God. The meaning is clearly that Christ, as a substitute, bore that wrath himself and so turned it away from us.

Reconciling

The third word group is 'reconciliation' and comes from the area of personal relationships. If our enemy becomes our friend, he is said to have been reconciled to us. In 2 Corinthians 5:20-21, where Paul uses this language, it is clear that a costly substitution is involved in the reconciliation process. Paul says: 'We implore you on Christ's behalf: Be reconciled to God. God made him who had no sin to be sin for us, so that in him we might become the righteousness of God.' There is the exchange, the substitution.

Imagine two little boys learning to write at an old-style school. The teacher says: 'You must finish this script, you must copy out this writing, absolutely perfectly, no mistakes.' One boy does it perfectly – his script is immaculate. The other boy has a few little problems: the pen nib does not work properly, he gets his sleeve in the ink, and by the time he has finished the whole thing is a mess. Before the teacher comes in, the boy with the perfect script gives it to the boy who messed his up, and says: 'Here, that's yours.' Then he takes the marred one out to the teacher as his own and receives the punishment.

That is a very simple picture, but that is what Paul says happened on the cross. There was an exchange. '[God] made him who had no sin to be sin for us, so that in him we might become the righteousness of God.' A substitution takes place, and it is on the basis of that substitution that God's anger is turned away from us, that we are redeemed from the slavery of our sin and that we are bought from its consequences under God's judgment and made God's friends again.

The New Testament presents these three word groups to give us its perspective, from a number of angles, on the same essential truth: that there is a costly substitution going on in the cross, which liberates us from the consequences of our sin and brings us back into a relationship with God, as friend with friend.

Rooted in the Old Testament: Isaiah 53

All those word groups have a fascinating and extensive Old Testament background. Three passages are particularly important. First, Isaiah 53, which is where Jesus found his model of the suffering servant. It is very important to realize that Jesus did not dream this up for himself; he learned it from the Scriptures and was being obedient to what the prophetic passages of the Old Testament taught of his role as Messiah. We hear Jesus say in the gospels: 'The Son of Man *must* be crucified', 'The Son of Man *must* suffer'; and it is this Old Testament passage which lies at the root of that 'must' – the necessity he felt about the cross.

The key verses here are Isaiah 53:4-6: 'He took up our infirmities and carried our sorrows, yet we considered him stricken by God, smitten by him, and afflicted. But he was pierced for our transgressions, he was crushed for our iniquities; the punishment that brought us peace was upon him, and by his wounds we are healed. We all, like sheep, have gone astray, each of us has turned to his own way; and the LORD has laid on him the iniquity of us all.' The prophet was writing that in a situation where Israel was suffering a great deal and asking: 'Why is it happening?' He was looking into the future, to the coming of God's Messiah, and seeing that when Messiah came, people would be asking the same question: 'Why is he suffering? Surely God's Messiah ought to be a person of victory?' This is the paradox: he comes to be the costly substitute for his people's sins, and so he has to be a man of suffering. Isaiah saw that, as Jesus did too.

The Passover: Exodus 12

A second important passage in the Old Testament is very influential on the New Testament's way of describing these facts: Exodus 12 on the Passover. After the Jews had been enslaved in Egypt, Moses performed a number of miracles at God's instruction to try and persuade Pharaoh to let them go. Pharaoh would not. Finally, the crunch came: the last plague was going to be particularly devastating. All the firstborn children were going to perish in a single night, when the angel of death swept through the land.

The key to this event is in verses 12 and 13:

'On that same night I will pass through Egypt and strike down every firstborn – both men and animals – and I will bring judgment on all the gods of Egypt. I am the LORD. The blood will be a sign for you on the houses where you are; and when I see the blood, I will pass over you. No destructive plague will touch you when I strike Egypt.' The blood there is the blood of a lamb; they were instructed to take and kill a lamb and to smear the blood on their doorposts, so that it would be a sign for them.

On the face of it, the Passover seems complicated. We might think that if God wanted to distinguish the fate of the Egyptians from that of the Israelites, he might do it in a straightforward way, on ethnic grounds. Why all this ritual – especially when God is omniscient and does not need a red mark on the doors to identify the houses of Jews?

The answer is that this is not a simple example of racial discrimination. The Jews could not escape the judicial execution that God had planned simply because they were Jews. That is the whole point, for in their own way they had been just as obstinate and unbelieving as anybody else in that land. God could be as justly angry with them as with the Egyptians. Yet, of course, they were his elect people, the ones to whom he had made the promise. How could God be faithful to those promises and yet wipe them out in the way that he was planning? If justice demanded that the Jews be punished too, surely there was no alternative but to include them in this appalling holocaust.

That is where the surprise comes in. That is where the experience of Passover develops the meaning of the words of the Old Testament and provides a searchlight on the New. God does not pretend that the Israelites are innocent; such a verdict would be contrary to truth. Neither does he issue some cheap, blanket decree of pardon that would make a mockery of his own righteousness. Instead, he makes a provision, which would avert the judgment when it fell, for any who had faith to appropriate it. 'Each man is to take a lamb for his family, one for each household' (Exodus 12:3) – but what difference did the lamb make?

It is not hard to see, once we imagine the situation as they experienced it. Inside every Egyptian home that morning there was a dead son; inside every Jewish home there was a dead lamb. What conclusion would they draw from that? The obvious one, surely, was that the lamb died in place of the son. The passage goes on to impress this, saying that there must be a precise equivalent between the number of families and the number of lambs. Why? Because each lamb represented that family's firstborn son; each lamb substituted for that family's firstborn son; each lamb bore the judicial penalty of death that night instead of that family's firstborn son.

Every surviving eldest Jewish boy could say

that night, with indelible conviction: 'That lamb died for me.' When the angel of death came through, and saw the blood, it was a marker that in that home a death had *already* occurred and that God's justice had been satisfied as far as that family was concerned. It was not just an ethnic marker of the Jews. It was a marker of people who had taken God's word and believed it as far as the substitution of the lamb was concerned.

The day of atonement: Leviticus 16

One more passage in the Old Testament is vital in this whole framework of substitution: Leviticus 16, about the Day of Atonement. This also is an Old Testament ritual of immense significance, because it was the one day in the year when the sins of the Jewish people were ceremonially taken away. The way it happened was this: the High Priest had to take the blood of an animal, to carry it inside the temple, inside the tabernacle as it was in the wilderness, into the Holy of Holies. That was the very dark place which no one could enter, except the High Priest once a year. There he had to sprinkle the blood of the animal on the Mercy Seat – the gold covering of the Ark, the big box where they kept the Ten Commandments, which was kept in that holy place. We may well wonder what all that ritual was about.

The key to it is to realize that the blood was sprinkled there, in the sanctuary which symbolized God's presence. It was taken into a place which nobody else could see. Even the High Priest would have had a hard job to see anything there, because the place was in almost total darkness. It had no windows in it, it was a place of deep mystery. That blood had to be sprinkled in God's presence. It is terribly important to realize that the blood was there for *God* to see. In fact, the same point is made in the Passover: 'When *I* see the blood...' (Exodus 12:13).

This points to the fact that this blood is not working a subjective change in the people. It is not changing the way they feel about their sins. Maybe it is doing that as well, but that is not its principal purpose. The point of that blood is for *God* to see it, because it makes a difference to him. That is the purpose of the ritual. A death has occurred. Satisfaction to God's justice has been offered. Once again comes this thought of costly substitution – an animal having to die in order for God to be able to pardon his people.

Again and again throughout the Old Testament we find this idea of substitution. Again and again we find New Testament references to these three key things. The *suffering servant* of Isaiah occurs, for instance, in 1 Peter 2, as well as many other places. The *Passover lamb*, of course, is at the centre of the Lord's Supper. It was a Passover supper that Jesus celebrated when the holy communion began. He did not take a lamb from the table, as was happening in every other Jewish home, he took bread from the table and said: 'This is *my* body ... this is *my* blood.' He offered himself to them as the Passover lamb. And the *Day of Atonement* occurs very much in the letter to the Hebrews, as the way into understanding the meaning of the death of Christ.

Whatever word group we take, whatever Old Testament passage we read, the New Testament homes in constantly on this thought: that the death of Jesus was a substitution which makes a difference to the way God sees our sins. Christ took on himself the damnation that was ours and suffered in our place.

Why did Jesus shrink from the cross?
That, of course, is why Jesus shrank from the cross – an observation that ought to strike us as most surprising. After all, many Christians have gone to their deaths singing hymns, rejoicing. Jesus went to his death in a state of gloom, despair and deep sorrow, spending a whole night before it immersed in depression about it all. 'My Father, if it is possible, may this cup be taken from me' (Matthew 26:39). Was Jesus a worse Christian than some of his followers? Could he not die more happily? His death, however, was a different death. His was a death no Christian has to die, for what he saw when he looked in that cup was our sin.

One objection is always raised against this argument that the Bible's way of seeing the death of Jesus is as a substitution for sinners – namely, that it is unfair. Surely it is grossly unjust for God to take an innocent person and punish him for all the sins of all of us?

Think back to that illustration of the two boys learning to write. Maybe you thought: 'Well, I'd consider it very unjust if they did that to my son – punished him for another child's mistakes. It would be scandalously unjust.' That is a fair and strong point, but it has a weakness which is simply this: when we look at Jesus, we are not seeing a third party as far as God is concerned. There are not three parties, only two: God – and us. Jesus was God on the cross. God was not punishing somebody else. That is why it had to be Jesus. He could not take a perfect angel and place the sin of the world on him. He could not even look around for a perfect man and make him the sin-bearer of the world. That *would* have been unfair. What God is doing on the cross is bearing our sins *himself*, so that Paul can say: 'God was in Christ reconciling the world to himself.'

Take another illustration. Imagine a married couple. Their marriage is going through a bad time and the husband decides that he wants to leave home. One day he walks out on her and goes off to sow his wild oats. In six months' time he comes back again. There he is on the doorstep; he says to his wife: 'I'd like to come back. I've changed my mind. I want to come home.' Think yourself into that wife's position: how does she react?

It seems to me there are only three ways in which she can react. She can say: 'I never want to see you again. Get out of my life.' She could probably say that in all justice. It would be perfectly just for her to say: 'Get lost.' But if she really loved that man, I don't think she would say that, would she? She wants him back. So 'Get lost' might satisfy justice, but it doesn't satisfy her love.

A second possibility would be for her to say: 'Well, yes, come in if you want. What do I care whether you come in or not? It makes no difference to me.' I cannot hear her saying that, not if her love is real. It does make a difference to her, for she has been grossly offended by what has happened, has been torn to pieces by it. She cannot say that she is indifferent. If there were indifference, there would be no love. That leaves only one other option.

If there is to be a reconciliation, the only way is if she says to that man standing on the doorstep: 'OK, you may come in. But you've got to realize how much you've hurt me.' Unless he realizes, deeply, how much he has hurt her by his sin against their marriage, there's no real possibility of reconciliation between them. No possibility of forgiveness. No possibility of beginning again. He must realize the seriousness of what he's done and how much it has wounded her.

The agony of sin to a moral God

That is exactly what God is saying to us in the cross: 'Your sins hurt me. You want to know how much they hurt me? Look at the cross and you'll see.' On the cross we see the Godhead stripped open, we see demonstrated the agony which the sin of the world is to a moral God. He did this to *demonstrate* his justice. No one can say to God, when he forgives you and me: 'God, you're being morally indifferent, letting that person go free. You don't care about his sin, do you?' God points to the cross. He says: 'I do care. That's how much I care. It's true that, in my patience, I have left sins unpunished. But that mercy I exercise toward men and women doesn't impugn my justice, because I have demonstrated that justice to the shock of men and angels. I have come down among men and borne the punishment they deserved, myself.'

That is why the cross is neither moral blackmail nor an irrational gesture. The cross is the place where God makes forgiveness, where he makes reconciliation, where he enables himself to be the justifier of sinful people.

God wants us to understand that the cross was an act of substitution on the part of Jesus for sinful men and women.

For whom did he die?

Now to the crunch question. For whom did Christ die in that way? If we had been satisfied with the moral example or the moral influence theory of the cross, there would be no problem. We could say: 'He died for everybody, he sets everybody an example. He has his moral influence on everyone.' That is because those theories make it all subjective. We have seen, however, that that does not do justice to what the New Testament says. There is an objective benefit in the cross for men and women. He is a substitutionary sacrifice *for* men and women there, not just an influence in them or on them.

May we then affirm, 'Christ died for everybody', when we are thinking about the substitutionary nature of the cross? We can quickly see that we cannot, for a very simple reason: hell is not empty. If Jesus died as a substitute for every man and woman in this world, God could not justly condemn any. He cannot and will not exact punishment for sin twice, which is what he would have to do if Christ took their punishment and then they had to suffer it as well. What kind of a universal redemption is it, if some are still in slavery? What kind of a universal propitiation is it, if some are still under God's wrath? What kind of a universal reconciliation is it, if some are still counted God's enemies?

That is our problem in arguing for a universal atonement or a universal death of Christ, once we have recognized its substitutionary character. The consequence of that is that everybody is actually saved – that is, universalism. Yet the New Testament makes it clear that hell is not empty. Nice as it would be to say to the world, 'Hell *is* empty,' we may not.

Two alternatives

What then are we to conclude? John Owen, in his famous book *The Death of Death in the Death of Christ*, points out that there are only two genuine alternatives. The first is that something is lacking in the death of Christ, which we human beings have to make up for ourselves. Those who succeed in making it up therefore go to heaven, and those who fail to make it up go to hell. That is why hell is not empty. Something is missing in the death of Christ, which human beings have to make up for themselves. If that is not right, we can come to only one other conclusion: Namely, that in the intention and purpose of God, when he thought this all out before the foundation of the world, Jesus' death on the cross was a substitutionary sacrifice not for everybody, but for a particular company, those whom the Bible often calls his chosen or 'elect'.

It is only to the Bible that we can go for help in sorting out which of those two is right. Take the tenth chapter of John's Gospel, for example, verses 14 to 16: 'I am the good shepherd; I know my sheep and my sheep know me – just as the Father knows me and I know the Father – and I lay down my life for the sheep. I have other sheep that are not of this sheep pen. I must bring them also.'

Jesus is talking specifically about his death and who it is for. He says it is for his sheep. Who are his sheep? Everybody? Talking to some of the Jews there, he said (verse 26): 'You do not believe because you are not my sheep.' We need to notice which way round he puts it. He does not say: 'You are not my sheep because you do not believe.' He says: 'You do not believe because you are not my sheep. My sheep listen to my voice; I know them, and they follow me. I give them eternal life, and they shall never perish.' When he talks here about his sheep, Jesus is distinguishing between two groups of people before him – those who are in his flock, and those who are not. And he says: 'I lay down my life for my sheep.'

The New Testament never speaks of Jesus dying simply to make salvation *possible*. The New Testament speaks about Christ dying actually to *secure* salvation for God's people, for the church.

Of course, there are any number of references where Christ's death is predicated of 'the world', or where we read that Christ died 'for all'. We must not deny or doubt that there are universal dimensions in the death of Christ.

Sometimes, when that phrase is used, 'he died for all', the passage is stressing the fact that Christ died for all types of people, all races of people, all classes of people, as distinct from just the Jews – which is what a lot of them would instinctively have thought. He died for everyone – all nations.

Sometimes when the New Testament speaks of Christ dying for all or dying for the world, it is stressing the fact that there is no limit to the power of Christ's death to forgive – it is sufficient for all men. Even if it is not *applied* to all men, it is *sufficient* for them. However, it is the *design* that God had in the death of Jesus that we are talking about here, not the worth of Christ's sacrifice.

Sometimes when it talks about Christ dying for the world or for all men, the Bible is making the point that there is no limit on the free offer of the gospel. In a true sense God desires all men to be saved, just as in a true sense God desires all men to be perfectly righteous. But God does not always decree that which he prescribes. God prescribes the remedy of Christ's atoning work for everybody, but it is part of the mystery of his eternal purpose that he does not apply Christ's atoning work to everybody.

Sometimes when the Bible speaks about Christ's death for all or for the world, it is hinting to us that there is a cosmic significance in Jesus' death. The angels are involved. Nature is involved. The whole universe is involved in this death on the cross, not just us. It is much bigger than just ourselves. It involves the cosmos.

But however we understand those references which speak of Christ dying for all or for the world, we cannot get away from those references where

the death of Jesus is described as definite or particular. 'Particular redemption' or 'limited atonement' are valid attempts to describe the truth that
Christ's work is effective for his sheep, his church.
Perhaps they now sound too negative, even miserly,
to do justice to the positive results of the cross. 'I
gave my life a ransom for many,' Christ says. Who
are the 'many'? It is the 'many' of Isaiah 53 –
God's people, God's elect.

Not a popular truth

We cannot pretend that this is a popular truth. The
whole idea of 'limited' atonement sounds narrow.

C H Spurgeon pointed out last century, however, that the people who actually limit the cross
of Christ are not those who hold this view, but the
other view. The Bible affirms that Christ's death
made certain the salvation of a great company that
no man can number. The other view is that Christ's
death made salvation possible for everybody, but
certain for nobody. In that case we have to imagine Jesus going up to heaven after he had died,
wringing his hands in anxiety in case his death
were all for nothing. If he had nobody specific in
mind when he died, there was no certainty in what
he did. In that case we destroy those two truths set
out in the first two chapters of this book.

We can no longer talk about 'unconditional
election', because this 'universal' view about the
cross makes salvation conditional on something

human beings add. We can no longer talk about 'total depravity', because man cannot be fully helpless, since there has to be this extra bit he makes up for himself in order to be saved. In fact we can no longer talk about assurance, because it is no longer a sufficient ground for my hope of heaven that Jesus died for me – according to this other view he died for many people who will perish, and I might be one of them.

It makes a big difference
What we believe on all this is not a matter of splitting hairs. It makes a great difference to the way we witness or preach. When I present the gospel on the basis of a definite atonement I can offer an all-powerful Jesus, who has accomplished salvation for sinners and offers it to them. If I present a 'universal' gospel I can only (if I am consistent), preach a rather pathetic Jesus, who is knocking wistfully on the doors of men's hearts like a salesman. Instead of preaching a total abandonment of self and a repudiation of all form of human merit, I would have to tell people: 'Look Jesus has done a great deal, but you've got to do just this bit to make it work.' Instead of talking about 'being rescued' in and from a state of hopelessness, I would have to start talking about 'making a decision' and 'committing yourself', as if people have something to contribute to their own salvation.

That, of course, means that when they get to

heaven, they can sit there with their hands in their pockets and say: 'Of course, you know why I'm up here, don't you? *I* believed, you see. Oh yes, Jesus did a tremendous lot. I'm not taking away from that. I wouldn't be here without him. But if I hadn't believed, I'd be down there with them. I did the extra bit. That's why I'm here.' In that case there would be boasting in heaven. We could feel a touch of pride – I believed, they didn't. That entirely misunderstands the nature of faith. It turns faith into a good thing we do, the merit of which earns us salvation. That is not the way the New Testament speaks about faith.

The cross and our worship

There is a still more important aspect of all of this, however. The way we see the death of Jesus, whether as a particular redemption or not, makes a radical difference to our worship. We began by seeing that Jesus' death has had a phenomenal impact. Moses, Buddha, Confucius, Muhammad – they were all great and admirable men, all of them. Why is Jesus' death so much more important than theirs?

It is all tied up with that verse: 'the Son of God, who loved me and gave himself for me' (Galatians 2:20). It is because Christians down through the ages have been captivated by that – 'he loved *me* and gave himself for *me*' – that the death of Jesus has the power it does in our lives. Yet that kind of testimony is only possible if you see the death of Christ as directed in God's purposes not just to men in general, but to 'me' in particular.

Questions on the death of Christ

Q: If God planned to save only a certain number, did he not fail? Did he not lose the rest to Satan?

A: The opposite is true. We can speak about God failing *only* if he intends or plans to do something, and fails to achieve it. We do not know why God did not plan to save everybody, but the Bible is clear that this is the case. If he had purposed the salvation of everybody and yet not all were saved, then he would have failed – the cross would have failed.

In fact, the view of the cross that sees Jesus as just making salvation *possible* – rather than as actually accomplishing it – opens up the possibility that it could have been a total failure, with no one saved at all. On that view we might all have said to God: 'No, thank you very much.' The truth is the other way round. We magnify the greatness of God in achieving his *purpose*. We may puzzle and wonder why his purpose was not different, and that is a dilemma; yet there is a limit to the type of questions we mortals may ask God. We may want to ask: 'Well, God, I understand what you purposed and I see you achieved it. But why didn't you purpose something else?' We may not ask such a question without being impertinent.

Q: The Bible says Christ died for sin, but did he die only for some sins (those of the elect) and leave out the others?

A: One very important dimension of the cross is that Jesus substituted himself for the sins of individual men and women. That is how God justifies them; he is able, without imperilling his own justice, to forgive those people, because his anger against their sins has been demonstrated against Jesus rather than against them. That is the effect, the logic of the cross. The substitutionary work of Jesus was for the sins – all the sins – of some men. Other sins were left out of that equation, the sins which take those outside Christ to hell.

Certainly there are some texts in the Bible which speak of Christ overcoming sin – as it were with a capital 'S' – sin almost personalized. The cross has cosmic dimensions in terms of conflict with Satan and overcoming Evil, with a capital 'E'. Those universal dimensions to the cross relate to Christ's conflict with Satan, Sin and Death. They do not obliterate this other, central dimension of the cross for us as individuals because the question is: whose side are we on, Christ's or Satan's, in that conflict? It is not Satan alone who falls under

Christ's victory on the cross. It is everybody who is on his side.

The individual and the cosmic are not two conflicting models or ways of understanding the cross. When Christ dies as our substitute, he dies also as our victor over Satan. And he dies to build a new world from which Evil and Sin and Death will be excluded. There is an entire new universe implicit in what Christ has done. All agree on that, but it is those for whom he died as substitute who have a place in that new universe – not everybody without exception. So some sins are left out of that victory, the sins of those who are outside Christ, together with the devil and all his angels, who are punished in hell. That is the message of the book of Revelation: 'Christus victor' reigns with his saints.

Q: If some sins were not included in the atonement, was it really sufficient?

A: We must not confuse sufficiency with efficiency. To be absolutely accurate, some sins are excluded from the substitutionary *purpose* of God. Christ was not substituting himself for all the sins of all the world, or else everybody would be saved. Some sins are outside that substitutionary purpose. But the work of Christ's death is *sufficient*; had God purposed to save the world, he would not have had to have a second cross to make up enough atoning blood. The sufficiency is there to save the sins of the world, if God had so purposed. That brings us back to his purpose, but there is no doubt that Christ's blood was sufficient for all sin.

Q: How does John 3:16 (so loved the world) relate to election?

A: One difficulty is that we all come to this verse and understand 'world' in a universal, statistical, numerical sense – i.e. the world's population through all the centuries. We need to look at the way John uses the word 'world', because the term can have more than one meaning in Scripture. Sometimes it means the inhabited universe, sometimes this present age and its moral aversion to God.

So how is John using the word through his gospel? The basic meaning of it in John 3:16 (in Jim Packer's phrase) is: 'For God so loved bad men everywhere'. Christ came for bad men, sinners. He loved them everywhere, indiscriminately, regardless of class, education, money, language, previous religion or anything else. (Jesus is speaking there to Nicodemus, a member of the Jewish ruling council, and is making the point that it is not just Jews who will be saved.) He loved bad men everywhere in such a way that whoever believes in him will not perish, but have everlasting life. He is saying that something of value is available to bad men everywhere. Therefore we can go with confidence to a 'bad man' and tell him that, if he believes, he will be saved.

That does not take away from the fact that only those whom the Father gives will come to Jesus or that none can come unless he is drawn. This verse gives full justice to the universal element in the atonement, but homes in on those who believe. We can tell people to repent and believe in the full knowledge that sinners everywhere will come. John 3:16 defines God's love as actually *giving* life to those who would otherwise perish. Others, as verse 20 says, do evil and hate the light and *will* not come. God is benevolent to all, but love in the Calvary sense is love that actually saves.

Q: Does not 1 Timothy 2:6 seem to say that Christ Jesus gave himself as a ransom for *all* men?
A: In the earlier part of that chapter Paul is urging people to pray for all kinds of people (for kings and those in authority), that we may live peaceful and quiet lives. He is envisaging prayer for society. He wants it to be ordered in such a way that there is peace and order, so that (among other things) the church can function. He is thinking about all kinds of people; every type of person who makes up society. He is saying that we can confidently pray for all in authority,

etc., because God ransoms all kinds of people (God obviously did not ransom all, or all would be in heaven). In this whole matter we do well to concentrate on the verbs – to save, to redeem, to give as a ransom, to be a sacrifice of atonement or to be a propitiation. They all mean what they say – that he saved, redeemed, etc., and did not merely make salvation possible. All the verbs used about atonement are definite; none of them says 'possibly', 'perhaps', 'maybe'...

Q: Are we not in danger of trying to explain away a text like Romans 5:18 ('justification that brings life for all men')?

A: This verse sees a parallel between Adam (and death) and Christ (and life). Adam did not by sin provide the possibility of death; he brought it about. So Christ did not die merely to bring the possibility of salvation – he secured it. The problem is in the two words 'All' - all in Adam, all in Christ. If Paul means the universal 'All' in both parts of the verse, then we have to conclude that all men will be saved. In that case, the text proves too much, for clearly not all are saved. The only alternative is that when Paul uses the word 'all' he is not speaking in terms of *all* men numerically, but of every type of person. Christ's death was not for one group out of humanity, in a social, financial, ethnic or educational sense, as a Jew might easily have thought. (When I say: 'Everyone come into the room for coffee', I do not mean the *whole* world! I have a particular setting in my mind. The same applies here.)

Q: What about the good shepherd who would leave the ninety-nine sheep in search of the one?

A: The point of that parable is that he *does* find the one. He does not just stand there wistfully wishing. He comes to 'seek and *save* the lost', not to seek and then make *possible* the salvation of those who are willing to co-operate.

Q: Is God unjust in punishing people and sending them to hell?

A: Not at all, because that is what all deserve. Paul asks and answers this very question in Romans 9:14. We labour under the liberal, humanist misconception that we are the measure of all things; we have to be humbled into realizing that we are creatures and that God does not owe us anything, even explanations. It is hard for us to bite that particular bullet, but that is what Paul is saying. We are creatures and God is God, the Creator. Indeed, God is magnified even in judgment. Far from seeing hell as God's failure, Paul sees hell as a triumph. It demonstrates God's righteousness (that evil is punished), even though the love of God has found another way to demonstrate it for his people.

A DEATH TO ABOLISH DEATH

Q: How does this affect our evangelism?

A: If I believe that Jesus's cross made up about ninety per cent of the way of salvation, and that anybody could be saved so long as they made up the additional ten per cent, I could never rest or have any peace. I would think: 'If only I could persuade them a bit better, if only I could manipulate them emotionally a bit more strongly, then maybe they'd make that ten per cent up and get saved.' I would be in a constant fever of anxiety as an evangelist, feeling that in the end it was all up to me. If I did not preach well, then people would go away saying: 'I'm not going to make up the ten per cent.' It would be all my fault for being such a pathetic preacher.

But thank God, that is not the way it is. My task as an evangelist (whether publicly or personally) is that of declaring to people the grounds on which they may come to salvation and assurance. I do this indiscriminately, *universally*, because that is what Jesus says I am to do – 'to all creation' (Mark 16:15). He does not tell me his secret plans. I do not know who is elect or who is not. He tells me to tell everybody and to declare to them that salvation is offered in this man, Jesus. When I see faith being generated under the word, when I see people coming to faith, I do not pat myself on the back, and say: 'That must have been a good sermon. You persuaded them really well there,

129

Clements.' I say to myself: 'Thank God. Here is a sheep hearing the Master's voice.' That is what Jesus said: 'My sheep listen to my voice' (John 10:27).

When I see somebody else who turns a cold shoulder and walks away, I do not crumple up inside and say: 'It's all your fault, Clements, for being such a terrible preacher.' I will seek to love them and win them. But people walked away from Jesus, and he said to them: 'You are not of my sheep.' Those truths make that kind of difference; they give the Christian and the preacher genuine confidence. This is the only reason why a true evangelist in a hard place keeps going.

What if you believed that it was all up to you (or up to them), because 'you've got to persuade them'? If you were in a place like Arabia, where you never saw a convert for thirty years, you would give up, wouldn't you? You would say: 'This is hopeless. I'm never going to get anywhere.' We must remember how God spoke to Paul in Corinth: 'Keep on speaking ... because I have many people in this city' (Acts 18:9-10).

That's the certainty, that's the logic: because God has got his people, preaching is bound to be effective, and we are on the winning side. There will be results, though they may take a long time to mature, though sometimes we will feel like Jeremiah, alone in the land. This confidence that God has his people will secure and encourage us, even when we may be going through a very unproductive period in terms of visible results. This is an incentive to evangelism.

Q: Why preach or witness, if the elect are going to be saved anyway?

A: The motive when we share the gospel is that they will be saved. But there's a higher motive: the glory of God. In no way is God more glorified in this world than through the salvation of his people, the accomplishment of the great pre-creation plan, the demonstration of his grace (Ephesians 1:6, 12-13). The extraordinary thing is that God has involved you and me in that purpose.

Paul does have a great desire for the lost (as in Romans 9:3), but what drove him to evangelism was not primarily the lostness of the lost. It was his wonder at the plan of salvation in Christ, and that he had been made a 'fellow-worker' in that. So he says: 'I planted the seed, Apollos watered it, but God made it grow' (1 Corinthians 3:6). That's the way he thought about evangelism. 'I and Apollos – we're nothing, but only God.' But if we do not believe that it is ultimately God who gives growth, we will become a mass of neuroses. We must be

4

An Offer You Can't Refuse

Roy Clements

Why is it that some people manage to believe things that others find utterly incredible? In the upside-down world of *Through the Looking-Glass* it seems that faith is all a matter of effort. Lewis Carroll's White Queen says that you can believe anything, if only you try hard enough, if 'you draw a long breath, and shut your eyes'. But on this side of the looking-glass we, like Alice, know that it is not so simple.

There is all the difference in the world between faith and mere wishful thinking. To fail to observe such a distinction is to confuse reality with fantasy. Holding your breath and shutting your eyes is not to believe – it is to make-believe. And, by definition, anything you have to make yourself believe cannot be real. For reality constrains belief effortlessly. As Alice puts it, 'There's no use trying, one can't believe impossible things.'

Yet, of course, Christians do. That is the mystery. Viewed in the cold, dispassionate light of reason, Christians believe in quite the most extraordinary things that it is possible to conceive – God coming down to live as a man. Alice could be excused for calling it impossible. Yet the Christian does not feel that he is *forcing* himself to believe it. He is not playing a game of 'let's pretend'. No self-hypnosis is involved. He believes under the constraint of what he feels to be the truth. How do Christians do it? It cannot be that they are just plain gullible. Some are pretty naive and credulous, but it won't wash to portray them *all* as dimwits or dupes. No, there's an enigma here, the enigma of faith. Some people have it, others haven't. The question we must ask is: 'Why?'

John 6 sheds light on it. At the very end of this long discourse or conversation Jesus says: 'There are some of you who do not believe' (verse 64). Some in that crowd listening to Jesus did not believe. On the other hand, Peter speaks on behalf of the disciples and says: 'We believe and know that you are the Holy One of God' (verse 69). So others there did believe. We must therefore seek the explanation for this division in Jesus's audience.

Why this division?

It is not hard to find. Jesus tells us, not just once, but three times in this passage. He reiterates it in slightly different ways. First, he says: 'You have seen me and still you do not believe. All that the Father gives me will come to me' (verses 36-37). Then: 'Stop grumbling among yourselves,' he says to these unbelievers. 'No-one can come to me unless the Father who sent me draws him' (verses 43-44). Finally he adds: 'There are some of you who do not believe.' Jesus had known from the beginning which of them did not and would not believe, and who would betray him. He went on to say: 'This is why I told you that no-one can come to me unless the Father has enabled him' (verses 64, 65).

Now those three statements of Jesus all set forth the teaching that theologians have called the doctrine of 'irresistible grace' or 'effectual calling'. Let me illustrate with a story I once heard from Dr Jim Packer (whose paperback *Evangelism and the Sovereignty of God* I also strongly recommend).

Headfirst into the water

He tells of how, when he was a student in Oxford, he had once gone punting on the river – and had fallen headfirst into the Thames. It was not, he said, a pleasant experience, because a mass of thick weeds entangled his legs and arms, and the water was very deep. For quite some time he was seriously afraid that he was going to drown; he just could not get to the river bank. He went on to imagine what his fellow students (who were safe and dry, still in the punt) might have said.

One might have said, as Packer gurgled away in the water: 'Oh, you'll be all right, Jim. You can get out if you want to. Just keep struggling.' A second might have said: 'Oh, I'd like to help you. But you see I've got this problem of conscience about interfering with anybody's free will. I can give you some tips about swimming if you like.'

Those two imagined reactions parallel two of the responses to Christ's work of salvation that history has thrown up. One is called Pelagianism, the other Arminianism – and they are both around today. Pelagians and Arminians both believe that the work of Jesus is very, very important; we cannot be saved without it. But they both also believe that if the work of Jesus is going to be effective in our lives, if it is going to be applied to us personally, then we have to make a little contribution of our own. The work of Jesus is not sufficient to save me on its own. I have to contribute something to get the work of Jesus out there on Calvary over here into my heart. And that contribution is *faith*.

'We all have the ability or the grace'

Pelagianism says that we all have the ability to believe in Christ's work of salvation if we want to, just by nature. Every human being has that natural ability. It is akin to the White Queen telling Alice: 'You can believe if only you practise a bit more. You've got it in you, Alice.'

Arminianism is slightly different. Arminianism agrees that we need supernatural help to respond to the gospel, but it says: 'God gives that help to everybody. It's just up to us whether we accept and use that help or not.' That is rather like the White Queen offering advice. Because God won't inter-fere with 'free will', he's still dependent on our *choosing* to respond to him. That is the element in both Arminianism and Pelagianism that we need to note. One way or the other, they are both say-ing: 'If you want to be saved, try harder. It is self-effort that will get you to the shore. You must choose, you must exert your will, you must try.'

That, however, leaves the question of what we do when, like poor Jim Packer, we're drowning and our strongest self-effort is not enough. As Alice says: 'It's no use trying, one can't believe impossible things.' What do you reply to someone who says to you: 'I'd like to be a Christian, but I just can't believe it'?

An actual rescue
Packer pursues his illustration a little further. When he actually fell in the river, he was immensely glad that the people in the punt were neither Pelagians nor Arminians, but Calvinists. What actually happened was that a friend of his jumped into the river, overcame his helpless struggles, pulled him free of the reeds, brought him to shore, gave him artificial respiration – and put him back on his feet. 'That,' said Jim Packer, 'is what I call a rescue.'

According to John 6, that is what Jesus calls a rescue too. He is not content to say: 'Well, I'll do this much. But you've got to do that bit.' He is fully aware of the insuperable obstacles that prevent sinful men and women from believing on him as the bread of life. Yet he's not discouraged by that, because he knows that salvation is not a matter of self-effort – not ten percent, not even one per cent. It is all a matter of grace, irresistible grace. This grace, he says, *draws* men and women; gently, with the wooing magnetism of a lover, not the brutality of a rapist (verse 44). It enables men and

139

women to come to him, giving them what they need to engage with Christ, illuminating their minds to understand him, renewing their affections to love him, liberating their wills to move to him (verse 65). Grace, so that they do not have to make themselves believe, but embrace Christ by faith spontaneously, intuitively, effortlessly, irresistibly.

'I confess that God is God'

That, I suggest, is actually the way it happens. C S Lewis's autobiography *Surprised by Joy*, has a lovely section which speaks to my heart because it is very much the way in which I was converted. Lewis tells how he fought tooth and nail against the idea of becoming a Christian. But then, he says, there was one night when it came to the crunch for him; he knelt down in his room at Magdalen College in Oxford: 'I gave in, and admitted that God was God.' He added, 'The Prodigal Son at least walked home on his own feet. But who can duly adore that love which will open the high gates to a prodigal who is brought in kicking, struggling, resentful, and darting his eyes in every direction for a chance of escape?' Those words in the parable, 'Compel them to come in', were sweet words to him, because that is how he experienced it. There was an irresistibility about God's grace.

Now we must be careful not to misunderstand the word 'irresistible'. We must not think that God coerces, brutalizes or dehumanizes us in the act of conversion. Quite the opposite. A moving incident in the Bible shows that this irresistible grace of God is gracious as well as being grace. It is the story of Lydia (Acts 16). She was a dealer in purple cloth, a business woman, a sophisticated lady from the city of Thyatira. We read: 'The Lord opened her heart to respond to Paul's message' (verse 14). Notice the gentleness of that description: 'He opened her heart.'

Which side is the handle?

Evangelistic speakers often speak as if the door handle to our hearts were on the inside. They talk about *us* opening *our* hearts; it is not wrong to do that, in the sense that that is what it often *feels* like. But when Luke is inspired by the Holy Spirit to express it, he does not say: 'Lydia opened her heart' to respond to the gospel. He says: 'The Lord opened her heart.' That is the way round it is, for that is where the initiative really lies. The handle is on the outside and the Lord opens it. Our hearts are locked tight against the gospel by nature. It is not just that we do not want to open our hearts to Christ; we could not, even if we wanted to. 'No one can come to me,' said Jesus, 'unless the Father who sent me draws him' (John 6:44). Yet there is nothing brutal, nothing cruel, about this opening of the heart.

This is how C H Spurgeon put it:

> When you see a casket wrenched open, the hinges torn off, the clasp destroyed, then you discern at once the hand of a thief. But when you observe a casket deftly and smoothly opened, with a master key, you discern the hand of the owner.

In the same way, he says, conversion isn't a violent wrenching open of the heart, in which the will and the reason and the judgment are all ignored or crushed. God does not plunder human lives; that is the devil's way. God opens hearts, not like a beast his prey, but as the owner his own treasure. He comes to us as the Creator to his own creature and deals with the human heart according to its inner nature. God does not enslave the will, he frees it. He does not blind the reason, he enlightens it.

That is what we mean when we talk about irresistible grace or effectual calling. We mean that Jesus does not just abandon his work for us to accept or reject it as we will. He actually applies that work to men's hearts. This is the particular role of the Holy Spirit in the plan of salvation. God the Father planned the work of Salvation; Jesus the Son accomplished it; and it is the distinctive work of the Holy Spirit to apply it to our hearts, to make it real to us individually. And we must never, never steal that prerogative from the Holy Spirit.

Is there an alternative?

Obviously not all believers accept this teaching. There are real born-again Christians who (whether they know these titles or not) are Pelagians and Arminians. How do we relate to them? Is there an alternative to the teaching we have been setting out? I am a man whose heart is for gospel unity with all true born-again believers.

However, God does want us to think things through biblically, while always rejoicing in the great truths we hold in common. And big issues are involved in this matter of grace that affect us and our churches very practically. We must each decide, in our own conscience and heart, with the help of the Holy Spirit, as we study the Scriptures, where we stand on these issues of grace. In particular, we must ask what happens if we take a Pelagian or an Arminian view of salvation.

The answer is, and it is a serious charge, that we thereby subtly resurrect a religion of works. Consider, for example, Paul's teaching in Ephesians 2:8-10:

> It is by grace you have been saved, through faith – and this not from yourselves, it is the gift of God – not by works, so that no-one can boast. For we are God's workmanship, created in Christ Jesus to do good works, which God prepared in advance for us to do.

What the apostle is saying there is that salvation is

one hundred per cent grace – and that includes the faith through which we are saved, and the good works which follow from our salvation.

He is saying that the whole work is grace. You have been saved, totally, by grace. There's not an ounce of good works in it, and because of that there is not a single opportunity or excuse for boasting. Everything – the faith by which we appropriate salvation, and the good works that express it – is all God's workmanship, his creation, his deed. It is all by grace.

We don't like charity

People, however, do not like such grace. They do not like charity, and for two reasons. First, because we're naturally cynical: we don't trust 'something for nothing'. The story goes that a man stood on Westminster Bridge, trying to sell golden sovereigns at a penny each. By the end of the day he had hardly sold any. Nobody believed that he was selling genuine golden sovereigns. We distrust charity. We feel there is a catch in it.

Secondly, because of our pride; we do not *want* charity. We want to be independent, to pay our own way. We don't like being put in a position where we owe anybody anything. Take Christmas cards: 'I'd better buy a few extra, because if somebody sends one to me, and I haven't sent one to them, I shall have to get one off pronto, shan't I?' We don't want to be one down, we like to keep the score

even. We want to 'pay' for what we get. We do not
trust charity and we do not *like* charity.

That is why the history of the church has seen
many people trying, one way or another, to twist
the gospel to get the grace out of it, or to push the
grace into a more acceptable shape. In Paul's own
day such an attempt was made in the church by a
group of legalists – people who had played down
grace and played up rules. They probably had their
roots in the Jewish faith. They tried to say: 'Of
course, the work of Jesus is great. But you have to
add *your* contribution. You have to have circumci-
sion, you have to have the works of the law. Jesus's
work is fine, but it's not enough on its own – you've
got to do your bit too.' Paul withstood that kind of
legalism in the church very emphatically. 'The
gospel is *free*,' he said. 'You do *not* contribute *any*-
thing. It is not of works.'

After legalists, the sacramentalists

What Paul said on this point is so strong and clear
that we might think that nobody would ever get it
wrong again.

Sadly, it was not so. Once legalism had stopped
threatening the church, a new kind of perversion
crept in during the Middle Ages: sacramentalism.
What the medieval Roman Catholic did was to say:
'Yes, of course, the grace of God is there. But how
is it mediated to the individual? How does the individual get hold of the grace of God in Christ?

145

He does so through the sacraments of the church.'

There were seven sacraments – baptism, confirmation, the mass, penance, holy orders, matrimony and extreme unction. Through these seven pathways the grace of God comes to you. And so you have a chance to do your bit. By coming to the mass, by going to confession and doing your penances, you make your contribution to getting hold of the grace of God and making it your own. It was not until a monk called Martin Luther stepped on to the scene that this particular heresy was broken – for heresy it is. The Roman Catholic Church likens the sacraments to the veins of the body of Christ. Grace is a fluid that flows through this ecclesiastical plumbing to people.

That was how Martin Luther was brought up to think. He was a man of great sensitivity and moral conscience, not unlike the apostle Paul; and he was burdened with a sense of personal guilt. Being a good Catholic, he tried the sacraments, because the church told him: 'That's the way you get hold of the grace of God, that's the way you find forgiveness.' He tried them all. He went to mass regularly, he did penance until he was exhausted with it and had exhausted his confessors.

One day, in a thunderstorm, terrified by what he took to be the signs of God's judgment, he decided he would have to become a monk and he took up holy orders. But even that sacrament did not help him. He still felt burdened with his guilt.

Only matrimony and extreme unction were left –
and, as he had vowed monastic celibacy and was
not dying, they were not available to him!

Indulgences

Only one thing was left for him in the Catholic
system – what are called indulgences. Indulgences,
according to the Roman Catholic Church, are special remissions of guilt, which the church has available to give. They are the result of the good works
of all the saints down the centuries – their good
deeds so outweighed their sins that they created a
kind of moral surplus to share out. Indulgences
were given on performance of certain special works
of piety – such as giving money to build St Peter's
in Rome, or going on a pilgrimage. Luther went
out to obtain indulgences. He went on pilgrimages
to Rome. He did all those things a true Catholic
was supposed to do. At the end of it, he still knew
he was guilty and hell-bound. The sacramental
system had not worked.

Such additions to grace, such as Pelagian or
Arminian contributions, which you have to do to
be saved – they never do help. All they finish up
doing is to plunge people into a total lack of assurance. You can never feel saved if you're a legalist
or a sacramentalist. You are always tormented by
the thought: 'Have I done enough? Have I done it
right?' The turning point of Martin Luther's life
came when his father-confessor in the Augustin-

147

ian priory told him that the only thing for him was to go to university and do a degree in biblical studies. 'Maybe,' he said, 'if you use your brain and get stuck into some academic work, you'll have less energy for all this morbid introspection.' So Luther, one day early in the 16th century, was in his study reading Paul's letter to the Romans. He came across that famous phrase: 'The gospel is the power of God to salvation, for in it the righteousness of God is revealed from faith to faith.'

He saw, as in a flash of light, that Paul was there talking about salvation, without sacraments! He was talking about the grace of God being given direct into the hands of faith, without any church ritual intervening. He suddenly saw that he had been on the wrong track all those years. It was a revolutionary insight for him. Suddenly he discovered for the first time the experience of peace of conscience. Though an impeccable Christian, all his striving to earn grace had just made him more and more and more discontented. Now he realized that in salvation grace is given into the empty hands of faith. He did not need sacraments, he did not need to do anything in order to earn it. It was given to him. At last he found peace. Salvation is not something we attain by religious techniques or earn by good works; it comes to us by grace alone.

That is all very interesting, you may feel, but it is all history. Why should we be talking about legalists in the early church or Catholics in the medieval church? We're neither legalists nor Catholics. We're Protestants and, after Martin Luther preached this wonderful Reformation gospel of: 'By grace alone, through faith alone', this attempt to get round God's charity has at last ended. We're not guilty of any of this. But we are. Let me describe the typical gospel message in a hundred evangelical churches today: 'God laid down the Ten Commandments. Do these, he said, and you'll be OK, you'll go to heaven. But unfortunately we couldn't keep them. So God decided that this was no good; there would be no way of saving anybody if it was just up to the Ten Commandments. He decided he'd have somehow to lower the demands. So he sent Jesus. And as a result of what Jesus has done, God can now offer salvation cutprice. Instead of keeping the Ten Commandments, all you have to do is believe.'

Subtly wrong

As you will notice, something very subtle is wrong with that presentation of the gospel. It is in severe danger of turning faith into a good work. The Catholic turned the sacraments into a good work, without which we could not obtain grace. The legalist turned obedience to the law into a good work, without which grace was no good to us. And some Protestants turn *faith* into a good work, on the merit of which we obtain the grace of Christ. That means we are back to religious technique again; and all

149

down history it has had exactly the same consequences. It means that people do not feel secure in Christ, they lack assurance. Just as Luther lamented that he had never performed enough penances, so I find people who all the time are tormented by the fear that they have not believed enough. They go to evangelistic meeting after evangelistic meeting, making one 'decision' after another because they never feel sure.

The reason why they do not feel sure is that the teaching they have received leads them instinctively to regard faith as a good work, to which they must contribute to make salvation theirs. They are never sure that they have done it right, properly or thoroughly. They are never sure they've done their five per cent. Therefore they fear that one day they may forfeit eternal life. The sad irony is that they are in precisely the same spiritual unrest as Luther was, and for exactly the same reason – that the gospel of grace has been corrupted with the idea that we have to do something to make it ours.

A matter solely of God's generosity

As we saw, Paul in Ephesians 2:8-10 is saying the very opposite: salvation is totally a matter of God's generosity. Everything in salvation comes from God. I mean everything, including the faith that receives it. Jesus did not just keep the Ten Commandments, die for us and leave us on our own to the business of believing in him. If that were so, faith would be our good work and we would have ground for boasting. But no, he says, 'By grace you have been saved, through faith', and this whole matter is not from yourselves, it's a gift. It's not a work, it's a gift of God's grace, one hundred per cent charity.

'Irresistible grace' or effectual calling is simply teaching that. God did not leave the work of salvation for us to appropriate for ourselves. He applies it to our souls, so that we cannot pat ourselves on the back in any way whatsoever. Even faith is a gift. It comes to us in the context not of self-congratulation, but of God-glorification. Think of Peter, when he first got an insight into who Jesus was: 'You are the Christ, the Son of the living God.' What did Jesus say to him? 'Well done, Peter. You did well to work that out'? Not at all. 'Blessed are you, Simon ... for this was not revealed to you by man, but by my Father in heaven' (Matthew 16:16-17). Jesus saw that this illumination, this faith of Peter's, was a gift – a gift of God's grace. So it is always. It is the Lord who opens the heart to respond to the message. And that is what irresistible grace is all about.

There are problems

All these truths have problems for us, however, because of our limited understanding. In particular, there are three problems that seem to recur constantly and cause people anxiety. These have been touched on already, but need to be faced squarely.

The first is: 'Surely this contradicts free will?' The second is: 'Surely it means people are predestined to hell?' And the third is: 'Surely this discourages evangelism?'

The fascinating thing is that Paul faces all three in his letter to the Romans, chapters 9 and 10. The problems arise for Paul as he considers a fact about which he feels very intensely: the fact that his fellow Jews are not Christians. That makes him upset, indeed brokenhearted. He says, 'I could wish that I myself were cursed and cut off from Christ for the sake of my brothers, those of my own race' (Romans 9:3). He would go to hell, if that would send them to heaven. It is important to realize that for Paul the Jews' unbelief was not merely an emotional problem. It was a theological problem.

At the end of chapter 8, Paul had been showing that we can be sure of going to heaven because our salvation does not depend on ourselves, but on God's eternal purpose and electing grace. God has predestined us. God has this great purpose in which Christians are involved. Therefore we can be sure, whatever happens to us, that nothing can separate us from the love of God. We may have this security, because it does not in any way depend on us. It hinges on God's purpose, his election.

Now the problem is that the Jews rejected the

Christian message, when surely they were God's elect too. Yet, despite all their privileges as members of God's elect people, the Jews do not believe. How then can the Christian feel secure in his salvation? If the covenant with Israel proved so unreliable, why should he feel so sure that nothing can separate him from Christ's love? The Jew seems to illustrate the very thing that Paul (at the end of Romans 8) says *cannot* happen – the promise of God failing. Can a people be God's elect and then, by their own decision, reject his blessing? That is the question we all want to ask. Can God elect a person who then rejects his election? Can God fail in his purpose? If he can, there is no assurance in the fact that he has a purpose, because we can thwart it. That is the problem which Paul perceives and feels: an intensely emotional problem and, beyond that, an immensely theological one – the problem of the unbelieving Jews.

'God's word has not broken down'

The way Paul answers is as significant as the content of his answer. The first point to notice is the answer he rejects. He will not allow that God's word has broken down. 'It is not as though God's word had failed' (9:6). In saying that, he is rejecting what we may call the 'free will defence'. That is, he does not use the solution which an Arminian or a Pelagian would put to this problem.

On their view, God's purpose to save is always

conditional on man doing his bit, on man's own inherent power of choice. God cannot save men in spite of themselves, according to the Pelagians and the Arminians. With gentlemanly reserve, he refuses to exert his power in such a way as to contradict man's free will. 'So,' they say, 'election (which Paul is talking about in Romans 8) is not an act of omnipotence.' To them (as chapter 2 showed) it is merely an act of omniscience. God foresees who is going to decide to believe. He does not do anything about it, he simply knows it beforehand. He foresees who is going to be saved by virtue of their own response to the gospel, and he elects them. So run the Arminian and Pelagian views of election. 'The Jews have simply chosen not to believe,' they say; 'There's nothing God can do about that.'

To Pelagians or Arminians three statements are enough to sort out Paul's problem. The free will defence is: (a) it is the Jews' own fault; (b) they should have believed; (c) they didn't and there's *nothing* God can do about it. You can't blame God. Now that free will defence was available to Paul. He was no idiot; he could think that through. If he had believed that to be the situation, this whole problem would have been solved by the end of verse 6. He feels it necessary to go into this very difficult chapter because he does not believe the free will case.

Paul was neither an Arminian nor a Pelagian.

'It is not as though God's word had failed', it is not as though human choice has thwarted God's purpose. That is not the way it is. That would be an easy and convenient answer, but that it is not true. It would be very nice, very logical, very tidy for us all, if we could see that as the answer to the problem. But the apostle, this man inspired by the Spirit of God who constrains us by his authority today in the word of God, says that that does not fit the facts. It is *not* as though the word of God has failed, or the will of man triumphed.

God's purpose has triumphed

What then is the answer? It is quite clearly that God's purpose has triumphed, but not in the way that some anticipated. He points out that not all who are descended from Israel are actually Israel. There are in fact two Israels. One is the political nation, to whom the covenant of temporal blessings and the physical land of Canaan were given; the other is the spiritual people, who have inherited the spiritual blessings of forgiveness and eternal life. The covenant was never a blanket arrangement, by which everybody who claimed physical descent from Abraham could share the relationship with God that Abraham knew. Those who knew those blessings were always an elect group within the Jewish nation as a whole.

To prove his point, he cites two examples. Firstly, Isaac and Ishmael, both children of Abraham: one was a participant in the promises, one was not. 'It is not the natural children who are God's children, but it is the children of the promise who are regarded as Abraham's offspring' (9:8).

Secondly, Jacob and Esau, the twin sons of Isaac, of whom only one was elect. 'Rebecca's children had one and the same father, our father Isaac. Yet, before the twins were born or had done anything good or bad – in order that God's purpose in election might stand: not by works but by him who calls – she was told, "The older will serve the younger"' (9:10-12). Paul is pointing out that God makes this declaration before the children were born, so that no one can say that they were elected because of the kind of person they were. 'It is not by works,' he says, 'but by him who calls' (9:12). God made his choice before they were born or had done anything good or bad.

In both cases, God contradicts the natural choice of men. With Abraham he ignores the existing child and miraculously enabling a barren woman to bear. With Isaac, he chooses the less attractive person in human terms, and ignores the human rules of primogeniture and inheritance. He does this to assert his own purpose over and against human purposes.

So there are two Israels, he says, the physical and the spiritual. Only the latter is the true elect of God. They have not rejected the Messiah, they are like the 7,000 who did not bow the knee to Baal in the days of Elijah. There is still a remnant of the

Jewish nation who have been saved by God's grace. The purpose of God has not failed, he says. On the contrary, it continues to achieve its goals with infallible certainty.

Is God unfair?

That is Paul's answer, but it still leaves us with other problems. Uncannily, Paul anticipates them. He is not so stupid as not to know what people will say when he rejects the free will defence and asserts this instead. He raises the objections himself. 'What then shall we say? Is God unjust?' (9:14). 'One of you will say to me: "Then why does God still blame us? For who resists his will?"' (9:19). He is getting at the very subject of irresistible grace. 'God's election is arbitrary, irresistible.' Therefore, they say, 'God is unfair to act in this way.'

It is when Paul responds to those two arguments that our submission to the authority of Scripture is supremely tested. For his answers are not palatable – and that's an understatement. Many human minds regard Paul's reply to these objections as totally repugnant.

He simply repudiates the charge that God is unfair: 'Is God unjust? Not at all' (9:14). He gives two grounds for denying the charge. The first is the nature of God's grace. It is the essence of mercy to be free. '[God] says to Moses, "I will have mercy on whom I have mercy, and I will have compassion on whom I have compassion"' (9:15). That is putting it positively. When Moses asked for some assurance of God's favour to the chosen people, God replies in effect: 'That's my business. I support whom I choose. It is of the nature of mercy to be free.'

What's more, Paul also puts it negatively, citing the example of Pharaoh. 'For the Scripture says to Pharaoh: "I raised you up for this very purpose, that I might display my power in you and that my name might be proclaimed in all the earth"' (9:17). Once again, it is God's prerogative to be free, whether in bestowing mercy or in withholding it. Verse 18: 'God has mercy on whom he wants to have mercy, and he hardens whom he wants to harden.' This is not God being arbitrary, this is the essence of mercy. Justice is about what people deserve. If we want to come to God on the basis of justice, then we can go to hell, because that is what we deserve. If we come to God on the basis of mercy, then we have to accept that he has the sovereign right to bestow it or withhold it, as *he* chooses. That is what mercy is. He does not owe it to us. We have no right to it. The first point that needs to be proved by those who want to accuse God of injustice is that we have any claim on God's mercy at all. But we have none. Should God deny us mercy, we would have no valid complaint against God, because he would be just. We are not asking for wages, but for charity.

'He doesn't deserve to be let off'

The point is made in a story from Napoleon's day. A soldier had committed some crime, and Napoleon said that he deserved to be shot. His mother came and begged Napoleon: 'Sire, have mercy! Please let him off this terrible punishment.' To which Napoleon replied: 'Why? He doesn't deserve to be let off.' 'Sire,' she responded, 'if he deserved it, it wouldn't be mercy.' That's exactly it – if he deserved it, it wouldn't be mercy. That is Paul's first answer to those who accuse God of injustice.

Paul's second ground for rebuffing the thought that God is unfair concerns man's nature as a creature. 'One of you will say to me: "Then why does God still blame us? For who resists his will?" But who are you, O man, to talk back to God? Shall what is formed say to him who formed it, "Why did you make me like this?" ' (9:19-20). Here is another crunch issue. Ultimately it is not so much the arbitrariness of God that offends us as the implied contradiction of our human self-determination. It's nice to know that God has the world under his control, it's comforting to know that history has a purpose. We are happy to see the universe in that way, but there has to be a reservation for human independence, one little sacrosanct sphere of human autonomy, where we insist that self-rule prevails and where even omnipotence may not invade. God cannot contradict our free will –

we say that with desperate confidence.

Paul, however, replies quite simply, 'Why not?' To accuse God of injustice in this matter is not only foolhardy, he says, but also impertinent. 'Shall what is formed say, "Why did you make me like this?" Does not the potter have the right to make out of the same lump of clay some pottery for noble purposes and some for common use?' (9:21). We must not misunderstand Paul with this potter and clay analogy. He is not saying that God superimposes some external constraint on human beings and forces them to go against their nature. Martin Luther wrote a great tract *On the Bondage of the Will*. But when he said in it, 'I deny free will', he knew that man does have the psychological freedom to act according to his own nature and desires. He was not denying that – only a fool would. It is obvious that we have that freedom. What Luther was saying is that, first of all, the human will is corrupt; and precisely because it is corrupt, our freedom is in fact a curse, for our free will disobeys God. The essence of our rebellion is that we live as if we could choose to live outside God's will, when we cannot.

The other thing Luther was saying is that God's providence includes everything. If God so wants, he can take away our health, our sanity, our life. Why then do we pretend that there is something inalienable, untouchable, about our power of choice? Every atom in our brains is sustained by

God. Every neuron firing away as I think is sustained by God's providence. We cannot take one breath without our Creator's personal permission. How much less can we make a decision independent of him?

Based on a myth

The idea of free will is based upon the myth that God is excluded from some corner of the universe and that his providence does not extend there. It is not so. The only unconditionally free agent in this universe is God. All the freedom we have lies within the permissive limits of his sovereign purpose. That is not tyranny, that is just deity. It is part of what it means to be God that he 'interferes' with everything and can do nothing else. Our role is to accept that interference, not to begrudge it to him. The truth is that we resent God's deity and are jealous of our free will, because we are not content to be creatures. That is the pride that ruined Adam, the arrogance that still grasps at divine prerogatives ('you will be like God' Genesis 3:5) and the insane ambition that still haunts us. Says Paul, we have to learn better, the gospel has got to teach us better, we have to be willing to be creatures.

Outrageous arrogance

It is therefore not so much that Paul rejects the free will defence, as that he refuses even to contemplate it. He sees it as an act of outrageous arrogance. Man is not on this earth to question God, but to worship him; not to accuse him of injustice, but to bow wonderingly at the complexity of his intelligence. This free will defence is unacceptable precisely because it reduces God. It excludes him from the human heart, saying: 'God, you can't interfere there, because that's my business, that's my private life, that's my territory. You can't interfere there, God.' Paul's answer is simply, 'Why not? You are a creature; you are not a god.'

I said that we would not like it. But we need to keep the balance that Paul sets, because unbelievers can press Paul's argument too far and say: 'Oh well, if I'm predestined to be saved, I shall be. What's the point of bothering?' Or believers can press it too far and say: 'Well, what's the point of evangelizing? If they are going to be saved, they will be.'

It is very important to see that Paul also realized that people are likely to follow that line. So he follows up his very tough emphasis on the sovereignty of God, with a very strong emphasis on the responsibility of man. 'What then shall we say? That the Gentiles, who did not pursue righteousness, have obtained it, a righteousness that is by faith; but Israel, who pursued a law of righteousness, has not attained it. Why not? Because they pursued it not by faith but as it were by works' (9:30-32). We are tempted to think that Paul is going back on all that he has just said. Is he perhaps explaining the Jews' failure to be saved not on the basis of God's purpose any longer, but on the nature of their response? This looks like the free will defence coming in again by the back door, but it is not.

Paul here is giving us not the reason for God's election, but the reason for man's condemnation. He is not saying: 'This is the reason God chose you.' He is saying rather: 'This is the reason God condemns you.' Men and women are not sent to hell because they are unlucky enough not to be chosen; they are sent to hell because they are rebellious sinners who refuse to repent, who refuse to seek God's righteousness through faith.

This is not Paul being crafty with his words: it is an important point. The Bible says that people are saved by grace, but condemned by justice. Election has to do with salvation and it is a gracious work that God does not owe us, but which in freedom he elects to give. Condemnation is an act of justice. Hell is where people go by their own fault.

Responsible for our destiny
We must never so press the doctrine of grace, then, as to obscure the fact that human beings are responsible for their destiny. We may find it difficult to separate those two ideas, but we can see how that difficulty arises. It is rooted in wrongly associating two things: being responsible and be-

ing capable. We instinctively assume that if we are responsible for something, then we must be able to do it. If a man is not able to do something, he cannot be held responsible for not doing it, can he? The Bible's doctrine of salvation hinges on the fact that man is responsible to God, but that he does not have the ability to please God and will be justly punished for that failure.

A bankrupt may be totally unable to meet his debts and yet be still accountable for them. And sinners, who are quite unable to stop sinning, will not be able to offer their inability as a defence on the day of judgment. We will not be allowed to say, 'I couldn't help it', because deep in our hearts we will all know we are responsible for our actions. The weakness of our nature, the deprivations of our upbringing, the perversions of our culture and even God's decision to withhold the Holy Spirit from us – none of these will be an extenuating circumstance that we may plead. They are not valid excuses. Men are condemned because they are responsible for their actions.

As Paul spells out in chapter 10, we are responsible, among other things, to seek salvation. 'The word is near you.' It's not difficult to get saved, he says. It's not as if you had to go a hundred miles to find out about it or to get hold of it. It's right here. You're responsible to receive it. 'If you confess with your mouth, "Jesus is Lord", and believe in your heart that God raised him from the dead, you will be saved' (10:9). That is all God requires, he says – the sincerity and commitment of that confession. He will not give assurance to a hypocrite or a coward, but he will give assurance of salvation to anybody who makes that confession. He who believes in him will not be disappointed (10:11).

It is important to notice that Paul does not limit this promise to the elect. He insists that it is genuinely extended to every man or woman, irrespective of racial or religious background. 'Everyone who calls on the name of the Lord will be saved' (10:13).

Responsible to evangelize

This free gospel of mercy is something we have to offer people, to share with them. We have a responsibility to evangelize. 'How, then, can they call on the one they have not believed in? And how can they believe in the one of whom they have not heard? And how can they hear without someone preaching to them?' (10:14).

Irresistible grace must not be pressed to deny human responsibility. We have to hold these two Bible doctrines in tension, recognizing them both as true. We cannot believe in Christ without a work of grace in our hearts. Once that work of grace is in our hearts, nothing can stop us believing. 'All that the Father gives me will come to me,' says Jesus (John 6:37). There is no doubt about it. Yet we are responsible for our unbelief. We cannot use lack of grace as an excuse for our impenitence. Those two truths have to be preached together. The Scriptures themselves reject the simplistic answer of the free will defence, and say that we must seek an answer within the bounds of that difficult, but creative tension.

All through history men have been trying to obtain God's grace by way of human technique. 'Ah,' says the ritualist, 'you want God to bless you? You must have the right ceremony, offer the right sacrifices, say the approved liturgy, employ the official priest, make use of the appointed sacraments – that's the technique.'

'Ah,' says the moralist, 'you want to find God's grace? You must heed all God's commandments. You must make your life absolutely holy. You must say your prayers. You must love your neighbour. You must give to charity. That's the way of getting hold of God's grace.'

'Ah,' says the Arminian, 'you want to find God's grace? Believe, make your decision, exert your human free will to receive Christ, commit your life to him – and you will obtain the grace you want.'

In each case, the suggestion is that God responds to man's initiative. Like some mechanical blessing dispenser, God will churn out the spiritual goodies, if man inserts the right religious coin. It's a matter of technique. The ritualist puts his faith in ceremonial, the moralist in loving his neighbour, and the evangelical in 'faith'.

They are all caricatures of what the Bible says. Spiritual blessings do not come to us as a reward; the grace of God is, by definition, an act of unprovoked generosity. God is not responding to us. He is not being manipulated by us. When God gives his grace to a man, it is never because he must, but always because he freely chooses to do so. It's a matter of his election. That's why faith, properly understood, is not a technique for obtaining grace. Faith is not a good work, but a cry of helplessness. It is the confession that I have no good works to offer, nothing to bring. Faith is not a demand on God's justice, but an appeal to God's free mercy. Supremely, faith is not an achievement, but a gift of the Holy Spirit.

That is crucial. Naturally we want to complain about it, to say that it is unfair, that God is being arbitrary. We want to put God in the dock and demand: 'Why?' But we will never get an answer to that question, because our indignation is itself a confession of our human pride and arrogance. We are furious, because our human religious techniques have not worked. God has frustrated them. We call him 'arbitrary' because he does not keep our rules. We call him 'unfair', because he will not play the game our way. We had it all worked out: we did this and this and this for him, and he would do that and that and that for us. It was, we felt, a most satisfactory arrangement.

God has spoiled our plans

And now God has spoiled our plans, because he has rejected our bargain and refused our contract. In place of them, he offers a completely different route to grace altogether. He tells us that we must trust him, even though his actions are sometimes quite unpredictable (to us) and apparently irrational. He tells us that we must depend on his grace, a grace that seems to be dispensed entirely at his whim, and in complete disregard of any merit. He tells us we have to rely on his mercy, even though we have no right at all to expect to receive it, nor any means at our disposal to guarantee that we shall. No wonder we feel angry! We wanted to keep the reins of our destiny in our own hands, but God will not let us. He will not be our puppet; he insists on being our Sovereign. He will *give* us grace; he will not allow us to claim it.

There have always been two kinds of religion in the world: religions that seek to do God a favour, and religions that seek the favour of God. Religions that think to earn heaven, and those that know man can only beg for it. Religions of works and religions of faith. Religions in which men choose God and religions in which God chooses men. What God asks us is: 'What kind of religion is in the New Testament? What kind of religion is yours?'

Questions on God's grace

Q: If we can't help sinning, how are we responsible for it?

A: None of us will deny that we are responsible for our actions. When we stand before God on the last day, and he judges us for our sins, we will know in our hearts that we made sinful choices, and that we are responsible for those choices. Yet we are also, as a matter of human experience, in bondage to sin. Not one of us is sinless, or could be sinless, by our own natural ability. By nature we are sinners; we know that we are going to remain sinners and that we're caught in a web of sin, from which we cannot extricate ourselves.

We have referred to Pharaoh before, because he is one of the most telling examples. In Exodus the hardening of Pharaoh's heart is expressed in three different ways. (1) 'Pharaoh's heart became hard and he would not listen to them' (Exodus 7:13). That is a state of nature; his heart was hard – that's just how he was. (2) 'When Pharaoh saw that there was relief, he hardened his heart and would not listen to Moses' (Exodus 8:15). That was a voluntary decision on Pharaoh's part. He was responsible for the hardening of his heart there. (3) 'The LORD hardened Pharaoh's heart, and he would not let the Israelites go' (Exodus 11:10). To the state

169

of nature and a voluntary choice has been added God's judicial decree. God was confirming Pharaoh in that state.

If people go to hell, it is because God confirms them in their decision and in that natural state in which they already are. He gives them what they have already said they want. They want independence of him; he gives it to them. They want to turn their back on him, they do not want him in their universe – all right, they will not have God in their universe. He gives them what they want. Reprobation is not a decree of God in the same way that election is, because in order to save us, God has to reverse the situation completely. But hell is where we are going, where we want to go. All that God has to do to send us there is to say: 'You will have what you want.' But to save us, he has to do what he did for the Jews – work a miracle to bring them out of Egypt. And that requires a great saving act of his initiative.

Q: How free are our wills?

A: This question crops up under the heading of 'total depravity', but it also occurs under the theme of grace and it is worth setting out the two problems about free will. One is the fact that we are sinners: our wills are in bondage to sin and, when we choose, we always choose wrong. We are a little like people standing on a slope; it's always easier to go down than up. Adam was standing on the level. He was not corrupt, so his will was not inclined to evil in the way ours now is by nature. In that sense, he had a 'free' will, but his will became limited as ours is by the Fall. The second problem with free will is that we are creatures and cannot operate outside the sovereign providence of God. The ultimate fact that limits the freedom of the will is that we cannot choose outside the bounds of God's permission, because we are creatures – any more than anything else in this universe can happen outside the bounds of his permission. No one, Adam included, has or had free will of that second order. God alone has free will ultimately – which is why he can bestow grace.

Q: How does God's sovereignty relate to Romans 10:9: 'If you confess with your mouth, "Jesus is Lord", and believe in your heart... you will be saved'?

A: Believing in your heart is not earning you salvation. It is the confession of faith, which evidences regeneration in the heart. There is no way that a person can make that confession and say, 'Jesus is Lord', but by the Holy Spirit. Paul is here giving assurance of salvation: if a person sincerely and publicly makes that confession, that shows that there has been a work of grace in that person's life. They could not otherwise make that confession sincerely and publicly. By saying, 'Jesus is Lord', you are just stating a fact about what your heart now sees to be true.

Q: What if the Ethiopian eunuch had not stopped his chariot to be baptized? What if the woman with the issue of blood had not touched the hem of Christ's garment? What if Naaman had refused to dip himself in the Jordan? Would they have been saved?

A: God does require obedience from us and the benefits of salvation flow to us as we are obedient; there is no doubt about that. But, having performed those acts of obedience and of faith, did those who performed them feel that they had reason to congratulate themselves? Did the Ethiopian congratulate himself on his judgment? Or the woman go home patting herself on the back? No, she went home saying, '*Jesus is wonderful.*' God was working all along, not just in the moment when those people (and any others) 'came to faith' in conscious experience. It was not a question of either/or – either *God* stopped the chariot or the Ethiopian did; when God works, you cannot separate the two, for God is over all.

Q: What about people who have never heard the gospel (e.g. Romans 2:12-16)?

A: I do not think the Bible ever fully answers the question of the people who have never heard. There are one or two hints and this verse in Romans is the biggest. The Bible never says much about this question for this simple reason: anyone who has a Bible in their hands does not belong to that category. The Bible is not given to satisfy our curiosity and has no interest in answering all the questions that you and I might like to put. It is clear that God's judgment cannot, for those people who have never heard the gospel, be on the same basis as for those who have – though it will still be a judgment.

Q: Has it not been a great spur to missionary zeal that people have believed that there can be no salvation unless the gospel is preached?

A: Yes. Scholars have argued that if God so chooses, he can work through his Spirit without his word. It would be over-dogmatic to say that someone who has never heard cannot be saved, though we do not have any evidence that such have been. But, if they *are* saved, it must be by active electing grace through the Spirit alone in their lives, without a conscious response to a preached word. If God wants to save someone without his word, on what basis may we say that he cannot? But it is certainly true that the normal means of grace is the word, and Romans 10:14 must be our spur: 'How can they hear without a preacher?' It would be very dangerous to allow speculations (about 'what if?' and 'couldn't God?') to deter us from obedience to the way he says we must go about it.

Q: 'Grace' seems arbitrary. How can we present it to the non-Christian?

A: If a person is humble, there is great encouragement in grace for the seeking unbeliever. What do you say to the person who says: 'I'd love to be a Christian because I can see you Christians have got a lot, but I just can't believe'? If you do not believe in all-powerful grace, you can only say: 'Hard cheese. It's up to you. Try harder.' That does not help. But if you believe in grace, you can say something to them and do something for them. You can tell them to pray; you too can pray. You cannot pray, if God cannot interfere with a person's 'free will'. But we can pray for our unconverted friend, because grace is a gift; we can ask God, in his mercy, to give it to them. They can claim God's promise: 'Ask and it will be given to you; seek and you will find; knock and the door will be opened to you' (Matthew 7:7). They can ask God for faith. They can say: 'God, I don't even know if you exist. But something in my heart is calling me into this Christianity. If you're there, please make yourself real to me. Please give me this faith these Christians talk about.' God never denies that prayer. The mere fact that they have got to that point of seeking is evidence of a work of grace in their lives. I feel terrifically encouraged when someone says to me: 'I'd like to be a Christian, but I can't.' I know they would not want to be a Christian unless God were already down the road with them quite a few miles. Grace is not arbitrary; it is encouraging. It gives us something positive to offer.

Q: How does this view of grace relate to mass evangelism?

A: It puts some qualification on mass evangelism, but it would be wrong to exaggerate it. Nothing takes away from that hymn: 'O happy day that fixed *my* choice'. It's a conscious, personal choice – our wills are involved; but the ability and motivation to make that choice derives solely from God's grace. People have to make decisions to become Christians. And the preacher has to call on people in the imperative: 'Repent! Believe!' We issue a command. Do you know that picture in Ezekiel of the valley of dry bones? God says to Ezekiel: 'Now preach at them!' What a stupid thing to do! That is exactly what a preacher is doing, when unbelievers are present: he is preaching to dead bones. A very stupid thing to do? No. He is

175

preaching in belief that God the Spirit is going to accompany the word and bring new life. So 'get up out of your seats' is not too far from what Ezekiel told them to do.

But when a decisionist approach to evange-lism is pressed too far, it may communicate to the unbeliever that *he* can contribute something to his salvation. Instead of seeing himself as someone just holding out empty hands to God, he may be very subtly encouraged to see him-self as doing something for God: 'I did my bit for God tonight. I went forward.' If people go forward in that attitude of mind, (a) they may not be saved at all, or (b) they may be absorb-ing bad teaching in the way that they are being evangelized – teaching that can leave awful problems of assurance in the weeks that fol-low.

5

You'll Get There in the End

Greg Haslam

The fact and the implication of God's grace are tremendously liberating, but we all finally want to know whether grace has guaranteed our future. We sing hymns that ring again and again with affirmations of the perseverance of the saints. It makes a mockery of those words, however, if remnants of doubt linger in our minds about whether we will get to heaven. If we are not sure that we will, we are mouthing meaningless words as we sing.

The question therefore is this: now that I am a Christian, will I remain one for the rest of my life? The converted slave-trader, John Newton, was in absolutely no doubt that he would. His famous hymn 'Amazing Grace' closes with these words:

> Through many dangers, toils and snares
> I have already come.
> 'Twas grace that brought me safe thus far,
> And grace will lead me home.

That strikes a vital note of realism. When we think of the perseverance of the saints, we are not looking at the future through rose-tinted glasses, as if it will be free from trials and difficulties. What God does assert is that his grace is sufficient to see us through every last one of them. Another great Christian, John Charles Ryle (the first bishop of Liverpool last century), was in no doubt that he would get there in the end. He said that

There are two points on which the teaching of the Bible is very plain and distinct: one is the fearful danger of the ungodly, the other the perfect safety of the righteous.

A 20th-century writer, G I Williamson, puts the basic question and gives the biblical answer:

When a person has been regenerated or born again by the Holy Spirit and truly converted to Christ through repentance and faith, is it possible to again become a child of wrath and of eternal destruction? The answer of the Scripture is clear and emphatic: no, it is not possible.

The only result

This seems almost too good to be true. It looks as though we are taking all the positives and overlooking all the negatives – as though we are exaggerating the Bible's promises to us as Christians and ignoring its warning and cautions. We will look at those later, but the 'perfect safety' of the believer is only the result of all the truths we have already seen in earlier chapters.

If I believed, like a Roman Catholic or an Arminian, that in some way God's will is not completely sovereign, but that man's will can intervene to abort his purposes, then I would be entirely consistent to doubt my security. We have no reason to doubt the keeping power of God, but if we allow our security to depend in any way on our fickle wills, then we sense that we could very easily unsave ourselves. If we could decide against the purposes of God, we know that our future is very uncertain indeed.

God, however, remains invincible in his purposes. God is God. By his all-conquering resurrection power he drew us to himself. No power, outside us or inside us, is greater than that. Jesus said: 'No-one can come to me unless the Father who sent me draws him, and I will raise him up at the last day' (John 6:44). The one he draws on the first day of Christian experience he will raise on the last day. The Christian will stick at it to the end. That may astonish us, knowing ourselves as we do. It astonishes me, knowing myself as I do. But it is what the Bible emphatically teaches. You will never die, never perish. God will never cast you aside, never disinherit you from his family, never reject you. You are destined to spend eternity with Jesus Christ. That is the perseverance of the saints.

No matter what?

We need to be clear as to what that perseverance does *not* mean. It does not mean that every person who goes forward at the end of an evangelistic meeting, or makes some decision while sitting in their seat, or signs a card in a counselling room will be saved at the last. It does not mean that everyone who claims to be a Christian and says, 'Yes,

I'm a believer', will be saved, no matter what happens. It does not mean that everyone who has been christened as an infant, or baptized by immersion on profession of faith, or joined the membership of a church will eventually be in heaven. It does not mean, by contrast, that only the super-saints will get there – the heroes and martyrs, the outstanding godly people in all those biographies.

It means positively that true believers – simple, ordinary Christians, known and unknown – will get to heaven, all of them. We can feel fairly sure about elderly Christians, those who are teetering on the edge of eternity and have just a few weeks or days left. It is reasonably certain that they will stay in the faith.

I knew a man who came to the Lord and then was taken into eternity less than a fortnight later. It is not hard to be certain that he died secure, but then we think: 'Well, I'd be pretty assured about my own future if I were to die in the next fortnight. But I may have fifty years ahead of me. How can I possibly predict how it will be with me then?'

Now and then
The Bible shows that you can know now how it will be then. The perseverance of the saints does not relate merely to the aged or those about to die. This does not mean that temptation will never come your way, that you will never encounter difficulties, never lapse, never grow cold, never prove

unfaithful in this area or that. This truth does not mean that you will be free from terrible assaults of the devil on your faith, or from gross doubts and fears. The Bible is replete with examples of believers who endured tremendous difficulties and fell in the face of fierce temptations – Noah got drunk; Abraham lied out of fear for his own and his wife's safety; Jonah ran away from the clear and declared will of God; David, the great king and anointed one of Israel, committed adultery; and Peter, in an act of supreme cowardice, denied the Lord before a servant girl. The examples are numerous.

We will not necessarily be preserved from such gross lapses into sin. Grace is available to make a way of escape from temptation, but that is not the point of this doctrine. John Murray has said:

> It is true that the believer does sin. He may fall into grievous sins and backslide for lengthy periods. But it is also true that a believer cannot abandon himself to sin. He cannot come once more under the dominion of sin. He cannot be guilty of certain kinds of unfaithfulness.

Perseverance does not mean a life free from the pain of failure or the pressure of temptation.

These are some negatives; now to the positives. This is how it will affect our experience as believers in Christ: God will ensure without a shadow of doubt that we will never fall absolutely headlong, never fall completely and finally away from him. If we trip up or seriously lapse in our Christian living, we will sooner or later rise again from those lapses to a fresh walk with God, to a renewed commitment to Jesus Christ, and to the true discipleship from which we temporarily departed. We can never be lost: the saints – those called by God, to whom faith is given by grace – will persevere to the end. Two parties are involved in this: God and ourselves. The supreme and conclusive reason why we can never be lost is that God has guaranteed to preserve us. It does not rest on us in the first – or final – instance.

God continuously at work

What the Bible says about our responsibility to continue always assumes that God is continuously doing the greater work for us. God will preserve us; that is why we will make it in the faith. The first focus is on God's work – he preserves; and he works so that our responsibilities may come to the fore – we persevere. These assertions are all consistent with the other great truths in this book. That is fine, but the important question is not whether they are logically consistent with each other, but whether the Bible teaches them. So we turn directly to its pages.

The Scriptures demonstrate that God's work runs concurrently with ours. They do not give any credit to us, but show that the grace of God elicits some activity from us and in us, as he preserves and keeps us. Put at its simplest, he preserves and we persevere. We persevere because he preserves. Many passages hold these twin truths together. 'Keep yourselves in God's love', states our duty to persevere. 'To him who is able to keep you from falling and to present you before his glorious presence without fault' (Jude 24), states his power to preserve. Revelation 3:10 makes the same two points: 'Since you have kept my command to endure patiently, I will also keep you from the hour of trial that is going to come upon the whole world'. Philippians 2:12 exhorts us to keep going: 'Continue to *work out* your own salvation with fear and trembling' (italics mine) and then it adds the reason, 'For it is God who *works in* you to will and to act according to his good purpose.'

The Bible's evidence of this double-sided truth is absolutely overwhelming, but it does not present it as a fifty/fifty proposition – as though we do half and God does half. God does it all; when we get to glory it will be one hundred per cent due to God. We persevere only because he preserves us, but that is why it is also one hundred per cent us. The decisions we make, the resistance we offer to temptation, the way we walk with God – our perseverance rests one hundred per cent on those, as they rest one hundred per cent on him. So we need to be persuaded of the preserving power of God.

This is clear as daylight in Philippians 1:6. As

Paul writes from a prison cell to encourage Christians and to sort out their difficulties, he strikes this positive note: 'Being confident of this, that he who began a good work in you will carry it on to completion unto the day of Jesus Christ.' Paul would not allow his readers (then or now) to add any 'Yes, but' at the end of that sentence. The same concept is repeated: 'He will keep you strong to the end, so that you will be blameless on the day of our Lord Jesus Christ' (1 Corinthians 1:8). He *will* keep you strong.

Rescued from every attack

This is reinforced: 'The Lord will rescue me from every evil attack' (2 Timothy 4:18). In Paul's experience, 'every evil attack' included the hostility of men. He knew, however, that there were subtler, stronger attacks as well. He was writing from his final dungeon cell in Rome, waiting to be beheaded by the Roman authorities. He knew that 'our struggle is not against flesh and blood, but against ... the powers of this dark world and against the spiritual forces of evil in the heavenly realms' (Ephesians 6:12). He had in mind the final onslaughts on his soul which would surely take place as he awaited martyrdom. He knew the devil's sharp desire to make this great apostle tremble at the very last and denounce the faith at the Roman executioner's block. But his assurance was this: 'The Lord will rescue me from every evil attack, and will bring me safely to his heavenly kingdom.'

His assurance echoes in his prayer for the Thessalonian believers:

> May your whole spirit, soul and body be kept blameless at the coming of our Lord Jesus Christ. The one who calls you is faithful and he will do it (1 Thessalonians 5:23-24).

Hebrews 13:5 says the same: 'God has said, "Never will I leave you; never will I forsake you."' Particularly fascinating is Romans 8:29-30, because it takes us through the themes of this book:

> For those God foreknew he also predestined to be conformed to the likeness of his Son, that he might be the firstborn among many brothers. And those he predestined, he also called; those he called, he also justified; those he justified, he also glorified.

We have seen that this is called 'the golden chain of salvation', with five links: God foreknows us; God predestines us; God calls us; God justifies us; and God glorifies us. Astonishingly, these verses take us from eternity past to eternity future, through five profound words. Each of those words focuses on God's elected, redeemed people, the uncountable multitude for whom Christ died. In eternity past God foreknew and predestined us. Then he began to work out his purposes in time in our own experience. He gave his effective call that brought us to faith in Christ. At the same moment he justified us.

What is left after that? Our whole lifetime, of course. But Paul does not mention that, and we want to say to him: 'Hold on, Paul. I do know about forgiveness, I do hear what you say about being justified. But what about my whole life ahead of me? What about all its ups and downs, its temptations and trials?' Paul's thought leaps right over this life to assure us that our glorification is already achieved and settled. It is not that Paul ignores this life and its human uncertainties; it is just that the one crucial factor is what God has done, is doing and will do. That is why he jumps from justification to glorification, for the glory will simply be our sanctification completed. What God starts he rounds off. Those chosen in eternity past are taken through time to glory, with no exceptions, no failures, no dropouts.

That is the golden chain of salvation. Everyone who believes has been justified. Every justified person has been called. Everyone called was predestined. Everyone predestined to glory will get there. None can fall short. The basis for this exhilarating fact is Romans 8:28: 'We know that in all things God works for the good of those who love him, who have been called according to his purpose.' In *all* things: in everything that enters your mind, or happens to you, or comes into your experience, or puts pressure on you. In all things God is working for the good of those who love him. If God is working for us, who can be against us? (Romans 8:31).

Another guarantee

All this is bound up with another guarantee which God has made to us. We are safe because God has pledged himself to the legal covenants and promises that he has made to us. God has sworn a legally binding covenant towards us and confirmed the same with oaths. This comes out in Jesus' teaching. He always spoke the truth, but he prefaced certain statements with a solemn and binding phrase: 'Verily, I say unto you,' or (as the NIV puts it), 'I tell you the truth.' He wanted to draw our attention to what he said, but he also wanted solemnly to affirm that he bound himself to what he said. In John 5 Jesus says three times, 'I tell you the truth' (5:19, 24, 25). In effect he is saying: 'This is worthy of the weight of your whole trust. I am going on record as telling you the truth.' He goes on: 'Whoever hears my word and believes him who sent me has eternal life and will not be condemned; he has crossed over from death to life' (5:24). These are guarantees that the Son of God has made to us; he cannot go back on his word.

Hebrews 6 is a difficult passage, talking about 'if people fall away'. We will return to that chapter, but it is significant that the writer says: 'Even though we speak like this ... we are confident of better things in your case – things that accompany salvation' (Hebrew 6:9). How can he be confident, in view of potential falling away? Because of 'what has been promised' by God (6:12) and because 'he confirmed it with an oath' (6:17).

> Men swear by someone greater than themselves, and the oath confirms what is said and puts an end to all argument. Because God wanted to make the unchanging nature of his purpose very clear to the heirs of what was promised, he confirmed it with an oath. [The oath was 'I will surely bless you and give you many descendants.'] God did this so that, by two unchangeable things in which it is impossible for God to lie, we who have fled to take hold of the hope offered to us may be greatly encouraged (6:16-18).

It is not simply that God has told us: 'I will surely bless you' – though that secures all the future God has for his people, the sons and daughters of Abraham by faith. It is not merely that a God who cannot lie has said this to us – though it would be enough if he only said it once. God has done more. So that our sceptical, unbelieving, doubting, introspective minds may be assured, God said it once and then confirmed it with an oath. By two unchangeable things, his word and his oath – in which it is impossible for God to lie – we who have fled for refuge may be greatly encouraged.

That is an understatement; 'greatly encouraged' means 'absolutely assured'. God said it on oath.

On oath

Now people can bend laws, wriggle out of sworn statements, twist the rule book and generally find ways round undertakings they do not want to keep. Not so with God. When God gives his word and oath, he will not go back on it and no human or demon can change his mind or get him to bend. So Romans 8:31-34 begins with this challenge: 'What, then, shall we say in response to this? If God is for us, who can be against us?' If God is for us – that is the all-important thing. Only those called and justified can say 'Yes, God is for me'.

There is Paul imagining us in the law courts. He is throwing out a challenge on behalf of all God's people, all the elect, every believer, you and me. He is challenging all the forces in all creation – death and life, angels or demons, present or future, height or depth. 'Who,' he demands, 'will bring any charge against those whom God has chosen?' In other words, who can bring evidence to persuade God to reject us? We say: 'Well, I could bring charges myself ... my conscience ... my past ...' It does not matter at that point what our conscience says, what our family could tell about us. Most of all, it does not matter what accusations Satan can hurl against us. If God is for us, who can be against us? If God has declared us not guilty, no charges can ever be brought against us, because Jesus has already answered them for us.

Paul draws his conclusions

Paul draws certain deductions from this: nothing can separate us from the love of Christ, because that love has been legally pledged to us. No upset can surprise God. We often feel that we may fall, because we cannot predict what temptations the devil will throw at us or for how long. But God cannot be taken by surprise about our future. God knows the whole sweep of our earthly existence and will never allow the prosecution to succeed against us.

'God's gifts and his call are irrevocable' (Romans 11:29). That statement is about God's unchanging purposes towards the Jews, but it is a general truth also. It applies to us. God does not give with one hand and take back with the other. He does not bestow now and reclaim later. Someone has called this the 'syllogism of security'. The ancient Greeks argued by syllogisms: each would have a major premiss, a minor premiss, and a conclusion. For example: 'All men are mortal. Socrates is a man. Therefore Socrates is mortal.' Here it is as though Paul is saying: '*Major premiss*: God's gifts and his call cannot be revoked. *Minor premiss*: salvation is the gift and call of God. *Conclusion*: therefore salvation cannot be recalled.'

A further ground for our security is in the imperishable nature of the eternal life God has granted to us. John 11:25-26 reads: 'I am the resurrection and the life. He who believes in me will live, even though he dies; and whoever lives and believes in me will never die.' Do we believe this? We possess, as believers, nothing less than the life of Christ indwelling us - our body, mind, heart, soul, spirit. God imparted this life to us, as the letter to the Romans teaches, because of the union we have with Christ.

That union means intimate involvement in everything Christ has done. All Christ's saving acts are passed on to our benefit because of our union with Christ. For this reason it is impossible to have died with Christ when he died, to have been buried with him in a tomb, to have been raised along with Christ, and yet to fall short of being more than a conqueror through him who loved us. If Christians can finally fall away before they get to heaven, then all Christ's saving work can be frustrated by you or me, by some lapse on our part. I, for one, find that impossible to believe. It is declared in 1 Peter 1:23: 'You have been born again, not of perishable seed, but of imperishable, through the living and enduring word of God.' Indestructible life is ours.

The sealing of the Spirit
The sealing of the Spirit confirms this assurance. Whatever our views about when that sealing takes

place, it certainly has to do with our conscious knowledge that we have eternal life. Paul writes in Ephesians 1:13:

> You also were included in Christ when you heard the word of truth, the gospel of your salvation. Having believed, you were marked in him with a seal, the promised Holy Spirit.

This includes the assuring witness of the Holy Spirit to our hearts that we are the children of God. We are sealed also in the sense that our salvation cannot be tampered with; we are sealed for delivery to glory.

If it is possible for the believer to fall away, it makes a mockery of the seal of the Holy Spirit. A seal means ownership, security, assurance. The seal of the Holy Spirit is God's witness to us that we are his saved children. But the Holy Spirit is lying, if it is possible for a believer to fall away; he says one thing, but things are not what they seem.

It is sometimes like that with street sellers. You can go shopping in a big city, particularly before Christmas, and as you walk down the street, you may see many unlicensed salesmen offering goods marked with famous brand names. The name on the perfume and the packaging look just right. You soon discover that they are a cheap imitation; the aroma does not last long, even though the perfume is in a 'Chanel No 19' box and bottle. The Holy Spirit plans no such confidence trick on the believer, labelling us as secure in Christ, yet knowing that the life within us may fade as that perfume did. If the Spirit has sealed us and been given to us as a guarantee of promised glory, the Spirit is no liar. The Spirit's sealing in our hearts is evidence enough that God is going to keep us.

All this positive affirmation of God's power and promises goes hand in hand with God's expectation that we persevere in the faith. John Calvin, the great 16th-century Reformer, spoke of the 'perseverance of *the faith* of God's elect'. The balance between the preserving power of God and the concurrent persevering in faith on our part is in 1 Peter 1:3-5:

> He has given us new birth into a living hope ... and into an inheritance that can never perish, spoil or fade – kept in heaven for you, who through faith are shielded by God's power until the coming of the salvation that is ready to be revealed in the last time.

Those verses make three points relevant to our theme. First, that we are kept; we have seen the evidence for that. Secondly, that we are kept through faith. Thirdly, that this keeping and believing are *until* the final revealing of our salvation. God will keep us until Christ returns or calls us home; and it is through faith that we are being kept until that same event. Our faith will endure until the end. We are not kept by God, irrespective of whether we do or do not believe. On the contrary, the keeping power of God is there to ensure that we keep on believing.

Christ interceding

This is enforced by another passage, which illuminates that most consoling truth – the intercession of Christ. It tells us what Jesus Christ is doing, now that he has risen from the dead and ascended to heaven. He still has involvement in our lives and concern for our temptations here on earth. Anything else would be unthinkable for the One who loved his own to the end. The writer to the Hebrews is at pains to demonstrate that Jesus Christ in heaven is doing a great deal for us, even now in our current lives on earth. In particular: 'He is able to save completely [i.e. right to the very end] those who come to God through him, because he always lives to intercede for them' (Hebrews 7:25).

At this very moment Jesus Christ has your name on his lips as he presents your concerns and your welfare to the Father, as he intercedes for you. If we want to know the thrust of his intercession, the only hint Scripture gives is the kind of praying he did for his disciples while still on earth.

Before his arrest and betrayal, for example, he turned to Simon Peter and said: 'I have prayed for you, Simon, that your faith may not fail' (Luke 22:32). The timing of that prayer tells us something vital. Within hours Simon Peter had lapsed badly, had fallen into a terrible state of cowardice and denunciation of Christ, even with swearing. Had Christ's praying failed? (If it did for Peter, it might for us.) The Saviour's interceding could not go unanswered. This helps us to understand that our security rests ultimately not on our avoiding a fall, but on the intercession of Christ.

To take another example, our Lord prayed as our high priest, as John 17 records. There he makes many requests for all God's people through all time:

> Protect them by the power of your name ... Protect them from the evil one ... I want those you have given me to be with me where I am, and to see my glory (John 17:11, 15, 24).

Jesus has prayed then and is praying now that we may be with him where he is, and see his glory, that we may get to heaven. It is unthinkable that a Saviour, who lives always to intercede for us, could have his prayers unheeded and see us finally in hell. Impossible. The intercession of Jesus shows that our security is not in the absence of danger, but in the presence of God through those dangers, guaranteeing that we are maintained in the faith.

Robert Murray McCheyne expressed the confidence this brings: 'If I could hear Christ praying for me in the next room, I would not fear a million of enemies. Yet the distance makes no difference; he *is* praying for me!'

To say that a believer could stop believing because of some extreme pressure or danger is to deny not only the power of Christ's intercession, but the very nature of the gospel.

> In the gospel a righteousness from God is revealed, a righteousness that is by faith from first to last [from faith to faith], just as it is written: 'The righteous will live by faith' (Romans 1:17).

Paul there is setting the keynote for the gospel he is going to present in his first eight chapters. At the outset he puts in a nutshell what he understands to be the essence of Christianity: something (a righteousness from God) that is by faith and is from first to last.

The quotation he uses, 'The righteous will live by faith' comes from the Old Testament prophet, Habakkuk (2:4). That was written against the backdrop of Babylon's impending invasion of Israel. The prophet wonders how a holy God could use such an unholy instrument to chasten his disobedient people? He is absolutely rocked by God telling him that Babylon (the Chaldeans) – that murderous, cruel Third Reich of the ancient world – is going to invade the holy land of Israel to plunder, ruin and take captive. But God tells him it is so, and gives this word: 'The righteous will live by faith.'

God is saying that, despite all the tribulation that will come, the righteous will endure. A sift-

ing and chastening work will go on. But the righteous will stick at it, they will endure through it all.
How? By faith. If the righteous are to endure, their
faith must keep being exercised. That's why Paul
quotes this, because the gospel is a donation of
righteousness to a responding faith in our hearts –
a faith that God guarantees from first to last.

Incredible - a rich reward
Knowing our weakness, it is incredible to think
that our faith will last, but it will. That Habakkuk
reference occurs also in Hebrews 10:35 and its use
there clinches the fact that our faith will endure:

> So do not throw away your confidence; it will be
> richly rewarded. You need to persevere so that
> when you have done the will of God, you will
> receive what he has promised. For in just a very
> little while, 'He who is coming will come and
> will not delay. But my righteous one will live by
> faith. And if he shrinks back, I will not be pleased
> with him.' But we are not of those who shrink
> back and are destroyed, but of those who believe
> and are saved.

Sinclair Ferguson has said: 'There is no such thing
in Scripture as perseverance without faith ... but
those who have faith will persevere.'

All this seems almost too good to be true. So
we must now try to relate it to the various objec-

tions that are brought, from Scripture and experience. Which of us has not been horrified to see an apparently keen Christian, perhaps even a leader or prominent figure in the church, initially drifting, then falling and finally even denouncing the faith and denying Christ. We cannot credit this; how can it happen? We must turn to some of the difficult passages of Scripture, aware of the background from which we come. Our 20th-century Christianity has been shallow, with a great deal of easy believism, which has seen a high proportion of professing Christians falling away. Our day therefore has a distaste for strong, assertive statements about our security; and it has a very man-centred view of the Christian life that says: 'It's all up to me.'

The passages we must look at are best seen as safeguards against any distortion of the truths of God's grace. They show what those truths do not mean, as we saw earlier. They warn us against glibly presuming on grace. They alert us to the possibility that people can delude themselves about their salvation. They remind us that God's sovereignty does not eliminate our human responsibility. They are rather like what Paul said about the storm-tossed sailors in the impending shipwreck: 'Unless these men stay with the ship, you cannot be saved' (Acts 27:31). They were saved by means of staying in the ship. Many sobering passages are there to ensure that we stick to the means of getting us to heaven (our enduring in the faith, 'staying with the ship'). We get to the shore as we respond seriously and obediently to those warnings. They do not imply that Christians can fall away; they are preservatives, to keep us from falling away.

The backslider

What then of a passage like Hebrews 6? There are in general in the New Testament three types of trouble into which professing believers can fall. Most of the warning texts deal with one of these three categories. The first is the backslider. Galatians 6:1 describes him as a saint who has been overtaken in some trespass, and exhorts fellow Christians: 'Brothers, if someone is caught in a sin, you who are spiritual should restore him gently.'

Every believer has at some point in his Christian life backslidden, though there are degrees of backsliding. The backslider's fellow Christians have brotherly responsibilities of exhortation and admonition, and then sometimes of church discipline. That may mean telling the church and even, in extreme circumstances, having him put out of the church with a view to his restoration. The Bible has many examples of backsliders, but they are always eventually restored, as was Jonah.

Dr Martyn Lloyd-Jones had a moving story of a man who had backslidden for twenty years. He had fallen into adultery and abandoned his wife and children. He walked into Westminster Chapel on the very evening when he was contemplating suicide, just at the moment the Doctor was praying: 'Lord, restore the backslider.' He was restored and gloriously brought back to faith in Christ.

The reject

The second is the reject or castaway. 1 Corinthians 9:27 is a very alarming text which reads: 'I beat my body and make it my slave so that after I have preached to others, I myself will not be disqualified for the prize.' I think I can show that Paul is not talking about losing his salvation at all. That is far from his mind. He has rather been speaking of his ministry as an apostle of Christ. He is saying that it is frighteningly possible for a Christian in service for the Lord, through moral lapse or doctrinal deviation or unwise entanglement with others, to be disqualified from his ministry.

It is possible for him, as it were, to be put on the shelf, to be taken out of that work for the Lord, perhaps never to re-enter it. For example, if the minister of a church fell into adultery, or some kind of sexual promiscuity, and it was discovered, he would have to be put out of the ministry, and unless there was a proper process of repentance, accountability to others and evident recovery it would be extremely unlikely that God would permit him to re-enter it. Paul was afraid that he would be disqualified from his ministry – a reject. He was not thinking about losing his salvation, but about proving derelict in his duty and therefore forfeiting his privileges as a minister of Christ. So he disciplined himself – he pummelled his body.

The apostate
After the backslider and the castaway, the third category is the apostate. Certain passages describe him: Hebrews 6:4-8, Hebrews 10:26-31 and 2 Peter 2:20-22.

> It is impossible for those who have once been enlightened, who have tasted the heavenly gift, who have shared in the Holy Spirit, who have tasted the goodness of the word of God and the powers of the coming age, if they fall away, to be brought back to repentance, because to their loss they are crucifying the Son of God all over again and subjecting him to public disgrace (Hebrews 6:4-8).

These passages warn us of a falling away from spiritual influences that entails no possibility of restoration. That is very important. The passage is emphatic: there is no possibility of restoring *these* people. That is why they cause such trouble. I do not believe that these passages are hypothetical. They are not dealing with a man of straw, as if this could never actually occur, as though the writer were just putting something up to frighten us. The language is too strong and too terrifying to be merely painted fire. It is a very real danger. The passages are describing more than an occasional lapse, even into very serious sin. They picture more than Abraham's lying, or David's adultery, or Peter's cowardice under pressure. All of those were restored; all of these it is possible to restore. What the writer is describing is enforced by the word he uses in Hebrews 6:4 – a participle from a verb *piptein*. The verb means to fall headlong, to fall absolutely, to fall without remedy and beyond all recovery. A Christian cannot do that.

The sin described is delineated very clearly in Hebrews 10:29:

> How much more severely do you think a man deserves to be punished who has trampled the Son of God under foot, who has treated as an unholy thing the blood of the covenant that sanctified him, and who has insulted the Spirit of grace?

The sin delineated is a knowing, wilful, deliberate, calculated, complete rejection of Jesus Christ. It is a wilful turning aside from that which you have been convinced is true. It is to rid yourself entirely of the whole of Christianity, in full awareness of what you are doing. It is a hard-faced impenitence in the light of all the warnings of God and the exhortations of others. It is to remain faithless to the day of your death and so prove finally damned.

Can a Christian possibly do that? The answer is

emphatically: 'No, he cannot.' Many of the people whom the writer to the Hebrews addressed were just Jews, who were convinced that Christianity was true, but had not entered into the good of it. That is why Hebrews 3:7-47 is a long exhortation to them to enter into God's rest. 'You're convinced Jesus is who he says he is? Well, enter into God's rest,' he says to them in effect. This ought to alert us that it is possible to be very near to full faith in Christ, but finally to fall short of it. Certainly the description in Hebrews 6:4-6 looks as though it cannot be of anybody else but a Christian!

Five features
But what do the five points mean, which are true of these people who possibly fall away? They were *once enlightened*. Now, as someone has said, all who have been regenerated have been enlightened, but not all those who have been enlightened have been regenerated. 'Once enlightened' means to be intellectually lit up with the gospel, to perceive it in some way, to come to some grasp and understanding of it and to be convinced that it is true. We have all come across people who can say: 'Yes, I can see that.' They do not have overwhelming intellectual barriers to faith, so we ask: 'Why won't you believe?' But they will not. So near, but so far – enlightened. More than this, they have *tasted the heavenly gift*. Tasted – yes; swallowed – no. They have sensed the power of God's truth and even felt

the presence of Jesus. But, as Jesus said to the crowds in John 6:36, 'You have seen me and still you do not believe.' You see, you can have your emotions powerfully affected and yet not believe.

Shared in the Holy Spirit is perhaps the most difficult phrase of all. It is not the same as indwelt by the Holy Spirit, as in Romans 8:9. It means taken up in some way in partnership with the Holy Spirit, perhaps even used by him. In the Sermon on the Mount Jesus said:

> Many will say to me on that day, 'Lord, Lord, did we not prophesy in your name, and in your name drive out demons and perform many miracles?' Then I will tell them plainly, 'I never knew you. Away from me, you evil doers' (Matthew 7:22-23).

It is possible to be used by God and not be a Christian.

You can *taste the goodness of the word of God*, you can sense the powers of the spoken word of God and experience the miraculous interventions of God in your life. You can *feel the powers of the coming age* – just as if there were an exposed live cable by your feet. You could go near it and a spark could leap from the gap from the cable to your fingers. You could momentarily feel the power that was pulsating continuously through that cable. But only the cable is permanently connected to the power station, to the source of supply. You would have had only a temporary influence, on the side, as it were.

It is perhaps like the hundreds of people who pass through our services and become affected, to one degree or another, in the ways the writer of Hebrews has described here. People can come into congregations and feel a temporary influence of the gospel that is so convincing that they are in no doubt that the gospel is true. Then they just turn aside and say: 'I don't want anything to do with it.' That is what is being described in these verses. There is no change of heart. They have had a mild dose of the real thing, but it has only inoculated them against full conversion.

This is warning us that we can have very high privileges, but we have a high responsibility to act on those privileges. It is telling us very solemnly that we can come within the gateway of the city of refuge and still perish, because we have never entered fully in. John Murray has said:

> These passages advise us of forces that are operative in the kingdom of God and of the influences those forces may exert upon those who finally demonstrate that they have never been radically and savingly affected by them.

Never savingly changed

Examples like Simon Magus or Judas Iscariot all fall within the category of people who were greatly affected by the gospel, but were never savingly changed by it. The statement that sums this up is in 2 Peter 2:22, which speaks of a dog returning to its vomit, and of a sow that is washed going back to her wallowing in the mud. The dog never had its nature changed, neither did the sow: there was only an external change in their lives. Bruce Milne says:

> Anyone who returns wholeheartedly to sin, renounces former Christian ways, manifests no remorse in so doing and continues in this apostasy to the end of his life, was, *despite initial appearance*, never truly born of God.

The perseverance of the saints is not in spite of what we are. It is because we continue in the faith that we persevere. The true explanation of those who fall away is in 1 John 2:19:

> They went out from us, but they did not really belong to us. For if they had belonged to us, they would have remained with us; but their going showed that none of them belonged to us.

There was no genuine faith from the start, despite all they professed.

If you and I do not persevere in the faith, what kind of God is it that we follow, whose will could be thwarted by ours? What kind of Saviour do we trust?

Are not his mighty incarnation, his radiant and holy life, his infinitely valuable death on the cross, and his all-victorious resurrection enough to guarantee that we will get into heaven? The gospel we preach magnifies the irresistible and keeping grace of God, that will bring all his own to heaven.

If Jesus does indeed 'save to the uttermost all who come to God by him' then let this truth affect you radically and visibly.

Stop idling! The Christian life is no quiet life, no passive and indolent existence. It is intended to be a life of dynamic and energetic activity, a determination to pursue God and to live productively for his glory.

Be liberated! Shake off nervous introspection and the anxious 'pulse-taking' of a spiritual hypochondriac. Realize your security in God and allow that realization to set you free to serve him and minister to others.

Be obedient! All the truths we have surveyed have not been to provide excuses to live careless and indifferent lives, but rather to supply you with the greatest incentives to please God and obediently implement his will in your day-to-day pilgrimage to your certain goal. Go for gold!

Be optimistic! Never give up in despair over a backsliding friend, and never despair of yourself. Be humble, but confident. You will make it to the end, and praise God, so will your friend.

Therefore, my dear brothers, stand firm. Let nothing move you. Always give yourselves fully to the work of the Lord, because you know that your labour in the Lord is not in vain (1 Corinthians 15:58).

Questions on perseverance

Q: Is it unnatural for a Christian ever to wonder if he is saved?

A: No. Most (all?) Christians have at some time doubted their salvation. But your very concern over it is almost certainly an indication that you *are* saved. Why else would you bother?

Q: Did Paul leave sanctification out of the 'golden chain of salvation' in Romans 8:29 because glorification does not depend on sanctification?

A: The thief on the cross had no opportunity to be sanctified, but he was saved. His glorification did not hinge on his inward holiness. Our perseverance does not ultimately depend on the level of our sanctification. We must persevere in faith, but holiness of life is very difficult to gauge and at some points may seem to be non-existent. Holiness is crucial – God has elected us 'to good works' (Ephesians 2:10). Holiness affects rewards, but salvation depends ultimately on grace and God, not us.

Q: If some can come so near as to have the experiences of Hebrews 6:4-6, and still not be saved at the end, how can any of us know we have been saved?

A: The only answer to that is by looking to Christ. Our assurance is not based in the last analysis on our experiences or obedience; it is based on Christ and what he has done. A Christian ought to have little difficulty in knowing that he is saved just by looking to Christ and what he's done. Such looking to Jesus has an accompanying witness of the Holy Spirit to the heart. No man can call Jesus 'Lord' except by the Holy Spirit. Do you look to Christ and say 'Jesus is my Lord'? When you look up to God, do you have a cry in your heart: 'Abba, Father'? Do you know he's your Father? Don't focus on yourself, focus on Jesus, focus on the Father. That's how I know I'm a Christian – primarily because I'm looking to Christ. That in fact is what the writer to the Hebrews majors on in the last half of chapter 6.

He does bolster them up by pointing out that they have suffered and endured so much: he was encouraged by that, but he will not let them base their assurance on what they have performed in their Christian life. He wants them to see what their hope is in the promises of God: 'Let us fix our eyes on Jesus, the author and perfector of our faith' (Hebrews 12:2). Assurance is derived primarily and sufficiently from Christ and only secondarily from any kind of change of life or obedience on our part.

Q: Does a backslider have to be restored while on earth in order to receive a place in glory?

A: Whatever a backslider is, he is not out of faith. This is proved by the fact that no one is more miserable on earth than a backslider. He can fully go back in all external appearances, but he is miserable because the seed of faith is within him. It is like a spring of water in the earth. You can block up the hole with all kinds of filth and dirt, and the spring can apparently stop flowing. But one day it's going to push through again. Christians have the responsibility to do what God has told them: 'As long as it's called today exhort one another daily, lest some of you become hardened through the deceitfulness of sin.' If we use the means that God has given – exhortation, rebuke, admonition, and even church discipline - and if he is genuinely a child of God, he will be restored.

Q: What is the unforgivable sin? Can a Christian ever commit it?

A: The term Jesus used is the 'blasphemy against the Holy Spirit'. 'Blasphemy' meaning 'to speak evil against'. The Pharisees were attributing to the devil the works Jesus was performing in the power of the Spirit. The blasphemy against the Holy Spirit, therefore, is akin to the terms in Hebrews 10:29, namely, to trample under foot the Son of God, to treat as an unholy thing the blood of the covenant that sanctified, and to insult the Spirit of grace. It is the mentality of an avowed, wilful, knowing rejection of the Holy Spirit's teaching, instruction, promptings, leading, conviction – a deliberate rejection of all of that. A Christian can never do that. The love of God is within him and there is a sin that he cannot commit. As John Murray said: 'There are certain types of unfaithfulness the Christian cannot commit.' And one type is trampling under foot the Son of God. However far a Christian may go, however much he may backslide, he cannot wilfully and knowingly trample under foot the preciousness of the blood of Christ, and say: 'No, Holy Spirit! I don't want anything to do with you or your religion again!'

Q: Is it possible for someone to have and use the gifts of the Holy Spirit and not be saved?

A: Not only can the Holy Spirit use graceless Christians in the gifts of the Spirit – he can also use non-Christians. Many will say to Jesus on the judgment day: 'Lord, Lord, did we not prophesy in your name, and in your name drive out demons and perform many miracles?' (Matthew 7:22). Judas Iscariot, presumably, went out on all the missions with the apostles and was given along with them the ability to preach and to do miraculous works.

He came back with the rest of them saying: 'Lord, even the demons submit to us in your name' (Luke 10:17). Jesus said: 'Do not rejoice that the spirits submit to you, but rejoice that your names are written in heaven' (Luke 10:20). Our security in the Christian life is not dependent on any gifts or abilities, even if given by the Holy Spirit. The least graces are better security for heaven than the most powerful gifts. The Holy Spirit may temporarily use non-Christians in works and gifts.

Q: Can you explain 2 Peter 1:5 – the exhortation to 'add to our faith'? How does this bear on perseverance?

A: The opening verses (1-4) of 2 Peter 1 speak about what God has done for us ('his divine power has given us everything we need for life and godliness'). The promises of God, all his resources, are at our disposal. Therefore verse 5 says: 'Get cracking! Make every effort to build – add to – furnish out – your faith' – as a couple would when they move into a house, first cleaning it out and then furnishing and decorating. Peter is saying: 'Here you are in the house of salvation. The house is swept clean. Well, now furnish it out!' The reason is (verse

10): 'Be all the more eager to make your calling and election sure. For if you do these things, you will never fall, and you will receive a rich welcome into the eternal kingdom of our Lord and Saviour Jesus Christ.' Our salvation is not conditional on our obedience to verses 5 to 9, but our sense of welfare, well-being and that kind of 'rich welcome' are. Do you want Jesus to say to you on that day: 'Well done, good and faithful servant?' Well, for this reason, make every effort to furnish out your faith.

Q: Is it possible for a Christian to commit suicide? If so, how does that affect his standing before God?

A: It is very hard to understand the mind of a suicide, but perhaps more people than we may suspect have, in depression, entertained the thought. That does not mean that faith in Christ has died within them. It does not mean that the suicide has necessarily died outside the faith. Judas Iscariot, by contrast, seems to have died outside the faith; he had remorse for what he had done, but no repentance. Peter, who denied Jesus and went away, was different, for he wept bitterly. There is no indication that Judas was repentant at the last. He died the apostate, unbelieving suicide's death, the death of a man in absolute despair. He is different from the Christian. Suicide is horrendous, but a Christian may not be in complete control of his faculties – for example, through the debilitating effects of prolonged mental trouble. Many factors drive a person towards suicide, but we are not warranted to say that such a person may have been an unbeliever. Their faith may have been too low to encourage them out of that depression, but not so low as to be non-existent.

Q: God does not base salvation on our works, but what place does he give to works in the Christian life?

A: A very high place indeed. Hebrews 6 is a rebuke to those who are lapsing from an energetic outworking of their faith. 'Let us leave the elementary teachings about Christ and go on to maturity' (6:1). His concept of maturity is a fruitful life of blessing to others – the life he delineates in Hebrews 13 by all his practical exhortations. '[We are] created in Christ Jesus to do good works, which God prepared in advance for us to do' (Ephesians 2:10). The practical thrust of all Paul's letters exhorts us to fruitfulness and energy in the Christian life. The *motive* for such exertion is not that our salvation hangs in the balance if we do not put our backs into it. It is precisely because our salvation is secure that we do and always want to 'give ourselves fully to the Lord' (1 Corinthians 15:58). If I thought that there were some uncertainty about my salvation, I think I would give up. But if I know I am saved, that makes me all the keener for the Lord.

For Further Reading

Among the many books relevant to the subjects covered in these pages are the following:

General books on God and grace
D A Carson *Divine Sovereignty and Human Responsibility* (Marshall Morgan & Scott)
S B Ferguson *The Christian Life: a doctrinal introduction* (Hodder & Stoughton)
E F Kevan *Salvation* (Evangelical Press)
J I Packer *Knowing God* (Hodder & Stoughton)
J I Packer *Evangelism and the Sovereignty of God* (IVP)
George Philip *The Apostles' Creed* (Christian Focus Publications).
A W Pink *The Sovereignty of God* (Banner of Truth)

Reference books
L Berkhof *Systematic Theology* (Banner of Truth)
L Berkhof *A Summary of Christian Doctrine* (Banner of Truth)
B Milne *Know The Truth* (IVP)
R. Shaw *Exposition of the Westminster Confession of Faith* (Christian Focus Publications)

Historical background
For a celebrated collection of the statements of many of the major Reformed writers of the 16th and 17th centuries, see the volume *Reformed Dogmatics* by Heinrich Heppe (Baker Book House, USA).

Specific themes

(1) Man

For an excellent general survey of what the Bible says, and what Christians have thought down the centuries, see *The Christian View of Man* by H D McDonald (Marshall Morgan & Scott).

On Marxism, see *The Challenge of Marxism* by Klaus Bockmuehl (IVP) and *Karl Marx* by David Lyon (IVP/Lion).

On existentialism and humanism, see the books listed in McDonald (above) *and Christianity: the true humanism* by J I Packer and T Howard (Word).

On the image of God in man, see McDonald and, for a more detailed study, *Man: the image of God* by G C Berkouwer (Studies in Dogmatics; IVP). See also *Sin* by G C Berkouwer (Studies in Dogmatics; Eerdmans).

On holiness and wrath, see: (a) *The Cross in the New Testament* by L Morris (Paternoster); (b) Volume 4 of *God, Revelation and Authority* by C F H Henry (Word Books); and (c) *The Book of Leviticus* by G Wenham (New International Commentary Series; Marshall Morgan & Scott).

On Romans 1, see the multivolume series on Romans by D M Lloyd-Jones (Banner of Truth).

For two classic works on man's condition, see *The Bondage of the Will* by Martin Luther and *The Freedom of the Will* by Jonathan Edwards.

(2) Election

G C Berkouwer *Election* (Studies in Dogmatics: Eerdmans)

R Sheehan *Chosen For Glory* (Christian Focus Publications)

B B Warfield *Biblical Foundations* (IVP; essay on 'Predestination')

(3) The cross

D Bridge *Jesus - The Man and his Message* (Christian Focus Publications)

R A Finlayson *The Cross in the Experience of our Lord* (Christian Focus Publications)

D M Lloyd-Jones *God's Way of Reconciliation* on Ephesians 2 (Banner of Truth)

D M Lloyd-Jones *The Cross* (Kingsway Publications)

J Murray *Redemption accomplished and applied* (Banner of Truth)

J Owen *The Death of Death in the Death of Christ* (Banner of Truth)

J I Packer *What did the cross achieve?* (Tyndale Bulletin, 1974)

A W Pink *Seven Sayings of the Saviour on the Cross* (Christian Focus Publications)

R C Sproul *Mighty Christ* (Christian Focus Publications)

(4) Grace

J Boice *The Grace of God* (Baker Book House)

J Cheeseman and others *The Grace of God in the Gospel* (Banner of Truth)

(5) Perseverance

D M Lloyd-Jones *Assurance* on Romans 5 (Banner of Truth)

D M Lloyd-Jones *The Final Perseverance of the Saints* on Romans 8:17-39 (Banner of Truth)

Focus on the Bible Commentary series

Focus on the Bible is a series aimed at providing in-depth studies of the Bible in a readable and non-technical fashion. The series covers both Old and New Testaments. It is useful for both pastors and Bible Study leaders as well as helping individuals understand the teachings of the Bible. The authors come from different countries, but each is committed to an evangelical understanding of Scripture.

Jonah, Micah and Nahum
John L Mackay
ISBN 1 85792 03 09   *240 pages*   B format

Haggai, Zechariah and Malachi
John L Mackay
ISBN 1 85792 06 78   *350 pages*   B format

Both above commentaries are written by the Professor of Old Testament in the Free Church College, Edinburgh, Scotland.

Mark
Geoffrey Grogan
ISBN 1 85792 114 3   *224 pages*   B format

Geoffrey Grogan was the Principal of the Bible Training Institute, Glasgow (now Glasgow Bible College). He has written several books including *Wrestling With The Big Issues*, a study of the ways Paul dealt with the various problems he faced. It is also published by Christian Focus Publications.

Romans
R C Sproul
ISBN 1 85792 077 5   *250 pages*   B format

Ephesians
R C Sproul
ISBN 185792 078 3   *160 pages*   B format
R C Sproul is Professor of Systematic Theology at Reformed Seminary, Orlando, USA. He is the author of numerous books.

Philippians
Hywel Jones
ISBN 1 85792 046 5   *160 pages*   B format
Hywel R Jones is Principal of London Theological Seminary and has pastored churches in both London and Wales.

James
Derek Prime
ISBN 1 85792 129 1   176 pages   B format
Derek Prime, formerly pastor of Charlotte Baptist Chapel, Edinburgh, is the author of numerous books and is in considerable demand as a speaker and lecturer.

Other titles are currently in preparation and will be published in due course.

Peter Lewis is Minister of Cornerstone Evangelical Church in Nottingham, and his preaching ministry is respected at conventions and churches throughout the country. He has written *The Glory of Christ* and *The Lord's Prayer*.

Roy Clements is Pastor of Eden Baptist Church in Cambridge. He preaches at many conventions, including Keswick and Word Alive. Several of his books are available and Christian Focus Publications have two of them. *The Strength of Weakness* is an exposition of 2 Corinthians and is particularly suitable for those in leadership. *Songs of Experience* looks at ten well-known psalms, each of which describes a different but common Christian experience such as guilt, anxiety, joy and praise.

Greg Haslam is Pastor of Stanmore Evangelical Church in Winchester, and he too is respected for his preaching ministry. He is the author of *Could You Fall Away?*, which examines the Bible's teaching on backsliding and apostasy.

Lilian Jackson Braun composed her first poem at the age of two. She began writing her *Cat Who...* detective series when one of her own Siamese cats mysteriously fell to its death from her apartment block. Since then over twenty-eight *Cat Who...* novels have been published, all featuring the very talented Koko and Yum Yum, Siamese cats with a bent for detection. She is currently working on the next in this internationally bestselling series.

Lilian Jackson Braun and her husband, Earl, live in the mountains of North Carolina.

Praise for the bestselling *Cat Who...* series:

'Whimsical and wonderful . . . vive the cats!' *New York Daily News*

'The entanglements are better than a Christie and the cat descriptions are terrific' *Liverpool Daily Post*

'For all those cat aficionados out there, here are more quaint, small-town goings-on' *Library Journal*

'More twists and turns than a tabby's tail' *South Wales Argus*

'Cat-loving fans of Braun will enjoy the latest from Pickax' *Kirkus Reviews*

'Lilian Jackson Braun keeps both paws planted on the side of charming' *Los Angeles Times*

Also by Lilian Jackson Braun

Short Story Collections

Qwilleran's Short And Tall Tales

THE CAT WHO
HAD 60
WHISKERS

Lilian Jackson Braun

headline

First published in Great Britain in 2007
by HEADLINE PUBLISHING GROUP

First published in paperback in Great Britain in 2007
by HEADLINE PUBLISHING GROUP

1

Cataloguing in Publication Data is available from the British Library

ISBN 978 0 7553 3855 9

Typeset in Times by Avon DataSet Ltd,
Bidford-on-Avon, Warwickshire, B50 4JH

Printed and bound in Great Britain by Clays Ltd, St Ives plc

Headline's policy is to use papers that are natural, renewable and
recyclable products and made from wood grown in sustainable forests.
The logging and manufacturing processes are expected to conform to the
environmental regulations of the country of origin.

HEADLINE PUBLISHING GROUP
A division of Hachette Livre UK Ltd
338 Euston Road
London NW1 3BH

www.headline.co.uk
www.hodderheadline.com

Dedicated to Earl Bettinger,

The Husband Who . . .

ACKNOWLEDGMENTS

To Earl, my other half – for his husbandly love, encouragement, and help in a hundred ways.

To my research assistant, Shirley Bradley – for her expertise and enthusiasm.

To Becky Faircloth, my office assistant – who's always there when I need her.

To my editor, Natalee Rosenstein – for her faith in *The Cat Who* from the very beginning.

To my literary agent, Blanche C. Gregory, Inc. – for a lifetime of agreeable partnership.

To the real-life Kokos and Yum Yums – for their fifty years of inspiration.

PROLOGUE

Overheard at an alfresco party in Moose County, 400 miles north of everywhere:

WOMAN IN BLUE SHETLAND SWEATER: 'I have never heard of such a thing! And I've been a veterinarian for twenty years!'

MAN WITH LARGE MOUSTACHE: 'What can I say? I counted them myself.'

WOMAN: 'You might have miscounted.'

MAN: 'Would you like to count them yourself? If I'm right, you can report the evidence to a scientific journal. If I'm wrong, I'll take you to dinner at the Mackintosh Inn.'

WOMAN: 'Fair enough! We'll do it the next time you bring him in for a dental prophylaxis.'

One

The man with the large moustache (a well-groomed pepper and salt) was Jim Qwilleran, columnist for the *Moose County Something* and transplant from Down Below, as locals called the metropolitan areas to the south. They themselves, for the most part, were descended from the early settlers, and they had inherited the pioneer fortitude, sense of humor, and appreciation of individuality.

They enjoyed the Qwill Pen column that ran twice weekly . . . accepted the fact that he lived alone in a converted apple barn, with two cats . . . and admired his magnificent moustache.

3

James Mackintosh Qwilleran had entertained several ambitions in his youth Down Below: first to play second base with the Chicago Cubs, then to act on the Broadway stage, and later to write for the *New York Times*. He had certainly never wanted to be the richest individual in the northeast central United States! How it happened was a tale 'stranger than fiction'.

'Aunt Fanny' Klingenschoen probably knew what she was doing when she made him her sole heir.

Qwilleran established a philanthropic organization: the Klingenschoen Foundation, which went to work improving the quality of life in Moose County. Medical, scholastic, cultural, and infrastructural improvements were made possible by the K Fund, as it was known to one and all.

To everyone's surprise, other old-moneyed families were inspired to put their fortunes to work for the public good. A music center, two museums – one in a mansion – and a senior recreation facility were in the works.

Everything's going too smoothly, Qwilleran thought, with the pessimism of a seasoned newsman. 'What's your fix on the situation, Arch?' he asked his old friend from Chicago.

Arch Riker was now editor in chief of the *Something*. He shook his head morosely. 'When there's so much money floating around, somebody's gonna get greedy.'

(Visitors from far and wide – in formal attire – had paid five hundred dollars a ticket for a preview of the mansion, called the Old Manse.)

It was a late evening in August. Qwilleran and the cats had been enjoying a cozy evening in the barn. He had read to them from the *Wall Street Journal*, and they all had a little ice cream.

The barn was an octagonal structure of fieldstone and weathered shingles more than a century old. Indoors, all the old wood surfaces and overhead rafters had been bleached to a honey color, and odd-shaped windows had been cut in the walls.

Where once there had been lofts for storing apples, now there was a ramp winding around the interior, with balconies at three levels.

Later in the evening, the Siamese deserted the reading area and chased each other up and down the ramp, then dropped like flying squirrels onto the sofa on the main floor. The living areas were open plan, surrounding a huge fireplace cube, its stacks rising to the roof forty feet overhead.

It was almost eleven P.M., and Koko and Yum Yum were being unduly attentive; it was time for their bedtime snack.

Proceeding in slow motion, to tantalize the anxious cats,

he rattled the canisters of Kabibbles and dusted off their two plates with exaggerated care. They watched hungrily. Koko appeared to be breathing heavily.

Suddenly Koko switched his attention to the wall phone that hung between the kitchen window and the back door. He stared at it for a minute, twitching his ears nervously.

Qwilleran got the message. By some catly intuition, Koko knew the phone was going to ring. After a few seconds it rang. How did that smart cat know? Guessing that it would be Polly Duncan, the chief woman in his life, Qwilleran answered in a facetiously syrupy voice: 'Good evening!'

'Well! You sound in a good mood,' she said in the gentle voice he knew so well. 'What are you doing?'

'Nothing much. What are you doing?'

'Shortening my new dress a couple of inches.'

'Whoo-ee!'

Ignoring the comic wolf whistle, she went on, 'It's much too long, and I thought I'd wear it with some Scottish accessories Sunday afternoon, since the party's celebrating Dr Connie's return from Scotland. Would you consider wearing your Highland attire, Qwill?'

Although he had once rebelled at wearing what he called a 'skirt', he now felt proud in a Mackintosh kilt with a dagger in his knee sock. After all, his mother had been a Mackintosh.

'What was Connie doing in Scotland? Do you know?'

'She earned her degree from the veterinary school in Glasgow twenty years ago, and she goes back to visit friends. Did you know her cat has been boarding with Wetherby?'

'No! How does he get along with Jet Stream?'

'Connie introduced them when Bonnie Lassie was a kitten, and now Jet Stream acts like her big brother. And,' she went on, 'Connie brought Joe a lovely Shetland sweater as a thank-you for boarding Bonnie Lassie.

'Do you realize, Qwill, that the Shetland archipelago, where the wool comes from, has a hundred islands! . . . A hundred islands!' she repeated when he failed to respond.

'It boggles the mind,' he said absently, watching the Siamese trying to get into the Kabibbles canister.

'Well, anyway, I thought you'd like to hear the latest. *À bientôt*, dear.'

'*À bientôt.*'

After the Siamese had finished their bedtime repast and their washing up, Qwilleran escorted them up the ramp to their quarters on the top balcony. They looked around as if they had never seen it before, then hopped into their respective baskets and turned around three times before settling down.

Cats. Who can understand them? Qwilleran thought, as he quietly closed their door.

Returning to his desk at ground level, he wrote about it in his private journal. He was a compulsive writer! When not turning out a thousand words for the Qwill Pen column, he was writing a biography or history of interest in Moose County. And he always filled a couple of pages in his private journal. On this occasion, he wrote:

I've said it before, and I'll say it again: Koko is a remarkable cat! Is it because his real name is Kao K'o-Kung, so he knows he's descended from the royal Siamese?

Or is it because – as I insist – he has sixty whiskers?

He knows several seconds in advance when the phone is going to ring – and also whether the caller is a friend or a telemarketer selling life insurance or dog food.

When crazies bombed the city hall window boxes, Koko knew ten minutes in advance that something dire was going to happen. Why didn't someone read his signals? The police chief was sitting here having a nightcap, and neither of us got the message!

Oh, well! We can't all be as smart as a psychic Siamese!

Two

Qwilleran was a well-known figure in downtown Pickax: tall, well built, middle-aged, always wearing an orange baseball cap. He responded to casual greetings with a friendly salute and took time to listen if someone had something to say. There was a brooding look of concern in his eyes that made townsfolk wonder. Some wondered if there had been a great tragedy in his life. His best friends wondered, too, but they had the good taste not to pry. Once he had been seen to help an old lady cross Main Street. When observers commended him for his gallantry, he said, 'No big deal! She just wanted to get to the other side.'

At Lois's Luncheonette, where Qwilleran went for coffee and apple pie and the latest scuttlebutt, customers would say, 'How's Koko, Mr Q?' Humorous mentions about Koko and Yum Yum in the Qwill Pen were awaited by eager readers.

Moose County was said to have more cats per capita than any other county in the state. In Lockmaster County, horses and dogs were the pets of choice.

In cold weather, when the converted barn was hard to heat, Qwilleran moved his household to Indian Village, an upscale residential complex on the north edge of Pickax. There, four-plex apartments and clusters of condos had features that appealed to career-minded singles and a few couples. There was a clubhouse with a swimming pool, meeting rooms, and a bar. There were walking paths for bird-watching along the banks of a creek. And indoor cats were permitted.

The cluster called the Willows had four rather notable occupants: the manager of the Pirate's Chest bookstore, a doctor of veterinary medicine, the WPKX meteorologist, and – at certain times of the year – a columnist for the *Moose County Something*.

Also in residence were six indoor felines: Polly Duncan's Brutus and Catta; Dr Connie Cosgrove's kitten, Bonnie Lassie; Wetherby Goode's Jet Stream; and Jim

Qwilleran's Siamese, Koko and Yum Yum, well known to newspaper readers.

Wetherby Goode (real name Joe Bunker) had a yen for party-giving and a talent for entertaining at the piano. He played 'Flight of the Bumblebee' and 'The Golliwog's Cakewalk' without urging at pizza parties on Sunday afternoons.

Dr Connie's return from Scotland was a good excuse for assembling the residents of the Willows.

The guest of honor was wearing a Shetland sweater in a luscious shade of blue. The host was wearing the taupe sweater she had brought him from Scotland, and there were Shetland scarfs for Polly and Qwilleran.

'Connie, may I ask why you chose to get your degree in Scotland?' Qwilleran asked.

She said, 'The vet school at University of Glasgow is internationally known – and has been for many years. It's noted for teaching excellence and research. Early studies of animal diseases later resulted in advances in human medicine.'

Wetherby sat down at the piano and played a medley of songs from *Brigadoon* with the flourishes that were his trademark.

Qwilleran recited Robert Burns's poem 'A Man's a Man for All That'. Toasts were drunk. And then the pizza was delivered.

During the meal there was plenty of talk: mostly about Hixie Rice, who was promotion director for the newspaper and a resident of Indian Village. She was masterminding the new senior center on a pro bono basis ... She had worked so hard on the Fourth of July parade, and then it was rained out by the hurricane ... and then vandals had trashed the front of the city hall after she had done wonders in beautifying it. As for romance, she had been unlucky.

Qwilleran, who had known Hixie Down Below and had been instrumental in her coming to Moose County, had little to say.

She was unlucky, that was all. She was talented, spirited, and a tireless worker – but unlucky. There was a Hixie jinx that followed her, and now she was charged with the responsibility for the new senior center.

The *Something* had announced a contest to name it, with an entry blank printed on the front page.

Joe Bunker said, 'That was very clever of the *Something*. To make three entries, you have to buy three papers.'

Qwilleran said, 'You weathermen are too smart, Joe. We thought no one would notice our scheme.'

Polly said, 'The official ballot box has been in the bookstore, and it created a lot of traffic. Judd Amhurst kept moving it around so the carpet wouldn't wear out in one spot. Judd retired early from his job with Moose County Power, and he still had plenty of pep. He's manager of the Lit Club and he volunteers at the animal shelter, where he washes dogs.'

'What's next on the program at the Lit Club?' Qwilleran asked.

'There's a retired professor in Lockmaster who's an authority on Proust, and he's coming to lecture ... It would be nice, Qwill,' Polly said, 'if you'd put him up at the barn for one overnight.'

Qwilleran said, 'I'm sure it would make a good perk in addition to the modest stipend you can afford. Koko has been making aerial attacks. On ailurophobes. I hope this speaker likes cats.'

The foursome moved to the deck for coffee and Polly's homemade chocolate brownies. Jet Stream accompanied them on a leash, because of the recent scare about rabid wildlife. There had been a time when cats were free to visit the creek and watch the fish and birds. Now there was evidence of rabid skunks, raccoons, and foxes. What had happened?

Joe explained, 'Too many house pets are getting mixed up with rabid wildlife!'

Polly said she had never understood the nature of rabies.

'An infectious disease common to some forms of

13

wildlife,' Dr Connie said. 'It's transmitted through the saliva when rabid animals get into fights with household pets and bite them. The best safeguard is the leash or the cage. Otherwise they'll see something move on the bank of the creek and be off for some fun!'

Qwilleran said, 'We never had rabid animals in downtown Chicago – only kids with slingshots and careless truck drivers.'

Then Qwilleran broached the subject of Koko's sixty whiskers, and Dr Connie said, 'I can't imagine that Koko was enthusiastic about your counting them.'

Qwilleran said, 'I gave him a mild sedative that is used in the theater when cats are to be onstage.' He was the first to say he had to go home and feed the cats. The women said the same thing. As a farewell, Joe sat down at the piano and played 'Kitten on the Keys' very fast!

Someone said, 'We must do this again soon,' and everyone agreed.

Qwilleran escorted Polly to Unit One and went in to say good night to Brutus and Catta, as he always did.

After Joe's fast pace at the piano and after the nonstop friendly chatter, Qwilleran welcomed a quiet evening with the Siamese.

Driving home, Qwilleran remembered growing up in Chicago and hearing his mother play 'Kitten on the Keys'

– and marveling at how her fingers flew over the keyboard. Now Joe Bunker played it twice as fast! Where did he get his nervous energy? He grew up in the town of Horseradish, inhaling all those powerful fumes. Joe had a cousin with a PhD in corvidology, and she was as wacky as he was.

Entering the barnyard, he saw Koko cavorting in the kitchen window. He knew what that meant.

Two cats – Where's our dinner? We're starving!

One cat – There's a message on the phone.

The call was from Judd Amhurst, one of the three judges assigned to select a new name for the facility.

'Qwill! We've got the name! And it's perfect! It'll be in tomorrow's paper, but if you can't wait, give me a call.'

Judd lived at the Winston Park apartment complex – just across from the bookstore where the judging was scheduled to take place.

Never comfortable with unanswered questions, Qwilleran phoned him immediately. 'Judd, don't keep me in suspense!'

'Well, Maggie, Thornton, and I met in one of the community rooms at the bookstore. Big table! Bushels of entries! We started reading them aloud. Most were ordinary. Some were silly. A few had possibilities. Then

Thornton read one from Bill Turmeric of Sawdust City—'

'I know him!' Qwilleran interrupted. 'He writes clever letters to the editor.'

'You'll like this one! It's complete with a motto!' Then he read: 'Senior Health Club – Good for the Body, Good for the Mind, Good for the Spirit.'

'Sign me up!' Qwilleran said. 'Am I old enough?'

'I thought you'd like it, Qwill. We sorted through all of them, but this was the best.'

'What's the prize?'

'The paper's giving two hundred dollars, and there are gift certificates from merchants.'

'Well, thanks for tipping me off. I'll devote Tuesday's column to the Old Hulk – Its Past and Future.'

Qwilleran started making notes for his Tuesday column:

- Feed-and-seed warehouse.
- Served farmers for more than a century.
- Called the Old Hulk.
- Typical warehouse: flat roof, no windows, loading dock.
- Interior: nothing but open space with lofts for sacks of feed and seed, connected by ramps. In-town location no longer serviceable to today's farmers,

16

who prefer more accessible outlets located at handy locations around the county.

- Property vacant for several years.
- Will need public entrances, windows, five floors connected by stairs and elevators, plumbing, electricity, and a lot of paint and carpet and ideas!
- Why not a roof garden?

In his journal he would write:

The Old Hulk was a piece of abandoned property on the north edge of Pickax, recently purchased by the Scottish community and given to the city as a senior center, along with a grant covering complete remodeling, redecorating, and furnishing.

In the nineteenth century, Scottish shipbuilders had come to Moose County to build three-masted schooners using the two-hundred-foot pine trees for masts. When steam replaced sail, they turned to house building and did well, as attested by their mansions in Purple Point and their support of community projects. The senior center was to be their thank-you.

As for the property chosen, it had been a feed-and-seed depot and warehouse where farm wagons came to stock up. New modes of transportation had replaced it with several small depots around the county. The Old Hulk, as it was called, became a hangout for kids, feral cats, and who knows what else. Now, architects and builders were donating their expertise and the *Something* was offering the coordinating services of Hixie Rice to the project pro bono.

Later that day, Qwilleran had a phone call from Hixie Rice.

'Guess what? The dog table is back!'

Early in the year an heirloom auction had been staged to raise money for furnishing the new Senior Health Club. Old families donated prized possessions – everything from porcelain teacups to rare items of furniture.

One such was a six-foot library table of ponderous oak construction with bulbous legs at one end; the other end was supported by a life-size carving of a basset hound. It was donated by the office manager of the *Something*, inherited from her wealthy father.

Everyone said: 'It weighs a ton! Bet she's glad to get rid of it. Can she take it as a tax deduction? What's it worth?'

At the auction an unidentified agent made a sealed bid and won the table for . . . ten thousand dollars! It left town on a truck for parts unknown.

Now the dog table was back! . . . donated to the Senior Health Club by an unidentified well-wisher.

Qwilleran asked, 'How will it be used?'

'In the foyer, which is quite large. It'll be a focal point, with magazines on top, and a table lamp . . . Maybe we should have a cat lamp! An artist could do a sculpture of a cat sitting on his haunches and holding the socket in his paws! Do you think Koko would pose? Everybody would come to see our dog table and cat lamp!'

'Hang up!' Qwilleran said. 'You're hallucinating!'

Three

Qwilleran was half an hour late in serving breakfast to the cats on Monday morning. They attacked their plates as if they had been deprived of food for a week. At one point, though, Koko raised his head abruptly and stared at a spot on the kitchen wall. In a few seconds the phone rang, and he returned to the business at hand.

The caller was Lisa Compton, retired academic and wife of the school superintendent. She was also the chief volunteer at Edd Smith's Place, where preowned books were sold for charitable causes.

'Qwill, a chauffeur from Purple Point just brought

in a box of books that made me think of you.'

'The statement raises questions,' he said.

'You'll love them! They're all pocket-size hardcovers – the kind they had before paperbacks. Convenient for reading to the cats – and really quite attractive. Some have decorative covers and gold-printed titles on the spines.'

'What kind of titles?'

'All classics. *Kidnapped*, *Lorna Doone*, *Uncle Tom's Cabin* . . . and authors like Guy de Maupassant, Henry James, and Mark Twain.'

Qwilleran said, 'Don't let them get away from you! I'll be right there!'

'May I make a suggestion? Since the box is rather large, you should park in the north lot and come to the back door. It leads right downstairs into Edd Smith's Place.'

Qwilleran liked Lisa. She always thought everything through – not only selling him the books but figuring the easiest way of getting them to his car.

'And by the way, Qwill, there's some Lit Club business to discuss. If you have time.' She used a formal voice that indicated the other volunteers were listening. 'Do you have a few minutes?'

Always interested in a little intrigue, he said, 'See you in ten minutes.'

* * *

Later, in the private meeting room, Lisa said in a low voice, 'This is not for publication, but I'm giving up volunteer work and taking a paid job as manager of the Senior Health Club.'

'Well!' he said in astonishment. 'I'm shocked – and pleased! What does Lyle think about it?'

'He thinks the club is very lucky to get me.'

'I agree!'

'It's a big job of coordination: scheduling activities, handling memberships, finding instructors, finding new ideas—'

'Lisa, you're the only one who can do it. Let me know if there's anything that I can do to help.'

Famous last words, he thought on the way back to the barn. What am I getting into?

Qwilleran collected Famous Last Words and had his readers contributing them too. Someday, he told them, the K Fund might publish a collection. There were examples like:

'You don't need to take an umbrella . . . It's not going to rain.'
'The Road Commission says the old wooden bridge . . . is perfectly safe!'

'Let's not stop to buy gas . . . We're only driving over the
mountain.'

And for every gem that was printed, he gave the proud
contributor a fat yellow lead pencil stamped *Qwill Pen* in
gold – trophies that were treasured.

To Arch Riker it was just a lazy columnist's way of
letting his readers do all the work. The editor's huff was all
an act, of course, Qwilleran told himself with a complacent
shrug as the sacks of his fan mail filled the mailroom.

When Qwilleran brought the boxful of books into the
barn, Koko came running; Yum Yum came in a sedate
second.

Qwilleran placed the treasure trove on the bar, and Koko
proceeded to go wild with excitement, a performance
leading one to wonder where the books had been. When
they were unloaded, however, it became evident that it was
the box – not the books – that aroused the cat's interest.
Interest was a mild word; Koko went berserk over the
empty box, inside and out!

Qwilleran called the ESP. 'Lisa! Is it polite to ask who
donated these books?'

'Is it polite to ask why you want to know?' she asked
teasingly.

'Koko wants to know. It's not the books that interest him so much as the box they came in.'

'It's large,' Lisa said. 'Maybe he wants to set up housekeeping in it.'

'It's not only large – but plain. Just a brown carton without any pictures of Ivory Snow or Campbell's Soup.'

'That's funnier than you think, Qwill. The books came from one of the Campbell families in Purple Point.'

'I wonder where they acquired them. Do you know that family well enough to ask? Tell them Cool Koko wants to know its provenance.'

'They'll love it! They're all fans of the Qwill Pen.'

With shelf space found for the books and a session of reading from *The Portrait of a Lady*, Koko calmed down. The box itself was in the shed along with rubbish and a few garden tools. A do-not-discard note was taped to it; its provenance remained a mystery.

As for Koko, he behaved like a normal house cat for the rest of the day until four o'clock.

Late Monday afternoon, Qwilleran was lounging in his big chair when Koko suddenly appeared from nowhere and jumped to the arm of the chair. His lithe body was taut and his ears pointed toward the kitchen window.

Someone's coming! Qwilleran thought. The cat jumped down and ran to the kitchen, where he could look out the window from the countertop. Qwilleran followed him.

Outside the window was the barnyard – and then a patch of dense woods and a dirt road leading to Main Street and several important buildings. Surrounding a traffic circle were two churches, the public library, a theater arts building, and the grand old courthouse.

Qwilleran waited to see a vehicle coming through the woods. Nothing arrived, but Koko kept on watching. Qwilleran went back to his lounge chair.

At that moment the kitchen phone rang. It was the attorney.

'Qwill! This is Bart! I know this is short notice. Do you have a few minutes? I'm phoning from the court-house.'

Qwilleran was stunned into silence. Koko had known a call was coming from a building half a mile away!

'Qwill, did you hear me? I said—'

'I heard you, Bart. Koko was diverting my attention, that's all. Come on over.'

'Tell Koko I have a treat for him.'

'Your Uncle George is coming,' he told the cats.

Shortly, the attorney arrived and was joyously greeted by all.

The four of them proceeded single file to the conference table – Qwilleran carrying the coffee, Bart carrying his briefcase, and the cats carrying their tails straight up.

Opening his briefcase, Bart said, 'My wife sent a treat for the cats – something she makes for our brats. They like the sound effects when they crunch it.' He drew a plastic zipper bag from among the documents.

'It's like Italian biscotti but with seasoning of particular interest to cats – my wife says! She calls it biscatti.'

Koko and Yum Yum were allowed to sniff the plastic bag, but it was too early 'for their treat'.

Qwilleran said, 'While you're here, Bart, perhaps you could give me some information about the Ledfield house that's being opened as a museum. Not everyone knows it's called the Old Manse – and has been for the last hundred years. I'm wondering if Nathan Ledfield's grandfather had read Hawthorne's *Mosses from an Old Manse* and incorporated any ideas from his reading. If so, it's a suggestion for the Qwill Pen.'

'Would you like a tour of the house?' Bart asked. 'It can be arranged.'

Then he launched into an explanation of necessary changes in converting a private mansion to a county-owned museum.

'Nathan Ledfield had long employed two assistants:

Daisy Babcock, who handled financial matters, and Alma Lee James, in charge of his collection of art and antiques . . . You may know her parents' art gallery in Lockmaster, Qwill. Alma Lee is very knowledgeable, and her connection with the gallery resulted in some very favorable purchases for the Ledfield collection . . . Is there more coffee?'

As Qwilleran poured, he said, 'Leaving the mansion to the county must have entailed some drastic changes.'

'Not too drastic,' the attorney assured him. 'Alma Lee has been named director of the museum. That involves training museum guides as well as supervising maintenance of the building. Daisy Babcock will act as her assistant, since the finances will be handled by an investment counselor appointed by the county.'

'Then I should see Miss James for a tour of the Old Manse,' Qwilleran assumed.

'Yes, either she or Miss Babcock can show you around . . . If you'll pardon a little in-house gossip: Daisy Babcock resents being demoted to second-in-command. When Nathan Ledfield was boss, Daisy was his fair-haired girl! I wouldn't be surprised if she quits. She's married to one of the Linguini sons but uses her maiden name.'

'Wise choice,' Qwilleran murmured, reflecting that 'Daisy Linguini' would be a fetching name for a trapeze performer but not so good for a financial secretary to a billionaire.

Qwilleran asked, 'Are those the Linguinis who had the wonderful Italian restaurant?' It was a mom-and-pop operation. If a customer was having a birthday, Papa Linguini would come out of the kitchen in his chef's hat, get down on one knee, fling his arms wide, and sing Happy B-ir-r-rthday in an operatic voice. 'Apparently they retired.'

'Yes, and their sons preferred to open a party store and plant a vineyard. They also want to open a winery, but the neighbors along the shore are objecting.'

Before he left, Bart said, 'About visiting the Old Manse: either of the women could show you around and answer your questions, but it might be politic to work with Alma James. Let me break the ice for you. I know she's been dying to see your barn—'

'Half the Western world has been wanting to see my barn. That's okay. How do we go about it?'

'I could drive her over someday, then ease her out if she wants to stay too long.'

'Does she like cats?' Qwilleran asked. 'Koko has been known to react to ailurophobes in peculiar ways.'

'She's from Lockmaster and is more accustomed to dogs and horses.'

'I could put Koko and Yum Yum out in the gazebo.'

'No! No!' said Bart, a confirmed ailurophile. 'It's their barn! Let her adjust. If she begins to itch or sneeze, she won't want to stay so long.'

Qwilleran, detecting a lack of enthusiasm on the attorney's part, asked, 'How do you size up the two women in charge of the Manse?'

'Daisy is always relaxed and friendly. Alma – I never liked that name – is warm or cold, agreeable or reserved, depending on her mood . . . You'll have to excuse me; I grew up with an aunt called Alma, and she let her sons break my toys and squirt me with water pistols.'

That was what Qwilleran liked about Bart – he was human and *honest*.

On his way out, the attorney said, 'I almost forgot. My daughter asks a favor. She's making a survey and would like you to write two words on an index card.' He drew a card and a pen from his pocket. 'You write *cat* on one side of the card and *dog* on the other . . . Sign your initials.'

Qwilleran wrote *dog* on the first side in proper penmanship. On the reverse side he dashed off *cat* in a flamboyant script, crossing the t with a bar an inch long.

'I thank you. My daughter thanks you. She's quite serious about this study – her own idea – although it will never be published.'

'How old is she?' Qwilleran asked.

'Nine going on fifteen. Next summer she wants to extend the survey to Lockmaster,' he said, raising parental eyebrows.

Qwilleran found his copy of *Mosses from an Old Manse* and scanned it for references that might be linked with the mansion in Purple Point.

That night Qwilleran wrote in his journal:

Monday – I thought I had Koko all figured out. He knows when the phone is going to ring!

But today he knew Uncle George was coming from the county building *before the guy had announced his intentions*. What about the biscatti in the briefcase? Did Koko know about that, too?

I sound crazy, and sometimes I feel I'm slipping over the edge.

What I mean is: it's pretty well established that Koko (a) knows what's going to happen. Does he also (b) *make things happen*?

I won't go that far, but I admit he puts ideas in my head. That's nothing new; Christopher Smart knew that a few centuries ago.

But why does Yum Yum's buddy have more on the

ball than most felines? I still say it's because he has sixty whiskers! Regardless of what Dr Connie says and what the scientific literature says, I still maintain my opinion.

How far am I prepared to go?

Perhaps I'd better pipe down? They'll start counting my own whiskers. That would be a joke! Koko transmits, and I receive!

Qwilleran mused whimsically. What an investigative team we'd make! . . . Koko's whiskers transmitting inside information – and my moustache receiving the data.

Four

Qwilleran ended his Tuesday column with a few 'Famous Last Words' submitted by readers. These folk gems of humor arrived in the mailroom of the *Something* – on government postcards. Reader participation was a healthy sign for a small-town paper, and the 'Famous Last Words' obviously came from all walks of life. Almost all were printable, and the best would be published in book form, it was promised, with proceeds going to some worthy cause. The latest were:

> 'My new kitten is adorable . . . and they assure me he's housebroken.'

'I haven't had a drink for five years . . . so it won't hurt
to have a little nip.'

'My dog likes to play rough . . . and he never bites!'

'I'm sorry, Officer . . . I thought I had the green light.'

When Qwilleran delivered his Tuesday copy to the office
of the *Something*, he walked down the long hall of the
building and could hear the editor in chief shouting behind
closed doors. It was the kind of angry shouting that is
usually accompanied by waving arms. There was no clue
as to which staff member was getting a roasting.

Qwilleran stopped in the food editor's office. 'What did
you give your husband for breakfast, Mildred?'

'Tell you later! I'm on deadline!' She waved him away.

'What happened?' Qwilleran asked one of the reporters.

'Clarissa Moore went home to Indiana to attend a
funeral, and this morning she sent a wire: she's not coming
back! Arch is wild, and I don't blame him,' the reporter
said. 'For a J student right out of college, she got a lot of
breaks here.'

Qwilleran had done his part to encourage the novice,
and although she was a *good* feature writer, she was hardly
good enough to be forgiven for such cavalier behavior.

Qwilleran asked, 'Does anyone know if she took her
cat? If she took Jerome, she knew she was going for good;

otherwise, she would have left him in her apartment with her neighbors.' He made a mental note to ask Judd Amhurst at the Winston Park apartments.

He disliked unanswered questions.

Deadline for the Tuesday Qwill Pen was twelve noon, and Qwilleran filed his copy with the managing editor according to custom – not late, but not too early either.

Junior Goodwinter glanced at the transcript and rang for the copy boy, and said, 'Do you know a feature writer we could hire? Jill Handley won't be back from maternity leave for a few months.'

'How about running a series of guest features? Make it sound like an honor instead of an emergency, and they'll be vying for the privilege. For their cooperation you can make a contribution to their favorite charity. It would be invitational, of course. I can think of a dozen names without even trying. Bill Turmeric, Dr Abernathy, Mavis Adams, Dr Connie Cosgrove, Wetherby Goode, Thornton Haggis, Judd Amhurst, Polly Duncan—'

'Stop! I think it might work!'

'Whannell MacWhannell,' Qwilleran went on. 'His wife, the astrologer. Silas Dingwall. Maggie Sprenkle can write about the animal welfare program . . .'

'How about setting it up for us?' Junior asked.

Qwilleran said, 'I'm a columnist, I don't do setup.'

* * *

Qwilleran went home to give the cats their noontime treat and consider his own problem: how to write a column on the Old Manse for Friday's Qwill Pen.

His pet theory about the Manse and the Hawthorne book remained to be tested, and the sooner the better. The attorney had been frank about the mansion's personnel, but it wouldn't hurt to get a second opinion.

Maggie and her late husband had owned the estate adjoining the Ledfields'. They had dined together frequently, and Maggie could probably give him some tips.

Qwilleran phoned Maggie and was offered: a nice cup of tea! He said he would come up right away. (Someday the Qwill Pen would address the question of tea – and the difference between an ordinary cup of tea and a nice one.)

He biked to the rear of the Sprenkle Building and was admitted to the small elevator lobby, just large enough for his British Silverlight.

The upstairs apartment – over the insurance and real estate offices – was of Victorian splendor. The five front windows were occupied by Maggie's five 'ladies' from the animal shelter. Tea was ready to be poured.

After the niceties, Qwilleran broached his idea for the Old Manse column. She thought it was splendid.

He stated his case, and the practical octogenarian said, 'I never heard Nathan claim a connection between his grandfather and the author . . . but he never *disclaimed* one either!'

'Mr Barter advised me to arrange an appointment with Miss James or Miss Babcock.'

She paused significantly. 'I think . . . you would find Daisy Babcock . . . amenable to your idea. She's a lovely girl. Alma Lee is a little . . . *starchy*, although I must admit she's an encyclopedia of information on Georgian silver and eighteenth-century crystal. She's not there every day, so you have to make an appointment. She spends three days a week in Lockmaster, where her parents have a gallery of art and antiques.'

She said more, but Qwilleran had made up his mind to choose Daisy. He said, 'The Ledfields have been very generous to the community.'

'Nathan was always a good and generous soul. There was a couple that worked for him – Mr and Mrs Simms, and they were killed in an auto accident, leaving a seven-year-old daughter. Nathan found a good home for her with a family at the church. But he also kept in touch with her, checking her report card at every marking and giving her gifts for birthdays and Christmas – nothing inappropriately expensive but useful and thoughtful. After high school he put her through business school and then hired her to handle his correspondence and personal expenses.'

'Where is she now?' Qwilleran asked.

'His will stipulated that Libby Simms should continue to handle his private matters. He made sure that his lawyers knew her position in the family.'

'A touching story,' Qwilleran murmured. 'How old is she now?'

'Early twenties, I think. But this illustrates the Ledfields: fondness for children and their sorrow over not having any of their own.'

When Qwilleran phoned the Old Manse to request a tour of the building, he had his strategy planned.

He talked to a cheery individual whom he rightly guessed to be Daisy. Informed when Miss James would be in town, he scheduled an appointment for the day of her absence, saying he was on deadline.

Daisy said she could conduct him through the building the next day.

That evening at eleven P.M. it was Qwilleran's turn to phone Polly with news.

'I'm interviewing Daisy tomorrow. Have you met her?'

'Yes, she's friendlier than the other one. Married to one of the Linguini sons . . . Their parents retired from the restaurant business and now live in Florida, although they visit Italy every summer. The sons preferred a party store to a restaurant, and I don't blame them!'

Qwilleran said, 'Their store is the only place I can buy Squunk water by the case, and they deliver!'

'Are you looking forward to visiting the Old Manse, Qwill? I wish, now, that I had accepted Doris Ledfield's invitations . . .'

He said, 'Do you think it's crazy to think that Nathan's grandfather might have have been inspired by Hawthorne's book?'

'Not at all. *Mosses from an Old Manse* was much revered in the days when the house was being built . . .'

'Do you know what I heard today? Nathan's will stipulated that some of his small collectibles should be gradually sold off to provide ongoing funds for child welfare.'

And so it went until it was time for '*À bientôt.*'

He combed *Mosses from an Old Manse* for details that might appear in the Ledfields' Old Manse. He had read the book twice before – once in college and once when he received a copy from the library of the fabulous Agatha Burns.

Agatha was a favorite name in Moose County; after all, the great teacher had lived to be a hundred and had inspired several generations.

Late that evening – after the Siamese were escorted to their quarters on the third balcony, and after Qwilleran had treated himself to a dish of ice cream – he wrote in his journal:

Today I found another clue to the Mystery of the Corrugated Box!

First, I had brought it home from Edd Smith's Place, full of fine old books donated by the Campbells in Purple Point, and Koko went crazy, not over the books but over the box! Why?

Investigation indicated that the Campbells had bought something from the Ledfields, and it came packed in the large brown corrugated box. Now we hear that valuable items are being sold at the bequest of the Ledfield will!

I brought the box from the tool shed, where it sported a do-not-discard sign. I brought it in for Koko's scrutiny, and he went wild again! Why?

The Ledfields had no indoor pets, I'm told. Was there some other kind of aroma that might tickle Koko's whiskers? If so, what?

When I return from my assignment at the Old Manse tomorrow, *will that cat know where I've been?*

Tune in for the next installment.

As he wrote, Qwilleran became aware of thundering paws coming down the ramp from the third balcony. Koko had opened his bedroom door by hanging on the lever-type door handle, a technique he used in emergencies. At the same time Qwilleran heard fire sirens, and from the kitchen window could be seen a pink glow in the dark sky visible above the treetops. Another siren sounded – then another. It sounded like a serious conflagration downtown!

Qwilleran grabbed the phone and called the night desk at the newspaper. 'This is Qwill! Where's the fire?'

'Downtown! The Old Hulk! Can't talk now!' He hung up with a bang.

Qwilleran phoned the McBee farm on the back road, where both the farmer and his brother were volunteer firemen.

Mrs McBee said, 'It's awful! Someone torched the Old Hulk!'

After talking to Mrs McBee, Qwilleran wrote in his journal:

The Old Hulk is a big wooden box on the southwest edge of Pickax with the height of a five-story building and the shape of a coffin. No windows. It was once a depot and warehouse for feed and seed, and farmers came in horse-drawn wagons from three counties to stock up. The interior was a series of lofts connected by ramps. With the advent of paved roads and motor vehicles it was replaced by smaller depots around the county, but the dirty-tan exterior still said FEED AND SEED across the top in letters four feet high, and the eyesore became lovingly known as the Old Hulk. And the stories they tell about it are nothing you would want to tell to your kids and mother-in-law.

Despite the building's appearance and reputation, no one wanted the city to tear it down. But now it has burned down!

Five

Moose County was in shock. Police called it arson. Ruffians from Bixby County had torched the Old Hulk.

Qwilleran went to Lois's Luncheonette for coffee and the public reaction to the disaster. Although the Old Hulk was empty and only the shell of the senior center and could be rebuilt, it was the idea of the crime that rankled. When the newspaper hit the streets, there were statements from city officials, clergy, the donors of the property, retirees, students. Funds would be available to build the Senior Health Club from scratch, but it was the loss of the Old Hulk that hurt. Qwilleran was asked to write a special

Qwill Pen column – consoling, philosophizing, encouraging. At Lois's Luncheonette, the customers were angry and vengeful.

While the public grieved or raged about the arson – as well they might – Qwilleran looked for a constructive approach.

One day while cashing a check at the bank downtown, he stood in line just ahead of Burgess Campbell, lecturer at the local college and revered leader of the Scottish community. Blind from birth, Burgess was always accompanied by his guide dog, Alexander.

Qwilleran said, 'Burgess, do you have a minute to talk? I have a constructive suggestion.'

When their transactions were completed, they met in one of the bank's small conference rooms, and Qwilleran said: 'The K Fund could publish a small book on the Old Hulk, if your students would do some research. They could interview family members, neighbors, public leaders. It would be good experience. They could borrow snapshots and check the photo file at the newspaper. Then a postscript could put a positive slant on the subject by introducing the Senior Health Club.'

Alexander whimpered, and the two men considered that approval. He was a very smart dog.

* * *

Qwilleran had a bad habit of writing a news story before the news broke, or describing a building before it was built. Polly said he should be writing fiction. The products of his imagination always surpassed the actual thing.

As for the Old Manse at Purple Point, Qwilleran wanted to design it to match Hawthorne's book.

And the approach to the mansion signified he might be right . . . There was the iron gate between two rough stone gateposts . . . Then a long, straight driveway between two rows of poplar trees, with beds of daffodils here and there . . . ending at a large building with a prisonlike look: gray brick, plain windows, and a severe entrance door.

The make-believe script ended when he clanged the heavy brass door knocker.

He expected to be admitted by a butler with silver buckles on his shoes, but Daisy Babcock opened the door in a pink pantsuit and a flurry of excitement.

Merrily she said, 'You're Mr Q! Welcome to the Old Manse. Did you bring Cool Koko?'

Only devoted Qwill Pen readers talked nonsense like that. He liked her instantly.

He remembered meeting her at Linguini's Party Store when ordering Squunk water, but her informality came as a shock in a two-story foyer with marble floor, tall mirrors, brocaded walls, a mammoth crystal chandelier, and a stairway as big as the Bridge over the River Kwai.

Soberly, Qwilleran replied, 'Koko regrets that he had a previous appointment with his publisher. He hopes you'll call on him at the barn.'

'I'd love to,' she said. 'Alfredo has told me about it. He makes deliveries of Squunk water, he says.'

'It's a far cry from this little palace. Do you give guided tours?'

'Where would you like to begin?'

'As the King of Hearts said to the White Rabbit, begin at the beginning and keep going till you come to the end. Then stop.'

The loaf-shaped building with modest architecture was one of four wings surrounding a great hall with skylight and a fortune in large oil paintings importantly framed.

There was a music salon with two grand pianos, a dining room that would seat sixteen, and an extensive library upstairs. Every suite had a four-poster bed and an eight-foot highboy.

There was Mrs Ledfield's pride and joy – a large cutting garden that supplied freshly cut flowers for the silver and crystal vases throughout the house . . . and there was Nathan Ledfield's specialty: a formal garden of daylilies comprising five varieties compatible with a northern climate.

It was almost as if the Ledfields were still living there. In the music salon there was sheet music open on the racks, as if waiting for the pianist and violinist to make an entrance.

'And this is called the Box Bank,' Daisy said. 'It's not usually shown to anyone outside the family.'

It was a roomful of empty boxes of every size and shape that Nathan had used in buying and selling collectibles: shoe boxes, hatboxes, jewelry boxes, clothing boxes, and large cardboard cartons.

At one point, a young woman in denim came to Daisy and whispered something.

'I'll call him back, Libby. Get his number . . . Did you go to the doctor? I want to know what he said.'

The girl nodded and dashed away.

Daisy said, 'That is our office manager. She went into the garden this morning and was stung by a bee . . . She was Nathan's protégée, you know.'

Altogether, Qwilleran enjoyed coffee and cookies with Daisy more than the extravagances of the Old Manse.

Qwilleran said, 'Your husband is making a delivery from the party store tomorrow. Why don't you come along and say hello to Koko and Yum Yum?'

* * *

Qwilleran described the visit to Polly during their nightly phone call.

'You're a rascal,' she said. 'If Alma Lee James finds out Daisy has visited the barn first, she'll be furious!'

'How do you know?'

'One of the Green Smocks at the bookstore has a cousin who is a housekeeper at the Old Manse, and she says there is jealousy between Daisy and Alma.'

Qwilleran said, 'One of the office personnel came back from the doctor's office while I was there – allergic to a bee sting, they said.'

'Did you know that's how Maggie Sprenkle's husband died? He was working in his rose garden when he was stung and had forgotten his emergency kit. By the time he maneuvered his wheelchair into the house, it was too late. That's why Maggie sold the estate and moved downtown. By the way, what did you think of the Old Manse?'

He said, 'I've decided the Hawthorne connection is too esoteric for Qwill Pen readers. I'm going to leave the Old Manse to the feature writers when the preview takes place. Well . . .

'*À bientôt.*'

'*À bientôt*, dear.'

* * *

Late Thursday afternoon, Koko, who had been invisible for hours, suddenly made an appearance in the kitchen – not to order his dinner but to announce that someone was coming. He jumped on and off the kitchen counter overlooking the barnyard. He was right, of course. In fifteen seconds, according to Qwilleran's stopwatch, the Linguini truck emerged from the wooded trail and drove up to the back door.

Daisy jumped out and looked up at the barn in wonder. Her husband, Fredo, jumped out and started unloading two cases of Squunk water and boxes of cranberry juice, potato chips, pretzels, mixed nuts, and enough wine and spirits to stock the bar for Qwilleran's guests. Koko supervised.

'Is he your new bartender?' Fredo asked.

'No, he's from the State Revenue Department. We have a limited license.'

Daisy was wandering around, gazing up at the ramps, balconies, soaring chimney stacks, and six-foot tapestries hanging from the highest railings.

The Siamese followed her, and Yum Yum allowed her to pick her up while Koko demonstrated his flying-squirrel act, landing on a sofa cushion below.

Then Qwilleran conducted them to the formal foyer with double doors, overlooking the octagonal gazebo screened on all eight sides. It had a view of the butterfly garden, flowering shrubs, and birdhouses on the trail leading to the Art Center on the Old Back Road.

Daisy was reluctant to leave, but they had two more deliveries to make.

Before they left, Qwilleran said, 'It seems to me the Qwill Pen should do a column on vineyards. I've never grown so much as a radish, but grapes appeal to me as – what shall I say? – a satisfying crop.'

'My brother Nick can give you a conducted tour. He's the vintner. Say when!'

On the phone Friday morning, the attorney and Qwilleran plotted Alma Lee's visit to the barn. It would be brief: Bart had another appointment, and Qwilleran had to file his copy for the noon deadline.

When Bart and Alma arrived, the Siamese flew to the loftiest rafters, from which they could observe the first-time visitor.

Qwilleran met them in the parking lot and conducted them to the formal entrance on the other side of the barn.

'Where does this lead?' Alma asked.

'To my mailbox on the back road,' he said, omitting mention of such items as the butterfly pool and the Art Center.

She looked at the screened gazebo. 'Is that where one of your guests shot himself last year?'

'He wasn't a guest; he was an intruder, wanted by the police in three counties,' Qwilleran said, embroidering the truth.

Indoors, she looked up at the balconies and ramps, the large white fireplace cube with stacks rising to the roof forty feet overhead, the six-foot tapestries hanging from balcony railings. 'You could use some small art objects,' she said.

Qwilleran replied, 'The architectural complexities and vast spaces and walls of books don't leave much space for miscellaneous art objects. Apart from that, there's not much to see. It's an atmosphere you *feel*; you don't see it.'

Dropping her critical frown, she said amiably, 'Do you know what I'd like to see in this environment? Large vases filled with fresh flowers! Every area has an ideal spot for it, and you can get fabulous vases from the Ledfield collection in crystal, porcelain, and silver.'

Qwilleran and the attorney exchanged glances.

Qwilleran said, 'With two airborne cats, a vase of flowers would last about ten minutes.'

And Bart said, 'Come, come, Alma. Mr Qwilleran is on deadline at the newspaper.'

Opening her handbag, she found a booklet bound in black and gold. 'Here is the catalog of the Ledfield collection. The items with red stickers are already sold.'

Qwilleran thanked her and gave his wristwatch what was supposed to be a surreptitious glance.

Alma said, 'The most important item has already gone to an old family in Purple Point.'

Barter said, 'We won't have time to sit down, because I have another appointment, and I know you're on deadline, but thanks for showing Alma the interior.'

They were standing – awkwardly, Qwilleran felt – around the area with two large angled sofas.

Suddenly there was a scream as a cat dropped from the rafters onto the cushion of a sofa.

'Sorry,' Qwilleran said to his unnerved guest. 'That's Koko. He wants to be introduced.'

'We don't have time for formalities,' said Barter. 'We're holding up the presses. Thank you, Qwill. Come on, Alma.'

As Barter rushed Alma out of the barn, he looked back and rolled his eyes meaningfully.

As soon as they had driven away, Qwilleran checked the catalog for red-stickered items. He found: a fifteen-inch punch bowl of Chinese export porcelain. It was dated circa 1780. The design was elaborate and historical.

He called Lisa Compton at the ESP. 'Are you still there? Won't they let you go?'

'This sounds like Qwill. Tomorrow's my last day at the bookstore. What can I do for you?'

'About your rich cousins' . . . (Campbell was her maiden name, but she claimed to be from the poor side of the clan) . . . 'Do you happen to know what they bought from the Ledfield estate? Koko's still fascinated by the box the books came in.'

'It was only a punch bowl, they said.'

'Glass or china?'

'China, but quite old. Do you want me to find out the nature of the design? There's no telling what might light a fire under that smart Koko!'

After a little more nonsense common to the fans of 'Cool Koko', the conversation ended.

Qwilleran grabbed the black-and-gold catalog and found the punch-bowl listing: it had sold for sixty thousand dollars.

Six

As Qwilleran had once written in his private journal:

> Anyone who thinks it's easy to write a twice-weekly
> column is misinformed. It may be an enjoyable
> challenge, but it's never easy. Friday has a relentless
> way of following Tuesday, and next Tuesday follows
> this Friday inexorably.

Only the loyalty and enthusiasm of readers kept
Qwilleran's creative juices perking.

The Hawthorne idea had proved to be a 'no-story' – an

unfortunate situation to a newsman with a deadline to meet. He had to resort to his 'trash barrel', as he called the deep drawer of his desk. Postcards from readers, clippings, notes could always be made into a chatty Qwill Pen column with, perhaps, a saying from Cool Koko: 'Faint heart never won the softest cushion in the house.'

Polly said that Qwilleran made the same mistakes over and over again.

But doggedly . . . not stubbornly, he proceeded with another Qwill Pen idea, writing a story in his mind before researching it.

Moose County had a vineyard and a vintner! Qwilleran, Chicago-born, saw his first vineyard in Italy while a young foreign correspondent, and he had retained a romantic impression of the vineyard, the vintner – and perhaps the vintner's daughter.

First he consulted the encyclopedia, determined to avoid another no-story disappointment. He liked the words: *vineyard*, *viticulture*, and *vintner*. He had never wanted to be a farmer, but he wouldn't mind being a vintner. And there was more to viticulture than the making of wine; there were grapes for eating, juice for drinking, raisins for baking, and – his favorite spread for toast – grape jelly. It was an ancient culture, mentioned by Virgil, Homer, and the Bible. Thomas Jefferson tried it. Julia

Ward Howe referred to grapes in 'The Battle Hymn of the Republic'.

Qwilleran had new respect for the Linguini brothers. Nick was the vintner who helped with the store; Alfredo was the storekeeper who helped with the vineyard. He called and made an appointment.

So, on Saturday morning, he drove to the western part of the county, near the lakeshore, and visited Linguini's Party Store. There were quite a few cars in the parking lot. The party store was in a rustic building with a porch running the full width. Indoors, the goods were arranged casually, and the customers were not in a hurry. Some were wandering in and out of a back hall, smiling. It seemed, on investigation, that another homeless pregnant cat had wandered in from the highway and had been given a box and blanket – and had given birth to four minuscule kittens. The smiling customers were putting dollar bills in a pickle jar on the counter for their food, shots, and future expenses.

'Hi, Mr Q,' said Fredo. 'Want to cast your vote for the kittens' names? . . . Nick is expecting you! . . . Marge, ring the vineyard and tell him Qwill is here.'

While waiting for the vintner to come up with his Jeep, Qwilleran accepted compliments from readers, answered questions about Cool Koko's health and happiness, and generally made friends for the *Something*.

As for discovering another two thousand words for the Qwill Pen, however . . . it was another Good Idea That Didn't Work. But he heard some provocative comments from Nick that his sister-in-law, Daisy, had brought home from the Manse; they raised questions.

'Fredo and I think she should quit,' he said. 'Too much monkey business! Know what I mean? There's too much money floating around! Do you realize that a punch bowl sold for sixty thousand? What I'm wondering is, where is the sixty thousand? . . . That young girl who's supposed to be handling Nathan's personal accounts has been whispering suspicions to Daisy. See what I mean?'

Qwilleran agreed it was a sticky situation. 'As I understand it, the entire property has been given to the county. Somebody should blow the whistle! But who? Let me think about it, Nick.'

'Think fast!'

Qwilleran left the vineyard in the firm belief that Koko's curiosity about the large cardboard carton in the shed had some connection with Alma Lee; the cat had dropped from the rafters as if trying to frighten her. Then, when Qwilleran arrived at the barn, he found that the black-and-gold catalog had been torn to shreds!

No sane person would consider this evidence. It was

coincidence, and yet . . . stranger things had happened in connection with Koko! What to do?

While he was downtown with his car, Qwilleran stopped at Grandma's Sweet Shop to pick up ice cream – a gallon of particularly good butter pecan for himself and a quart of vanilla for the Siamese. A real grandmother presided over the cash register in the front, and her grandchildren waited on customers in the rear. Before he could place his order, he saw a waving hand from the seating area (old-fashioned ice-cream tables and chairs of twisted wire). It was Hannah Hawley, wife of Uncle Louie McLeod – with their adopted son, now about nine.

She beckoned to Qwilleran, and as he approached, the young man jumped up and politely added another chair to the table. (This was the waif who had never brushed his teeth or said his prayers when adopted!)

'How's Koko?' she asked. 'I'll never forget his performance at the KitKat Revue.'

'He really blew his cool, didn't he? I think he was expressing an opinion of rhinestone collars.'

Qwilleran inquired, 'How's everything on Pleasant Street?' He signaled for a cup of coffee.

'Pleasant,' she said. 'We're casting for *Cats*. Would you like to try out for Old Deuteronomy?'

'That's about my speed, but if you need a genuine feline, I can supply one.'

'How well we know!' she said. 'By the way, the rehearsal pianist we've had for years has left town, and we were really worried, but we were able to rent Frankie from Lockmaster.'

After two gulps of coffee, Qwilleran asked, 'Would it be naïve to ask who Frankie is – and why he has to be rented?'

'He's crazy,' said Danny.

'Dear, we don't use that word,' he was reprimanded. 'He's an eccentric genius. He can sight-read a musical score he has never seen before! Perfectly! But he'd do it for nothing, and people would take advantage of him, so he's under the management of his family. He's remarkable.'

'What is the family name?' Qwilleran asked.

'His last name is James, but there are lots of Jameses in Lockmaster – like Goodwinters here. All kinds!' She stopped suddenly and looked at the boy. 'Danny, take this money and pay our check at the front counter. Tell Grandma we enjoyed our lunch. And don't forget to count your change.'

When Danny had left on his important mission, Hannah said in a low voice, 'Louie says the Jameses include teachers and preachers, horse breeders, and train robbers. There's an antique shop that we think is way overpriced.

60

Frankie's managers seem to be a decent sort. They're looking out for his well-being, since he seems to lack a sense of money. He doesn't drive – couldn't get a license, they say . . .' Her voice trailed off as Danny returned to the table with the change. 'We like Frankie, don't we, Danny? He has a friendly, outgoing personality—'

'He has a girlfriend,' Danny interrupted.

Hannah stood up. 'So nice to run into you, Qwill. I'll tell Louie I saw you. Come on, Danny!'

Late that evening Qwilleran and Polly had their eleven P.M. phone chat. He asked, 'Did you have a good day?'

'We had a few interesting customers. Sales were about normal. Dundee ate something he shouldn't have and threw up.'

'I visited Linguini's Party Store. They have a new litter of kittens, and I contributed a name for one of them. I suggested Squunky. Nick showed me around the vineyard. I've decided my interest in vineyards, vintners, and viticulture is purely literary. I like the sound of the words and the quotations from the Bible and poets and playwrights . . . So I'm afraid it's a no-story again . . .'

'Oh dear! You've wasted a lot of time!'

'A writer's time is never wasted. We'll talk about it at dinner Saturday night. How about the Old Grist Mill?

We'll pay the new management the compliment of dressing up.'

Polly hesitated longer than normal. 'Oh, dear! There's a complication . . . You know my friend Shirley in Lockmaster?'

'We haven't met, but I know she's the Lockmaster librarian who quit when you did – and went into book merchandising, the way you did.'

'Yes, but her bookstore is a hundred years old and has been in the family all that time. Saturday is her sixtieth birthday. They're taking a private room at the Palomino Paddock. They want me to be there as a surprise! You're invited, too, but I think you wouldn't enjoy it. They play guessing games.'

'I think you're right.'

'Qwill, I hate to miss our Saturday-night date. It's the first time ever!'

'That's perfectly all right. I'll take Rhoda Tibbitt to dinner and talk about her late husband. Have a good evening. Better not drive back till Sunday morning. I don't want you to drive alone at night.' Then, since he had placed the call, it was his place to say, '*À bientôt.*'

'*À bientôt,*' she said. Did he detect a slight chill on the line? Surely she realized that Rhoda was the eighty-nine-year-old widow of the century-old historian of Moose County.

Polly's defection on Saturday night – in favor of dinner and guessing games in Lockmaster – was just what Qwilleran needed to launch the Tibbitt project. Rhoda was only too happy to cooperate. He picked her up at Ittibittiwassee Estates, where the other residents were thrilled to see one of their number go to dinner with Mr Q.

Qwilleran had made a reservation at Tipsy's Tavern, a roadhouse in a log cabin – with its own poultry farm. It was aptly named for the owner's cat, a portrait of which hung in the main dining room – white with a black patch slipping crazily over one eye. There was a private alcove overlooking the poultry yard that could be closed off for conferences after dinner, and the management was always proud to reserve it for Mr Q.

As for the food, there was no doubt that Tipsy's had the best ham and eggs and chicken à la king in the county – but nothing fancy – and the cook made no claim to being a chef.

Qwilleran said to his guest, 'We'll have dinner first and chat; then we'll clear the table and turn on the recorder.'

He said, 'I first met Homer at the Klingenschoen mansion when it was a museum. The cats and I were living there. Iris Cobb was housekeeper. There was a meeting room upstairs, with an elevator, and Homer was scheduled to speak, but he was late—'

Rhoda nodded and smiled. 'Homer said everyone should have a personal motto, and his was: *Always be late*.'

'Well, there we were, waiting,' Qwilleran said. 'Every time the elevator bell rang, everyone looked at the approaching car. The door would open, and it would be someone else. About the fourth time the bell rang, we all looked at the elevator door, positive that it was Homer. The doors opened, and out walked Koko, with his tail high.'

'I remember,' she said, 'and he seemed surprised that everyone was laughing and shouting.'

'Was Homer a good principal?' Qwilleran asked.

She said, 'We all had a crush on our principal. He was so elegant the way he was dressed and groomed, and he treated his teachers in such courtly fashion. He was the first to retire and went into volunteer work at the Lockmaster Mansion Museum. So when I retired, I went there to apply. Imagine my surprise to find *my principal* in old clothes, crawling around on hands and knees, followed by a belligerent-looking cat! . . . It turned out that the mansion was plagued with mice, and Homer said that it was necessary to find out where they were getting in. He claimed to have found *over a dozen* mouse holes and plugged them up, and the cat was furious because his source of supply was being eroded!

'It was another twelve or fifteen years before we were married, and Homer turned out to be a lot of fun . . . Do you remember the time, Qwill, when a delegation of us in ten limousines rode around the county dedicating bronze plaques?'

'I do indeed! The worse it got, the funnier it got . . . Here comes our dinner. We'll continue the reminiscences later.'

Dinner was served. Chicken, of course, but the conversation never wandered far from the Grand Old Man who had lived to be almost a hundred. There was one question Qwilleran saved until after dessert: 'What can you tell me about the Midnight Marchers?' He turned on the recorder.

'When Homer was nineteen, he used to call on a young lady in the next town – riding there on his bicycle and spending the evening on the porch swing, drinking lemonade and talking. Every half hour, he recalled, her mother came out to the porch to see if they had enough lemonade. At eleven o'clock she suggested that he leave for home, since it was a long ride.

'On one dark night, on the way home, he was mystified

to see a long line of small lights weaving across the nearby hills!

'What he did not know – and what it turned out to be – was the annual *ritual* of the Midnight Marchers. They were mourning the loss of thirty-eight miners in a mine disaster that orphaned an entire town.

'Furthermore, it was caused by a greedy mine owner who had failed to take the precautions practiced by competitors . . .

'Every year, the descendants of those orphans donned miners' hats with tiny lights and trudged in silent file across the mine site. They have done it for three generations now, first the sons of orphans, then the grandsons of orphans, and now the great-grandsons. It always made Homer mad as a hatter! He said it was silly schoolboy stuff – putting on miners' hats with lights and staging a spooky pageant. He said they should do something that would benefit the community – and do it in the name of the long-ago victims.'

'How did people react?' Qwilleran asked.

'Oh, he made enemies, who said he was disrespectful of the dead. But as the years went on, the Marchers sounded more and more like a secret society who got together and drank beer. And then Homer got a letter from Nathan Ledfield, that dear man! He said Homer was right. He asked for Homer's help in changing the purpose of the Midnight Marchers without changing the name. Mr Ledfield wanted the Midnight Marchers to benefit orphans. And it proved to be successful.

'The beauty of it is,' said Rhoda, 'that churches and other organizations got behind it, and the Midnight Marchers changed their purpose.'

'Hmmm . . . this sounds vaguely familiar . . .'

'Yes, other philanthropists have copied the Midnight Marchers – not only in Moose County, I believe.'

Qwilleran said, 'Homer must have been pleased to have his lifelong campaign succeed.'

'Yes, but he never wanted any credit.'

Strangely, Qwilleran's mind went to Nathan Ledfield's protégée, but it was getting late, and he saw Rhoda glance at her wristwatch. They returned to Ittibittiwassee Estates.

Seven

Expecting Polly home for Sunday brunch, Qwilleran biked downtown early for the Sunday *New York Times*, unloading such sections as Fashion & Style, Business, Sports, and Classifieds. Otherwise, it would not fit in the basket of his British Silverlight. There were always fellow citizens who were glad to get his leavings.

By the time he returned to the barn, Koko was doing his contortions in the kitchen window, meaning there was a message on the machine.

It would be Polly, he knew, announcing her arrival and making plans for the day . . . Instead, when Qwilleran pressed the button, the voice was that of Wetherby Goode: 'This is Joe. Polly called and asked me to give her cats their breakfast. She said to tell you she won't be home till late afternoon.'

Qwilleran fortified himself with a cup of coffee and dialed the weatherman. He said, 'Appreciate the message, Joe. Did she mention what was happening in that jungle down there?'

'Just what I was going to ask you, pal.'

'She went to a dinner last night, leaving her cats on the automatic feeder and expecting to drive back this morning for the usual Sunday activities. No telling what changed her mind.'

'Anything can happen south of the border.'

'You should know, Joe.' (He was a native of Horseradish down there.) 'Polly went to a birthday party for a friend who was library director of Lockmaster but left to manage the family bookstore.'

'Sure, I know the store. Bestbooks. It's been there forever. Why weren't you invited?'

'I was, but I declined. They play guessing games at their parties.'

'I know what you mean . . .'

'Stop in for a snort on your way to your broadcast tomorrow and I'll fill you in – on who won.'

* * *

During this conversation, the Siamese had sat side by side, quietly awaiting developments. He gave them a good brushing with the silver-backed hairbrush . . . then played a few rounds of the necktie game . . . then announced, 'Read!' Koko leaped to the bookshelf and knocked down *The Portrait of a Lady*. It had more gilt on the spine, he observed, than others that had come in the last purchase.

The first chapter was interrupted by the phone – and the comfortable voice of Mildred Riker, inviting him to an afternoon repast with the Rikers. 'But I can't find Polly,' she said. 'She wasn't at church.'

'She's out of town,' Qwilleran explained.

'Then you come, and I'll invite someone from the neighborhood.'

When he arrived an hour later, he was glad to see Hixie Rice, promotion director for the *Something*.

'Where's Polly?' she asked.

'In Lockmaster – probably up to no good. Where's Dwight?'

'In the same place, probably for the same reason.'

Drinks were served on the deck. They talked about the Old Hulk. The Scottish community was prepared to underwrite a new building. Volunteer carpenters, electricians, and painters were offering their services, proud to have their names on an honor roll in the lobby of the building.

The meal was served indoors, as usual.

Mildred said, 'I envy Qwill's screened gazebo. He can serve outdoors, and the cats can be out there without leashes.'

After dessert (peach cobbler with crème fraîche and pecans) the two men entertained with their favorite topic: growing up in Chicago. Hixie had not heard the story before.

Mildred said, 'Tell about summer camp.'

The oft-told tale went like this:

QWILL: 'My father died before I was born, and so Mr Riker functioned as dad for both of us – taking us to the zoo and parades, giving advice, discussing our report cards, getting us out of scrapes.'

ARCH: 'One year he decided we should go to summer camp and learn something useful like doing the Australian crawl, rigging a sailboat, climbing a tree, whittling a wood whistle . . .'

QWILL: 'But there's only one thing we remember. Every night we'd sit around a campfire, listen to stories, and sing camp songs loudly, but not well.'

ARCH: 'But the only thing that either of us remembers in detail is the campfire chant.'

QWILL: 'Not only do we remember every word, but it runs through the mind at the most inopportune times.'

ARCH: '—Like, when facing a traffic judge.'

QWILL: '—or getting married.'

ARCH: '—Would you like a performance?'

Hixie squealed, 'Please do!'

The two men sat up in their chairs, eyed each other for a cue, then launched into a loud, bouncy beat:

'Away down yonder not so very far off
A jaybird died of the whooping cough.
He whooped *so hard with the whooping cough*
That he whooped *his head and his tail*
Right off!'

There was a moment's silence, during which Polly always said, 'To quote Richard the Third, I am amazed.'

Hixie squealed, 'I love it! I wanta learn it!'

'Want to hear the second verse?' they asked. 'It's the same as the first.'

The party broke up at a sensible hour, and Qwilleran drove home to get up-to-date on Polly's escapade. He would ask her:

How was the party?

Were there sixty candles on the cake?

Who was there?

Were they dressed bookish or horsey?

Did they really play guessing games?

Who won?

What were the prizes?

What church do they attend?

How was the preacher?

He was a thorough interviewer, and she liked to be interviewed.

When he arrived at the barn, the cat-in-the-window message assured Qwilleran that someone had checked in. It was the weatherman.

'Polly's home, but she's beat! Call me, not her. She looked frazzled, Qwill, high on excitement, short on sleep. I told her to turn in and I'd notify you.'

Qwilleran said, 'She never drinks more than half a glass of sherry. She's known Shirley for years!'

'Yeah, but . . . something got her overexcited and maybe it interfered with her sleep. Too bad she had to drive home alone. We'll keep in touch. Don't worry.'

That evening, around eleven o'clock, Qwilleran was

reading in his lounge chair, and the cats were sprawled on his lap. Suddenly Koko was alerted! He looked at the desk phone. And it rang. It was Polly, reporting for their bedtime chat.

'Qwill!' she cried. 'I suppose you wonder what happened to me. I've never been so exhausted in my life! A cup of cocoa, a few hours' sleep with my cuddly cats, and I revivified . . . I hope you didn't worry about me.'

'We'll go to dinner tomorrow night, and you can fill me in.'

'I'll have something exciting to tell you,' Polly said.

'Give me a hint.'

'No hints. If you guess what it is, it won't be a surprise . . . *À bientôt!*'

'*À bientôt.*'

Eight

On his way to the radio station, Wetherby Goode often stopped at Qwilleran's barn for a pick-me-up, and the newsman enjoyed his impromptu visits – not only to get the inside track on the weather but to share neighborly news, and the neighbors at the Willows were always making news. Joe had been genuinely concerned about Polly.

When he arrived at the kitchen door and dropped on a stool at the bar, he was greeted by Koko and Yum Yum, who would not be surprised to receive a friendly cat snack from Jet Stream.

Qwilleran poured and said, 'Well, she survived!'

'She's a tough one! Never underestimate the power of a cup of cocoa!'

The male cat jumped to the bar top, hearing his name.

Qwilleran said, 'I expect to hear the whole story when we have dinner tonight. The problem is: Monday is not a good night for dining out. The Mackintosh Inn is too formal, the Grist Mill too festive, the Boulder House too far.'

'Why not get a picnic supper catered by Robin O'Dell, Qwill, and serve it in the gazebo? You don't know how lucky you are to have premises that are screened.'

Qwilleran said, 'Once in a while you come up with a good idea . . . Have another splash in your glass.'

'And if there's anything Polly doesn't know about those horse people in Lockmaster, call on me. I can give you some ancient history about Bestbooks, Qwill. It's been in the same family for a hundred years, you know. At one time they kept a bottle in the back room and had a men's club back there. Lots of loud laughter and bawdy jokes. Parents put the whole store off-limits to kids. Women wouldn't go in to buy a cookbook. They lost a lot of business to mail order and secondhand and the public library.'

Qwilleran said, 'The librarians of both Lockmaster and

Pickax became great friends at that time. That's why Polly was invited to Shirley's birthday party yesterday.'

Joe drained his glass and headed for the back door.

'Before you go, Joe, one question. Does Jet Stream accept food from the automatic feeder?'

'He'll take anything he can get . . . Why?'

'When Koko hears the little bell ring and sees the little door open, he looks at the food in disbelief and then looks up at me and shakes his right paw – then sniffs the dish again and shakes his other paw before walking away.'

There was time, before Polly came from the bookstore, to call Celia and order a picnic supper.

Celia said, 'Does she like cold soup? I have some lovely gazpacho. And I have individual quiches in the oven with bacon and tomato. For dessert, chilled Bartlett pears would be nice, with a bit of Stilton . . . Pat can deliver it after five o'clock, and I'll send a little goodie for the cats.'

When Polly drove to the barn around six o'clock, Qwilleran said, 'We'll have an aperitif in the gazebo. Will you take the cats?'

She knew right where to go for their 'limousine', a canvas tote bag in the broom closet, advertising the Pickax Public Library. Qwilleran carried a tray with sherry for her and Squunk water for himself. 'I want to hear all about the Birthday Party of the Century.'

'Well!' she said, promising a momentous report. 'You wouldn't have liked it, Qwill. The main dining room looked like a stable – tack hanging on the walls, waitresses in riding boots – everything but the horses! I thought the food was terrible! I ordered salmon; I don't know what they did to it.'

Parodying an old joke, Qwilleran said, 'Apart from that, Mrs Duncan, how did you like the party?'

'There were forty guests at long institutional tables . . . forty frosted cupcakes, each with a tiny candle, and a matchbook . . . forty gift-wrapped birthday presents, including one that must have been a refrigerator and one that was obviously a bicycle!'

'How did the guest of honor react?'

'Shirley is always charming. She told her son she would like everything trucked to her home – where she could open the small ones with her shoes off and her cat on her lap. She said she would send everyone a thank-you note suitable for framing. That means an original cartoon.'

'Shirley sounds like a clever woman. I'm sorry I never met her . . . What about the guessing games? You haven't mentioned them.'

'They were boring: Why does the firefly flash his light?

Who owns the Volvo company in Sweden? Who explored Idaho in the early nineteenth century?'

They were both accustomed to Literary Club questions. Who wrote these lines: 'She walks in beauty like the night . . .' 'Tomorrow, and tomorrow, and tomorrow, creeps in this petty pace from day to day . . .' 'Order is a lovely thing, on disarray it lays its wing.'

'The best part of the evening was the music. A young man played fabulous piano! Pop and classical. A young woman turned pages for him. They say she's also his chauffeur – or is it chauffeuse? He has some kind of disability and can't drive. He's also a piano tuner. He tuned Doris's piano at the Old Manse four times a year, including regulating and voicing. Mostly he plays piano for hire.'

When Polly stopped for breath he asked, 'Is his name Frankie? I believe he's rehearsal pianist for the production of *Cats*. All very interesting.'

Later Qwilleran asked about Shirley's ideas for a bookstore.

'Bestbooks and Pirate's Chest had entirely different problems. *They* had a hundred-year-old building with a boozy aroma in the rear and a questionable reputation – not to mention bad plumbing. With Shirley's know-how and ideas and an unlimited budget, Bestbooks was born again. Her first move was to hire a bibliocat, a brother of Dundee, and customers' frowns changed to smiles. Then, just as we have an actual pirate's chest hanging on the wall, Shirley introduced a favorite work of art . . . Are you familiar with the Rodin sculpture *The Thinker*?'

Qwilleran had never seen it but knew its pose: male model, seated, with fist on chin and elbow on knee.

'Shirley has never seen the original, either, but she has a photo enlarged and framed as a focal point of the store. Obviously it represents "Thinking, not drinking." And then a competition among customers named the official cat Thinker – a wonderful name for a feline.'

He said, 'I'm sorry I don't know Shirley. What's she like?'

'She has a commanding figure and is very pleasant. Just don't call her *Shirl*, that's all!'

Qwilleran said, 'There's something on your mind, Polly. It's been bothering you ever since Shirley's party. Would you like to unload?'

She looked relieved. 'How to begin . . . At the end of the dinner, Shirley's son, Donald, who has been functioning as president of Bestbooks, made a very touching speech about Shirley and how she gave up a library career three years ago to save a century-old bookstore that had been going downhill. In the last three years, Shirley's personality and brainpower have tripled the annual income.

For that reason the Bestbooks board of directors have voted Shirley a bonus: something she has always wanted – a trip to Paris. Shirley screamed – something she never does. Then Donald said that all expenses would be paid – *for two!* Shirley looked at me, and I screamed! Then we clutched each other and both cried.'

Qwilleran was stunned into silence but recovered to say, 'I'm very happy for you, Polly!'

She said, 'I only wish you were going with me.'

'So do I, dear.'

Polly said, 'At least I won't have to impose on neighbors and worry about Brutus and Catta. They can stay at Pet Plaza, and Judd Amhurst can manage the bookstore.'

She added, 'A Lockmaster travel agent will handle airline tickets, hotel reservations, and sightseeing.'

Later that evening, and in the days that followed, Qwilleran speculated that they could have been traveling about the globe together. Why had they both allowed themselves to be trapped in the workaday world? Now there was no telling whom Polly would meet. There had been that professor in Canada, that antiques dealer in Williamsburg, those attorneys and architects at the K Fund in Chicago.

And now there were all those Frenchmen! She liked men, and they were attracted to her agreeable manner, resulting from a lifetime career in a public library. Her musical voice might be interpreted as being seductive. She had a beautiful complexion – the result, she said, of eating broccoli and bananas. She dressed attractively – with individual touches of her own design. Altogether, Polly seemed too young for the silver in her hair. And when she entered a room wearing a Duncan plaid over the shoulder, pinned with a silver cairngorm . . . she stopped conversation.

And now those two likable and attractive women were going to Paris!

Nine

The next day, a Tuesday, Qwilleran met his Qwill Pen deadline but felt an underlying disappointment, although he kept telling himself to snap out of it. Everywhere he went, the entire population of Pickax seemed to know that Polly was going to Paris without him.

One conference was with Lisa Compton, who wanted to update him on the proposed program at the Senior Health Club. When given a choice of venue, she gladly chose the barn.

'How's your crotchety and lovable husband?' he asked. Lyle was superintendent of schools.

'Crotchety and lovable, in that order,' she said cheerfully.

They decided it was too good a day to sit anywhere but the gazebo.

He asked, 'Is there anything the Qwill Pen can do for you?'

'That's for you to decide, Qwill. I'll tell you where we stand. The building itself is progressing incredibly fast. With all-volunteer labor. We're selling memberships and collecting ideas for activities. I've never seen this town so excited. The wonderful thing is that they want to learn how to do things! Does the Qwill Pen have any suggestions?'

'As a matter of fact, yes! I've been thinking about it – and about the pleasure I get from writing a private journal. It's not like a diary, where you record daily events – but a place for thoughts and ideas, no matter how personal or crazy. No matter how amateurish, it's something to leave to future generations – something that will be appreciated. I'd be willing to introduce the idea, give a few tips – even read some of my own entries.'

'Qwill! This is more than I expected! You could introduce the idea now – in the community hall, and get them started. Is there anything I should be doing?'

'Just tell the stationer to lay in a good supply of ordinary school notebooks with lined pages.'

* * *

That night as Qwilleran sat down to write in his private journal, he had a flashback to his lean and hungry years as a young man in New York. He wrote:

My furnished room had an old windup Victrola and a single 78 record: Johnny Mercer singing 'I'm gonna sit right down and write myself a letter.' I played it every night because I couldn't afford to buy another one.

Now, three decades later, it runs through my mind every night when I sit down to write to myself in my journal.

Qwilleran's phone rang frequently the following day.

'Is it true about Polly?'

'Why aren't you going?'

'Why Paris?'

'Does she speak French?'

'Are you giving a big party?'

'How long will she be gone?'

Finally he remembered the advice of his childhood mentor: 'When fed up, take the bull by the horns.'

He went downtown to Lanspeak's Department Store and asked Carol about a going-away gift for Polly. 'Not another scarf! And certainly not a bottle of French perfume!'

She said, 'We have a wonderful travel coat – gabardine – with snap flaps on the patch pockets – with secret pockets in the lining – and a brimmed rain hat. Polly looked at it but thought the price a little steep.'

'I'll take it!' he said. 'In fact, I'll take two. Is there a choice of colors?'

Now, it seemed to Qwilleran, would be a good time to work on his senior program for Lisa Compton. It would be easy. He could tell an anecdote or two about Cool Koko . . . then show a stack of the school notebooks he filled with journal entries. Never a day went by without filling a page.

On some days there were brief entries:

When Yum Yum, my female Siamese, has access to a long hallway with many doors to bedrooms, bathrooms, etc., her performance is a wonder to watch. The doors are open; the rooms are unoccupied much of the time.

With stiff legs and resolute steps, she proceeds to walk the length of the hall down the exact center, looking straight ahead. At each open door she stops in her tracks; her body remains motionless except for her head, which swivels to look in the room. Only her eyeballs move as she appraises the interior. Then, finding nothing of interest, she switches her head back to the main course and trudges on to the next open door.

I have never seen her find anything of interest, but she continues her silent inspections.

There are times when I would like to redesign this barn and put the front door in the front and the back door in the back. But what is the back? And what is the front?

I stable my bicycles in the elegant foyer – and greet guests at the kitchen door.

I guess this is what happens when you convert a drive-through apple barn into a residence. And it reminds me of the pioneers who founded Pickax. Did they have a mischievous sense of humor when they put North Street south of South Street . . . and when they put storefronts facing the alley and loading docks facing the street?

Pickax is the quintessential absurdist city!

That evening, Qwilleran phoned the Comptons and told Lisa he was ready to talk to the seniors about private journals. He had some free time. He would read a couple of his own entries. They could start their own journals without waiting for the Senior Health Club to be finished.

Lisa said they would announce the date at the community hall.

'There'll be a crowd!' she said. 'We'll notify the Traffic Department.'

On Thursday, Qwilleran felt the need for lunch and camaraderie with Kip MacDiarmid. The editor in chief of the *Lockmaster Ledger* was one of his best friends, and Kip's wife, Moira, was the marmalade breeder who had presented the affable Dundee to the Pirate's Chest. Their favorite restaurant was in the old Inglehart mansion.

Kip's first words were, 'Moira says you and Polly must come to dinner soon.'

'Polly's leaving for Paris for two weeks,' Qwilleran said, 'with Shirley Bestover.'

When told the particulars, Kip asked, 'Who's planning their trip?'

'It appears there's a semiretired travel agent in Lockmaster, who will go along to see that they get the best of everything.'

'Him, I know him! He's an old roué, but I suppose Polly and Shirley can handle him. You might tip them off.'

They talked about many things. 'If you would syndicate your column in the *Ledger*, we'd run it on page one and it would double our circulation . . .'

'Want to know something, Kip? Our office manager at the paper says that most of the mail that comes addressed to Koko has a Lockmaster postmark . . . You've got a bunch of Koko-nuts around here.'

They mentioned the local election that was coming up. 'The incumbent is sure to win,' Kip said. 'The challenger is confident, but . . . as the saying goes, he couldn't get elected dogcatcher!'

Then Kip made a suggestion that launched Qwilleran like a rocket. It was just what he needed under the present circumstances. 'Were you ever involved in the Theater of the Absurd?'

'Yes, I was in New York and saw it at its best. I always wanted to write an absurdist play, but never did.'

'There's talk about a revival. Would you be interested?' Kip asked.

'How about an original absurdist creation? How about: *The Cat Who Was Elected Dogcatcher*?'

Then Kip changed the subject slyly: 'Moira wants me to ask you if you're still practicing medicine without a license. You could bottle this stuff and sell it.'

He referred to a humorous verse Qwilleran had composed for his last birthday. He brought a card from his vest pocket printed with a typical Qwilleran limerick:

An editor known as Kip
Is said to run a tight ship.
His heart is large,
He's always in charge,
But he won't take any lip.

The editor said, 'Whenever I'm feeling below normal, physically or otherwise, I read your prescription and it gives me a boost.'

Qwilleran said, 'I've been thinking of writing a book on the subject of humorous verse—'

'Do it! I'll buy the first copies and give them to all my friends.'

As they talked, Qwilleran's gaze was prone to wander across the room to a table where three women were lunching in unusual hats.

He remarked, 'Polly would go for those bizarre hats, and she could wear one well.'

The editor corrected him. 'Moira says they're called art hats.'

'I beg everyone's pardon' was the facetious apology. 'Do you know the women who're wearing them? They keep looking over here at us.'

'They're looking at your moustache. They all know who you are. They see your photo in the Qwill Pen on Tuesdays and Fridays . . . I still think you should syndicate it to the *Ledger*.'

'Pleasant thought, but it wouldn't work.' He grabbed the check when it came to the table. 'My treat. Tell Moira she can invite us to dinner when Polly gets back.'

The editor left, and Qwilleran signed the check and left a tip, noting that two art hats had left the room, and the other woman was still eyeing his moustache.

On the way out of the restaurant he said to the hostess, 'I'm embarrassed. I know that woman at the fireplace table, but I can't place her.'

The hostess's face brightened. 'There are usually three. The public library is closed on Thursday, and they call themselves the Librarians Who Lunch. That one is Vivian Hartman, the chief librarian.'

She looked very pleasant when he approached. Her hat, he noted, was brimmed and about a foot in diameter . . . two shades of velvet, and a large silk sash with a realistic peony.

'I beg your pardon, are you Miss Hartman? I'm Jim Qwilleran from the *Moose County Something*.'

'Yes, I know! Won't you sit down?' she answered, and he pulled up a chair.

'I must say I admire the hats you ladies wear.'

'We make them ourselves . . . in memory of your

93

Thelma Thackeray. Her brother Thurston had a veterinary hospital here. We're still grieving over both of them. Not to mention her loss of twenty-five art hats.' She looked for his reaction.

He nodded somberly. 'Did you know that they had been photographed just before the calamity?'

'No!' she exclaimed. 'No one in Lockmaster knew!'

'Our photographer was commissioned, and I went along to hold his lights. I could show you a set of glossy prints – if you would come for lunch at my barn next Thursday,' he said. 'Thelma had commissioned a California woman to write a book, but she lost interest when the hats were destroyed . . . Perhaps . . .'

'Yes . . . perhaps,' the librarian said, 'we might revive the idea.'

Ten

As F Day approached, Polly became more distracted. There was no time for dining at fine restaurants followed by a classical concert on the magnificent music system of Qwilleran's barn. She spent her days instructing Judd and Peggy to take over the Pirate's Chest in her absence. She spent her evenings making packing lists, reading about Paris, brushing up on her college French, having long telephone conversations with Shirley Bestover; Qwilleran felt left out. His offers of 'any kind of assistance' were appreciated but apparently unneeded.

* * *

That evening and in those to come, Qwilleran took the initiative to phone at eleven P.M., knowing that Polly would be distracted with last-minute considerations of all kinds. She had not yet told him when she was leaving, and he stubbornly refused to ask. He said not a word about his Theater of the Absurd project (she had always despised that kind of play) or the Librarians Who Lunch.

Polly told him, 'Wetherby Goode will take Brutus and Catta to the Pet Plaza and visit them twice a week. Isn't that thoughtful of him? Dr Connie will water my plants and take in my mail. We have such wonderful neighbors at the Willows.' (Qwilleran had no comment.)

She said, 'There's a five-hour difference in time between Paris and Pickax, dear, so we'll have to forgo our late-night chats.'

'I'll give you a pocket recorder to take along, and you can dictate a running account of your adventures to bring home.'

He told her, 'If any problems arise in Paris, don't hesitate to contact me collect – at any hour of the day or night, regardless of time differential.'

When his parting gifts were delivered (blue gabardine for her, khaki gabardine for Shirley), the two women were overwhelmed. It was not until they had left for the Lockmaster airport in Shirley's son's limousine that

Qwilleran felt at ease again, and not even lonely! After all, he had Koko and Yum Yum for companions, two columns a week to write for the newspaper. He was committed to deadline on Homer Tibbitt's biography. He was working on his program for the Senior Health Club, to be given at the community hall since the redesigned building was far from complete. Also, the Literary Club's visiting lecturer on Proust was scheduled to be his overnight guest at the barn. (He was said to be an ailurophile, so Koko's aerial demonstrations would be amusing, not threatening.) Plus, to write a play in the absurdist style. All this . . . and Polly would be gone only two weeks!

Later that evening Qwilleran called Kip MacDiarmid at home. 'Were you serious about my writing an absurdist play?'

'I think it would be a hoot,' Kip replied.

'Would you use the title I suggested?' Qwilleran asked.

'Why not? When can you do it?' Kip asked.

'I've just done it; it took half an hour. I'll send it to your office by motorcycle messenger in the morning.'

THE CAT WHO GOT
ELECTED DOGCATCHER

A Play in One Act by Jim Qwilleran

CAST

Man with dog on leash

Woman with cat in arms

Street sweeper with broom

SCENE

A park with trees painted on background . . . park bench in bright green, center front . . . trash barrel overflowing in rear.

WOMAN (to cat in arms): Stop complaining, Jerome! If I put you down in the wet grass, you'll only want to be picked up again.

Enter MAN (with dog tugging on leash): No, Eugene, it's against the law. (Sees woman.) Oh, hi! Hi!

WOMAN: Hi!

MAN: Is that Jerome? I thought he skipped town after the . . . incident.

WOMAN: He came back.

MAN: Does he have any means of support?

WOMAN: His constituents are raising a slush fund.

MAN: Is that what he eats?

WOMAN: He'll eat anything.

MAN: He looks as if he eats better than I do.

WOMAN: Do you have time to sit down?

MAN: They just painted the benches.

WOMAN: That was last week.

They both sit . . . and look surprised.

WOMAN: Oh, well, I wasn't going anywhere. How about you?

MAN: I had an appointment at the traffic court.

CAT: Yeowwww!

WOMAN: You're sitting on his tail.

MAN: Has the candidate ever held office?

WOMAN: Only as ratcatcher.

MAN: Why did he quit?

WOMAN: No reason.

MAN: What makes you think he could catch dogs?

CAT: Yeowwww!

WOMAN: See? He's quite confident.

MAN: I'm still sitting on his tail!

WOMAN: Jerome! The gentleman has offered to be your campaign manager!

CAT: (Hisses at man.)

WOMAN: Jerome! This gentleman is here to get you votes!

MAN: Frankly, I don't think his name is suitable for public office.

WOMAN: What would you suggest? Pussy?

MAN: I had in mind something strong like Tiger . . . OUCH!

WOMAN: Jerome! That's politically incorrect!

MAN: I'm not sure he's qualified.

WOMAN: Jerome! Behave! . . . He hasn't had his lunch. He knows you have a sandwich in your pocket.

MAN: It's only peanut butter.

WOMAN: He'll eat anything except spinach.

MAN: (Attempts to leave in defense of his sandwich.)

All three are stuck.

The End

That night Qwilleran added to his private journal:

Well, she's gone. There was no send-off. She just faded away. It would have been different if I were living at the Willows. But the weather's much too good at the barn. Carol Lanspeak said that the two mature women probably looked like the Bobbsey Twins with their blue and khaki outfits. Tonight I watched Koko at eleven o'clock to see if he expected a call. He ignored the phone. He knew she was on her way to France . . . if not already there!

When the Linguini Party Store truck delivered another supply of Squunk water and other treats, Qwilleran was pleased to see Daisy Babcock step out of the passenger side. She was waving a camera.

'Libby Simms at the Old Manse wants me to take a picture of Koko. She memorizes everything you write about him. I told her you wouldn't mind.'

'True! But Koko will mind. Whenever a camera is pointed in his direction, he crosses his eyes, bares his fangs, and scratches his ear . . . But go ahead. They're both in the gazebo.'

He helped Alfredo unload.

'I see your wife is still working at the Old Manse.'

'Can't pry her away from that place.'

'No more bee stings?'

'Well, the girl with the allergy is supposed to take a medical kit every time she goes in the garden, which is several times a day, and she forgets, so Daisy bought her a hospital jacket with big pockets in a bright color to hang just inside the garden door. She just grabs it when she goes out. The kit is in the pockets . . . That's the way my wife is – always thinking of solutions to problems . . . How long before you move back to the condo?'

'It depends on the weather. The leaves haven't even started to turn,' Qwilleran marveled . . . He walked around to the gazebo and found the two cats on Daisy's lap.

'No problem,' she said. 'Are you trying out for the *Cats* musical?'

'No, but I'll attend a couple of rehearsals, looking for cues for the Qwill Pen. I hear Libby's boyfriend is a terrific piano player.'

'Did you know he was the Ledfields' piano tuner? They're a darling couple.'

Then Alfredo appeared, and the party was over.

In preparation for the evening, Qwilleran gave the Siamese an early dinner, and they walked around it three times as if questioning the propriety of the timing. For himself he ordered soup, sandwich, and pie from Robin O'Dell Catering.

To get in the mood for the *Cats* rehearsal Qwilleran played a recording of the musical and was half wishing he were singing a role, when . . . he heard a sound that made the hair stand up on the back of his neck. It was Koko's death howl!

Starting with an abdominal guttural, it ascended through the cat's stiffened body and ended with a curdling shriek!

Qwilleran had heard it before, and it meant that . . . someone, somewhere was the victim of murder!

He mopped his brow as he considered the possibilities.

He phoned the city desk at the *Something*. 'Qwill here. Any foul play reported?'

'No, but someone died as the result of a bee sting. Bad scene. Must've been allergic. My kids are getting stung all the time.'

Later in the evening Qwilleran attended the *Cats* rehearsal at the community hall. (The new music center was still being adapted from a public school.) The McLeods' nine-year-old adopted son, Danny, considered himself in charge of the rehearsal: arranging chairs, handing out scores, asking if anyone wanted a drink of bottled water, asking Qwilleran if he wanted something to write on.

When Uncle Louie mounted the podium and rapped on the music stand with his baton, the nine-year-old ushered the singers into the proper sections. No one seemed to find the boy at all too young for the responsibility.

However . . . the grimness of the conductor's expression and the presence of a substitute pianist quieted the assembly quickly. When he had everyone's attention, he said, somberly, 'A fatal accident has robbed our pianist of his assistant and robbed our group of a cheerful and valued member. Libby Simms. Let us express our sorrow and sympathy by standing for a few minutes of silence.'

The chorusers stood, and Hannah, at the piano, played 'Amazing Grace'.

Qwilleran, glancing around the assembly of stunned singers, caught Daisy's eye; the men in her family were trying out for roles. She motioned toward the exit, and when he met her in the hallway, her face looked taut.

She said, 'Qwill, I've got to talk to you.'

They found a bench near the drinking fountain.

'A sad story,' he said. 'I thought she had an emergency medical kit.'

'She was supposed to keep it in a pocket of the jacket – I got hot pink, her favorite color. She sometimes wore the jacket when she went on dates with Frankie. She was young and forgot to check the pockets. It's hard to convince young people to be careful.'

'Has the kit turned up since the tragedy?' he asked.

'I don't know. I've been too upset to think straight. Fredo thought it would do me good to come to the rehearsal with him and Nick . . . but . . .' She burst into tears again . . .

Qwilleran gave her a small packet of tissues.

When Daisy's sobs subsided, she said, 'Fredo's right! I've got to get away from that place.'

'You have talents and personality that would be useful in the exciting community that Nathan has left us. It would please him if you were a part of it. Let me look into it for you. Think of it as the beginning of something, not the end of something.'

One evening Qwilleran phoned his longtime friend John Bushland at home. 'Bushy, do you still have the negatives of Thelma Thackeray's hats that you and I slaved over?'

The photographer, who was losing his hair rapidly, liked to thumb his nose at his misfortune with an impudent nickname.

'Sure thing! Why do you ask?'

'I have an idea for a public-library exhibit in two counties that would be good public relations all around. K

Fund will sponsor. But first, can I get a set of prints before Thursday? Eight-by-ten color prints. How they would be presented – will come later.'

'Sure thing!'

Bushy was always cooperative. And he and Qwilleran had shared experiences that had cemented their friendship – with one reservation: Qwill would never again go out on Bushy's powerboat!

Eleven

While Qwilleran waited for Polly's first postcard from Paris, imagine his surprise at receiving a letter!

Dear Qwill,
It's our first day here, and something funny happened that's too good to keep!

Shirley wanted to take a nap, and our travel agent went looking for a bar. I just wanted to walk around and pinch myself. Was I really in Paris?

I was standing on a kerb, waiting to cross the street, when a short middle-aged man came up to me.

109

He was wearing a T-shirt with a large American flag on the chest – and carrying a French-English phrase book. He pointed to one translation and read slowly.

'Pardonnez-moi. Où se trouve l'opéra?'

I couldn't resist the cliché: 'I don't know. I'm a stranger here myself,' I said.

Instead of being amused, he was obviously embarrassed, because he virtually fled from the scene. Too bad. It would have been fun to find out where he was from – Chicago? Denver?

Actually, I was flattered that he mistook me for a native! The Parisiennes have a definite chic!

And I've never seen such beautiful postcards!

Love from Polly

P.S. What made it so funny – I was wearing my blue gabardine coat and hat from Lanspeak's.

Wednesday morning, G. Allen Barter arrived for legal business at the barn, whistling 'Memory' from the musical *Cats*.

Qwilleran said, 'Don't tell me. You're singing Grizabella in *Cats*? I would have thought you were more the Rum Tum Tugger type.'

'Not guilty! My wife and I took our eldest to the tryouts. We saw you there, but you didn't sing. Did you get cold feet?'

When the bantering was over and the two men had trooped to the conference area with two tail-happy cats and a tray of coffee, Qwilleran said, 'Does the county still need a coordinator for community activities?' Where once there had been only a community hall and athletic field, bequests from old families had now made it feasible for a music center, a senior club, and two museums as well. And although the office of HBB&A had handled the transition, the time had come for citizen control.

Qwilleran said to Bart, 'Daisy Babcock has the intelligence, skills, and creativity to handle it. I suggest you call her to come in for an interview. The K Fund will back me up.'

'What does Koko say about it?' Bart joshed.

'He was the one who suggested it.'

There was the usual amount of joking and coffee swigging, followed by serious decision making and document signing. Then Qwilleran broke the news.

'How would the K Fund like to undertake a little two-county collaboration? That is, share an exhibit that has warm ties to both of them! We're usually competing, criticizing, or opposing in some way.'

After a pause to arouse Bart's curiosity, Qwilleran continued: 'I think you will remember that Moose County twins once returned to the north country in later life. Thelma Thackeray had a career in Hollywood; Thurston Thackeray had made a name for himself, in providing medical services for the horses and dogs of Lockmaster. The passing of the two wonderful people was deeply mourned and – because of questionable circumstances – not properly honored.'

He stopped for breath, and his listener was interested.

'The activity would center about the bookstore of Pickax and the library of Lockmaster, and there would be newspaper features and talks. The twins' father is buried in a hilltop grave, with a simple grave-marker inscription: *Milo the potato farmer*. Some believe he was a bootlegger.'

Bart said, 'Go ahead! Anything that launches the two counties in one direction will be okayed in Chicago.'

Qwilleran said, 'We'll start with the photo exhibit at the two locations. Research, newspaper coverage, talks, et cetera, will come later. Everyone will want to jump on the bandwagon.'

That evening Qwilleran received a surprise phone call from Judd Amhurst. The temporary manager of the bookstore said, 'Wouldn't you know the showcases arrived today! Polly's been expecting them for weeks . . . no, months! As soon as she left the country they arrived!' It was like this. The bookstore architects had designed a space for exhibits of a cultural nature.

Qwilleran asked, 'Did you and Polly plan exhibits in them?'

'We had lots of ideas, but perhaps you'd like to make some suggestions. Showcases, too. They're really elegant.'

'Good, I'll drop in at the bookstore tomorrow.' Qwilleran was a welcome visitor at the Pirate's Chest . . . and not simply because he always brought a box of treats from Grandma's Sweet Shop.

That night Qwilleran wrote in his private journal:

These are busy days in Moose County: new ideas, new activities, new people. And the same old gossips in the coffeehouses. They are not always right, but they are always provocative. And the best place to listen to the best scuttlebutt is Lois's Luncheonette downtown. The trick is . . . to listen without getting involved. While the pundits and the know-it-alls filled the tables and chairs, I preferred to sit at the counter with my back to the madding crowd, supposedly reading the daily paper but actually listening. This was a good idea that didn't work. The store clerks, truck drivers, and farmers at the table would catch sight of me and ask, 'What's your opinion, Mr Q? Should they fire the guy? Was he stealing the city blind? How did he get elected, anyhow?' It was impossible not to get involved, when all I wanted was a cup of coffee and a few minutes' rest after ending my beat or standing in line at the bank and at the office. One day I carried a New York paper instead of the *Moose County Something*. I sat at the counter to read with my back to the noise . . . and no one bothered me! How to explain it? A small-town phenomenon! From then on, whenever I had my nose in the *Times* or the *Journal*, no one interrupted!

Twelve

On Thursday, a handsome middle-aged woman with reddish brown hair, hatless, drove from Lockmaster to Pickax – turning off the highway on to a trail called Marconi between the public library and the theater arts building. It led through a patch of woods and emerged with a breathtaking view!

One came upon the barn suddenly – four stories high, octagonal, constructed of fieldstone and weathered shingles, with two Siamese cats dancing in a small ground-floor window.

Qwilleran went out to meet her.

'Welcome to the barn, Vivian.'

'One question! Why is this little lane named after the Italian inventor of the wireless telegraph?'

'It's named after an owl in the woods that hoots in Morse code . . . Now come in and meet Koko and Yum Yum.'

His guest said, 'They're still talking – at our Lit Club – about the talk you gave on Stephen Miller's book, *Conversation: A History of a Declining Art* . . . Kip thinks you belong in Lockmaster.'

'I appreciate the compliment,' he said.

'May I ask what brought you to Moose County?'

'An inheritance, and when I had the barn converted, I was hooked. I'll show you the interior. It was the last work of a very talented designer. I feel privileged to preserve his work. The acoustics are incredible.'

They went indoors and the guest gasped over the vast spaces, ramps winding around the interior, the views from the balcony levels – all the while followed by the Siamese like hired security guards.

'They like you!' the host said. 'Do you have cats?'

'We have one of Moira's friendly marmalades at the library – the staff named him Reggie – and I have a bossy Siamese at home, called Caesar.'

'How do you two strong-minded individuals get along?'

'Oh, I let him have his way . . . and he lets me have mine.'

While waiting for lunch to be delivered by the caterer, they had aperitifs in the gazebo. On the way she saw the British Silverlight in the foyer. She asked, 'Do you do cross-country biking?'

'No. Do you?'

'Not since my college days. Memorable times! Especially in the British Isles.'

She raved over the gazebo, screened on eight sides. Vivian had heard about Squunk water and wanted to try it. He recommended a drink he had created called 'Moose County Madness' that consisted of Squunk water and cranberry juice.

Qwilleran said, 'I'd like to put something to you, Vivian. There appears to be a big difference between Lockmaster County and Pickax. Would it be appropriate – or even desirable – for the two counties to close the gap with a show of art hats at each venue?'

Qwilleran went on: 'Once upon a time . . . I'm going to sound like a storyteller . . . there was a Moose County potato farmer named Milo Thackeray, who reared motherless twins, Thurston and Thelma. She was a little taller, stronger, bolder than her brother and always looked after him. They were quite different.

'Thurston went to veterinary college in the east, married another doctor, came home, and started an animal hospital in Lockmaster. They had one son. The more flamboyant Thelma went to California and had a successful career with a private dinner club – never married, but kept a protective eye on her younger brother. His son was a problem.

'Eventually, she retired and came back to Moose County to help, if possible, with her difficult nephew. She brought her rare collection of twenty-five art hats, which were to be the subject of a book and a traveling exhibit . . . All the plans were ruined by the nephew, who destroyed not only the family and himself but the collection of art hats. The family scandal left a stain on the good name of Thackeray. Even the hospital changed its name under a new owner.'

Qwilleran paused for her reaction.

'How very sad,' she murmured.

'But that isn't the end of the tale . . . The twenty-five hats were photographed before they were destroyed, and I can show you the prints!'

Then lunch was served, and they turned to the subject of Thelma Thackeray's dinner club. How as hostess Thelma had always worn a hat as she moved through the dining room, chatting with members . . . and how Thelma had always stolen the show with her exotic headgear at Pickax restaurants like the Old Grist Mill, and the Mackintosh Inn.

Qwilleran said, 'What I want to discuss with you is the size of the show. Someone once said that the more art you look at, the less you see. What I propose is two small exhibitions opening simultaneously at the Lockmaster Library and the Pickax gallery. At the end of a certain length of time, the two shows would be reversed, and showgoers would have yet another thrill.'

'You're absolutely right!' she said. 'Our exhibit case will accommodate a dozen photos without crowding, and I imagine that's true of the one in Pickax.'

After lunch the tables were cleared and the photos of the Thackeray art hats were viewed and lavished with praise and amazement.

Vivian said, 'The hats are much more dramatic than the ones we design here in the boondocks! Who was the photographer?'

'John Bushland. Had a studio in the Inglehart house before it was a restaurant. Now he's on the staff of the *Moose County Something*. I helped him take the shots, acting as photographer's flunky. For the exhibits he'll print them on matte stock and mount them on matte board with easel backs.'

'What information will be available for the identification cards?'

'Name of hat, artist, and date.'

'I'm weak with excitement!' she said. 'And to think that it happened on Marconi Trail!'

'One question,' he said. 'Thelma not only wore lizard-skin shoes, she kept her hats in lizard-print hatboxes, destroyed along with the hats . . .'

'That's part of the hat hobby. We make our own signature hatboxes. Mine are gray pinstripe. If we could find some lizard-print paper, we could make one of Thelma's signature boxes for each exhibit, as an accent.'

Qwilleran was enthusiastic; she was getting into the spirit. He said, 'If you need any help along the way, Pickax has a new coordinator of community activities. She has ideas and enthusiasm – Daisy Babcock. You are on the same wavelength. I'll have her phone you.'

Later, they returned to the barn interior.

'You don't have a piano,' she remarked, as if noting the absence of indoor plumbing.

'No. My mother was an excellent pianist and wanted to give me lessons, but I preferred sandlot baseball. The barn has a fantastic music system and brilliant acoustics. Lately I've acquired some CDs of the Ledfields playing violin and piano, which I'd like you to hear.'

'I wonder how a grand piano would sound in this environment? Frankie, the piano tuner, gives concerts, you know.' Hearing no reaction, she went on, 'My parents are retiring to Florida and liquidating their furnishings, including a Steingraeber & Söhne grand piano made in Bavaria. Perhaps you'd like to take it on trial. There are several spaces that would be suitable—'

'Hold on! Do you realize this barn is in deep freeze five months of the year? But I'm sure the K Fund would buy it for the forthcoming music center. They could have concerts called the Hartman Series featuring talent from both counties!'

That night Qwilleran wrote in his private journal:

There are times when I wish I had taken those piano lessons! I would have left the high-speed stuff to Joe and concentrated on numbers with crashing chords that would frighten the cats and knock the pictures off the walls.

For the next two weeks Qwilleran was busier than he'd ever been. When Mildred Riker asked, 'Have you heard from Polly?' he replied, 'Polly who?'

There were postcards from Paris, of course, but life in

Pickax was challenging in many directions. The Library Hat Show alone had enlisted his attention in several ways: lining up Daisy Babcock, working with Bushy on prints, finding some lizard-print paper to cover a couple of hatboxes . . . and, yes, lining up G. Allen Barter for the K Fund donation of a Steingraeber grand piano to the music center, not to mention finding Frankie a new page turner and driver, giving a talk to the Senior Health Club on private journals, writing a play titled *The Cat Who Got Elected Dogcatcher*. His Qwill Pen column had to come from the 'trash barrel', meaning bits and pieces of this and that that could appear fascinating to his readers. He hardly had time to feed the cats, let alone read to them from the *Wilson Quarterly*.

Meanwhile, those stunning green postcards from Paris were arriving all over town, and recipients were talking about the beautiful river, all those bridges, the Eiffel Tower and the Arc de Triomphe, and especially the stray cats in the cemetery.

People said, 'How come we don't have stray cats in the cemetery?' . . . It was seen as a cultural deficiency, so citizens proposed a committee to promote it. Qwilleran tactfully declined their invitation to champion their cause with Koko as mascot.

Thirteen

Late Thursday afternoon, when Vivian had returned to Lockmaster and her precocious Caesar, Qwilleran felt the satisfaction of a job well done: the launching of a two-county effort and the discovery of yet another librarian with intelligence, vocabulary . . . and cats.

He phoned the *Moose County Something* and was connected with John Bushland in the darkroom.

'I have news!' Qwilleran said. 'We're going ahead with Thelma's hat pix on matte mounts with easel backs . . . Also, we need to cover a couple of hatboxes in the lizard print that Thelma used. Have you seen any lizard-skin print lately?'

'Frankly, I haven't been looking.'

'It's worth doing, even if we have to have an artist simulate it,' Qwilleran said.

'Janice may have some ideas. She may know an artist in California who produces lizard print,' Bushy added.

Qwilleran said, 'If I can give you any menial help to expedite any of these things, I'm available. And don't forget: charge everything to the K Fund.'

Then it was back to the Qwill Pen until the caterwauling began again: it announced a truck coming through the Marconi Woods.

It pulled up at the kitchen door, announced by the cat ballet in the wide window. It was the Linguini truck, and Alfredo jumped out, reaching for a case of Squunk water.

Qwilleran went to meet him. 'Hey, did I order that? I didn't know I ordered any!'

'You didn't. This is a present – from Daisy and me! There's more, too!' Out came a carton of cat snacks and juices.

Fredo said, 'Daisy and I appreciate everything you did to get her out of that hellhole.'

'She and the new job are perfect for each other . . . How

about you and Nick? Did you get roles in the new musical?'

'Yes, we're doing Mungojerrie and Rumpelteazer. Any time you want to come and sing with us, you're welcome at rehearsal. Have you done any singing? Your voice sounds like it.'

'Only in college, but I enjoyed it! Is the pianist back on the job?'

'Frankie? Yeah, that was a crime what happened to little Libby!' Fredo gave his listener a swift glance. 'And I really mean *crime*!' He jumped into the cab. 'Thanks again from Daisy and me.'

'One question,' Qwilleran said. 'What is the arrangement you have with Frankie? I understand he doesn't drive.'

'We take turns picking him up . . . Wanna volunteer?' Fredo added in a jocular afterthought.

'I might do just that!' said Qwilleran. 'I have a lot of space to fill in the Qwill Pen, and I might find a story on piano tuning. Why does a grown man – with an assortment of talents – get called *Frankie*?'

'His dad is Franklin, and they're sort of an old-fashioned family.'

Fredo gunned the motor – and scatted the cats away from the window.

The conversation had reminded Qwilleran of all the half sentences and innuendos he had heard at Lois's Luncheonette.

The Siamese were waiting for him near their feeding station. He asked, 'What really happened to Libby Simms?'

They looked at each other and then jumped off the counter, and chased up and down the ramp.

Finishing his thousand words, the newsman took his New York paper and went to Lois's Luncheonette for some scuttlebutt.

Before he could take the end seat at the counter and open his paper, Lois lumbered up. With all due respect to the heavyset proprietress, that was how she moved about her premises – slowly and with grandeur. The columnist was one of her favorite customers; she served him not only coffee but a slice of chocolate cake and some turkey scraps for the cats on the house.

He opened his newspaper and tuned in to the babble behind him:

'The city's hired someone to keep a check on all the goings-on.'

'No kiddin'! Who?'

'Fredo Linguini's wife.'

'She's a lively one.'

'They're giving her an office in the old community hall
building.'

'I hope they fix it up for her. It's showing its age.'

'Aren't we all? All it needs is some paint. If they called
for volunteers, I'd sign up! We're lucky to have that
building. We had our wedding reception there.'

During Polly's absence, Qwilleran had plenty of dinner
invitations, and one evening he was dining with the
Bushlands. They discussed the forthcoming exhibit of
Bushy's hat photos. Janice, who had been Thelma's
assistant for years, was now assisting Bushy in the photographer's darkroom.

Qwilleran asked, 'Do you remember Thelma's lizard-
print hatboxes?'

'Yes, she had them custom-made. There's still some
lizard-print paper in her closet.'

'What!' Qwilleran almost dropped a forkful of sweet-
potato pie.

After that, everything happened fast. A motorcycle
messenger was summoned, and two rolls of the unusual
paper were dispatched to Lockmaster.

By the time he returned to the barn, there was a

message from Vivian on the phone: 'A miracle! How did you do it?'

He called Vivian back and said, 'Abracadabra! An old sideshow trick!'

'And Daisy Babcock is going to meet with me,' she said. 'On the phone she sounds charming!'

The venerable community hall was part of the City of Stone in downtown Pickax. Several generations had trooped in and out of its doors for meetings, lectures, parties, business luncheons, exhibits, cat and dog shows, and antique auctions. Several generations of janitors had shuffled chairs, tables, platforms, and runways accordingly. Although the rooms were plain – clean but plain – it occurred to Qwilleran that Daisy's presence would inspire changes: a little paint, some art on the walls, even background music.

It gave Qwilleran an idea!

The forthcoming publication of the Homer Tibbitt biography would no doubt be introduced by a program at the community hall. Homer had been born in Moose County, had attended college in Lockmaster County, and had been principal of Central High School there until his retirement.

Homer then returned to his home territory and served as honorary Moose County historian until his death at the age of a hundred. During that time he wrote hundreds of research papers now on file in the public library, and his feisty sense of humor made the citizens laugh.

Qwilleran's idea – to mark the publication of the grand Old Man's biography – was to rename the community hall the Homer Tibbitt Auditorium.

He proceeded circumspectly – pulled strings – and hinted at K Fund backing.

That evening, as Qwilleran gave the cats their bedtime treat, he mused at the changes awaiting Polly's return: the two-county show of art hats ... the Homer Tibbitt Auditorium ... Vivian's offer of a grand piano ... the young girl's death from a bee sting – just like that of Maggie Sprenkle's husband.

Koko interrupted with a loud 'Yow-w-w!' as if saying, 'Let's go! Let's go!'

The next morning, Qwilleran drove downtown to the department store. He and Larry looked at Polly's post-card of the Champs Elysées. Qwilleran told the joke about the tourist who thought she was a Parisienne in her Lanspeak's raincoat. Qwilleran bought an alligator belt for himself. He had always wanted one, but Polly didn't like them.

So far, so good, he told himself. And then he had a

phone call from Steve Bestover in Lockmaster . . . the attorney who was Shirley's son.

'Mr Qwilleran. I hope I'm not calling too early.' It sounded urgent.

'Not at all. It sounds important.'

'The girls have been in an accident. It could be worse, but they're hospitalized, and it changes their plans. They were due to fly home this weekend.'

'What happened?'

'They were in a taxi that was hit by a car exceeding the speed limit. Polly has a few bumps and cuts, but Mother has a neck injury that causes back pain. She says they're getting the best of care and not to worry, but they can't leave as planned. I will fly over when I get the signal and accompany them home.'

'Do you have a number I can call?'

'Polly says it will be better if she calls you. She'll phone collect when she has some information. The odd thing is that it happened in the Pont de l'Alma tunnel, where Princess Diana was killed.'

'Yow!' came a blast in Qwilleran's free ear.

'Was that your Koko?'

'He knows bad news when he hears it. Thanks for calling, Steve. Sorry we've never met. Keep in touch.'

Then Qwilleran regarded the cat strangely. He had been

jumping on and off the desk. It was only when he heard about the tunnel accident that he responded – did he know that was where Princess Diana was killed . . . or what?

Fourteen

In most communities, half the citizens like a change once in a while; the other half likes everything the way it is. It was no different 400 miles north of everywhere. The proposed beautification of the community hall was considered either a calamity or a delight. The town's leading designer was offering her expertise. Without charge. She was the daughter of Andrew Brodie, Pickax police chief, and Qwilleran found it an excuse to invite his chum to the barn for a nightcap.

Qwilleran refrained from using the the old cliché 'Long time no see', but the first words the chief said were 'Long time no see.'

Andy took a seat at the bar, and his host reached for the Scotch bottle. 'The usual?'

'Still drinking that stuff?' the chief said in disdain as Qwilleran poured Squunk water for himself.

'What do you hear about the new community hall, Andy?' Qwilleran asked, although he knew the answer.

'I hear they're changing the name. Keeping it secret. I hear they're using wallpaper and fancy things like that.'

'Whatever your daughter suggests will be in good taste,' Qwilleran ventured. 'It's generous of the stores to donate the paint – and some of our foremost loafers to donate their labor . . . What are you buying your wife for Christmas, Andy?'

Daisy Babcock, the new county coordinator, had been busy coordinating the details of the event: the building itself had a face-lift. Qwilleran would preview his new biography of Homer Tibbitt. Rhoda, his widow, would come in from Ittibittiwassee Estates with two busloads of her neighbors and would be presented with flowers. A baritone from their church choir would sing 'He's a Grand Old Man' to the tune of 'It's a Grand Old Flag'. Longtime friends would tell amusing tales from Homer's later years, including the Brown Paper Bag Mystery. A delegation of notables would christen the old hall the Homer Tibbitt Auditorium. It would be filmed.

Daisy Babcock, working with Fran Brodie, had planned a decorative scheme based on the Pickax High School colors: gray, black, and gold. The building was gray stone; the athletic team was the Gray Panthers. Rhoda Tibbitt's flowers were yellow roses. The commemorative programs with Homer's photo on the cover were also yellow.

The weatherbeaten sign across the top of the entrance had been replaced with HOMER TIBBITT AUDITORIUM in crisp black letters touched with gold. And the shabby wooden doors in the wide entrance were now shiny black with brass hardware.

Qwilleran had interviewed countless citizens in writing the biography and planning the celebration, but nowhere did he reveal the secret of the Brown Paper Bag!

In his private journal that night, Qwilleran reported:

Homer came from a family of teetotalers and throughout his life he was never known to take a drink, but he delighted in teasing folks. In his adult life and well into his nineties, he carried a brown paper bag in his pocket, and it contained a flask of amber liquid from which he was known to take a swig occasionally. Even his closest friends were never allowed to share the secret. When, at the age of ninety, he finally married, it was expected that Rhoda would track down the truth. She never did. He managed to keep his secret to the end. He had a great sense of humor and kept on laughing at folks.

During Polly's absence, Qwilleran received many invitations to dinner. One of them was from Lyle and Lisa Compton in their condo. For a fourth they invited a neighbor, Barbara Honiger. He knew the name. She contributed regularly to the Qwill Pen column and boasted to the Comptons that she had received enough yellow pencils from the Qwill Pen to build the foundation of a log cabin.

Barbara was not tall but had a commanding personality and sharp wit – an attorney with her own practice, specializing in real estate.

She had good-natured opinions on everything. A meal at the Comptons' was always a lively talkfest, even though Lisa made no claims to cooking skills. No one asked any questions about the casserole she served, although it tasted pretty good, and conversation never lagged.

LYLE: 'I like your alligator belt, Qwill. Lisa won't let me have one.'

QWILL: 'Polly dislikes them, too, so as soon as she left the country, I splurged.'

LISA: 'When are you closing the barn?'

BARBARA: 'How do you go about closing a barn?'

QWILL: 'Pat O'Dell and his crew swarm all over the place.'

LYLE: 'Better do it before we have zero temperature and four feet of snow!'

QWILL: 'I was waiting until after the Lit Club meeting. I'm putting up the speaker overnight.'

LISA: 'That's changed. There's been a death in his family. Could you speak to the Lit Club, Qwill?'

After a thoughtful pause for dramatic effect, he said, 'What would you think of forming a secret society named Word Tasters Anonymous? . . . Anyone can join . . . no dues!' There was a stunned silence, and he went on. 'It's a theory currently being tested. Words have flavor as well as meaning. Words can be enjoyed on many levels. Dickens is a master of the art. Consider the last lines in *A Tale of Two Cities*.'

He quoted: ' "It is a far, far better thing that I do, than I have ever done; it is a far, far better rest that I go to than I have ever known." '

Following nods and murmurs from his listeners, he went on:

'When I say those words, I can taste their exquisite sweetness . . . In *A Christmas Carol* I feel the crispy crunchiness of consonants, vowels, and diphthongs, delighting my taste buds.' He quoted: ' "Then up rose Mrs Cratchit, Cratchit's wife, dressed out but poorly in a twice-turned gown, but brave in ribbons, which are cheap and make a goodly show for sixpence." '

He explained, 'Everyone knows there are music lovers, but few know that there are word lovers too: aware of the taste and feeling and magic of words, not necessarily the meanings. One of our members is a successful business-woman who loved four words from Shakespeare: "Nothing comes from nothing." The arrangement of friendly consonants reassured her.'

Qwilleran said, 'Word tasting is not limited to the work of great writers. Mildred Riker gets a shiver of pleasure from a practice sentence used in high school when learning to type.'

Everyone wanted to know it, and he quoted: ' "The time of many murders is after midnight." '

Then, Barbara asked, 'I suppose you've all seen Thelma's hat photos at the bookstore?'

LYLE: 'I hear the locals like the new showcases better than the hats.'

QWILL: 'The hats were designed by California artists.

Their taste is a little sophisticated for Moose County. I had to gulp myself at some of their productions, but I hear the library-goers in Lockmaster are so excited they can hardly wait to see the other half of the show; they're coming up here to the bookstore to see it.'

Qwilleran enjoyed meeting Barbara. He liked attorneys. He looked forward to meeting Steve Bestover. He enjoyed his K Fund sessions with G. Allen Barter, who was less of a legal eagle and more of a brother-in-law.

On Mrs Fulgrove's last two visits to clean the barn . . . or 'fluff it up', as she said, she and her housecleaners covered the premises, frightening the cats . . . and then she always left a note. Qwilleran saved them for what he called the Fulgrove Witchery Collection. Her syntax was curious, to say the least.

Dear Mr Q . . . Koko broke a bottle on your bathroom floor which I saved the pieces of glass so you could see what it was.

It proved to be Scottish aftershave lotion from Canada that Polly had brought from one of her trips. The following week, a porcelain figurine of a bagpiper in shoulder plaid, kilt, and knee hose was found on the living-room hearth in several fragments.

Dear Mr Q . . . I think Koko did it . . . which he was hanging around, looking naughty. I told him he was a bad cat which he ran away. He never broke anything before . . .

> *Yours truly . . . Mrs Fulgrove*

Just as Qwilleran was beginning to suspect Koko of anti-Scottish tendencies, all of a sudden he witnessed a third misdemeanor. He saw Koko tear the cover of a book Polly had given him. It was only a paperback, but it was twentieth-century poems that they both enjoyed.

He thought, That cat is trying to tell me something. Does he think she should not have left Brutus and Catta with strangers? Who knows what enters his feline mind? The cats are probably eating better at Pet Plaza than they ever did at home.

Fifteen

And then Polly dropped a bombshell!

Dearest Qwill,
I have thrilling news, and I know you'll be excited for
me. Steven has come over to escort Shirley home, and
I'm staying here for a while!

An American firm with offices in Paris advertised
for a librarian to handle their commercial library,
which is extensive.

I applied and was given a three-year contract!
Can you believe it? It's technical, but I'm a fast

learner. I simply can't believe my good fortune!

I'm notifying Dr Connie to find a good home for Brutus and Catta, preferably together. And I'm asking Mildred to conduct a house sale and sell everything of mine to benefit the church. It's not very good stuff, having belonged to my in-laws for ages before I got it. I can buy all new things when I return.

I'll miss dining out with you and the musicals at the barn.

Love,
Polly

Qwilleran phoned Dr Connie to inquire about Brutus and Catta and learned they were living it up at the Pet Plaza and might never want to leave.

He read Polly's letter again to see if he had misunderstood. It was perfectly clear. He told himself he had been the recipient of a 'Dear John' letter for the first time in his life . . . Perhaps he had been too complacent . . . they had been 'together', so to speak, for a long time!

The Siamese hovered around. They knew something was wrong.

It soon appeared that Polly had notified everyone. Always businesslike and thorough, she had sent news releases to the *Something* and *Ledger*, resulting in front-page coverage. The headlines also started the gossip mills grinding.

At Toodle's Market: Did you know she spoke French? . . . She went to college Down East. Her family's not from around here . . . Her father was a professor . . . She married a student from Moose County; that's how she landed here.

At the drugstore: Did you know she was a widow from way back? Her husband was a volunteer fireman killed while fighting a barn fire . . . Wonder why she never remarried . . . She went to work in the Pickax library; that's what she was trained for. But she never remarried.

At Lois's Luncheonette: Looks like his girlfriend ran out on him . . . He won't have any trouble getting a replacement.

At the post office: She went to our church. He never came with her, but he was a generous giver . . . No wonder! With all that money he has to pay tax on! . . . I'd gladly pay the tax if I had all that dough!

And now everyone was phoning Qwilleran . . . neighbors at the condo . . . bookstore crew . . . Polly's hairdresser . . . No one knew that she was fluent in French. People thought that the French magazine that was always on her coffee table was only stage dressing, so to speak.

Qwilleran hurried to the bookstore and had a conference with Judd Amhurst; no problem there, other than shock . . .

The Rikers invited him to dinner – alone – and he declined, saying he had a deadline in connection with his next book . . .

In the days that followed, Qwilleran, who had once trained for the stage, acted as if nothing had happened.

Still, at eleven P.M., he found himself thinking: Let's face it. Everyone needs a late-night phone pal.

'. . . What are you doing? Did you have a good day? . . . What did the vet say about Catta's stomach upset? . . . Where would you like to have dinner Saturday night? . . . I finished reading my book. I wouldn't recommend it. Well, let me know about the plumber's decision . . . *À bientôt.*'

Then Qwilleran pulled a few strings.

Polly's unit at the Willows was up for lease; Barbara Honiger had mentioned that it would be nice living closer to town. Both Joe Bunker and Dr Connie thought an attorney would be an asset to the Willows.

Qwilleran looked up a phone number.

'Good evening, Barbara,' he said in his mellifluous voice. 'I hear you're moving into the Willows! We couldn't hope for a better addition. Is there anything I can do to expedite your move?'

The Willows celebrated the arrival of Barbara Honiger's cat, Molasses, with . . . not another pizza party but . . . a catered meal by the Mackintosh Inn, delivered by a busboy in a chef's tall toque.

Toasts were drunk to the new neighbor. She showed snapshots of Molasses, her marmalade. They were a congenial group. Joe Bunker played 'Kitten on the Keys' very fast. He said he had just had his piano tuned. Barbara was impressed by Joe's high-speed performance at the piano. Dr Connie gave the newcomer a token gift from Scotland, a Shetland-wool scarf. Qwilleran invited them to a performance of the musical *Cats*.

With a commanding stance and a grand gesture, Qwilleran declared, 'I consider it significant that Shakespeare made no mention of newspaper columnists in his vast work . . . or of veterinarians or meteorologists. But he mentions attorneys!'

There were cries of 'Who? Where? Which play?'

'In act two of *Henry VI, Part II* . . . "First thing we do . . . we kill all the lawyers"!'

The festivities lasted longer than the usual pizza party; the hotel had sent over four courses. Dr Connie showed the movie of her trip to Scotland. Joe's piano playing seemed particularly brilliant.

Barbara asked Qwilleran, 'Is that portrait of Lady

Mackintosh in the hotel lobby your mother?'

'Yes. Amazingly, it was done by a local artist who'd never met her or seen her photo. He was merely told she resembled Greer Garson. Yet the portrait doesn't look like a movie star; she looks like my mother.'

Joe said, 'I should have him do a portrait of my father – a horseradish farmer with a moustache and glasses. He looked like Teddy Roosevelt.'

Qwilleran accompanied the women to their units and went in to say hello to the new cat on the block.

Barbara owned one of Moira MacDiarmid's cats. 'Or he owns me. He's in the deepest tawny tone like a molasses cookie, so I named him Molasses, and he seems to like it.'

Qwilleran noted that his markings, tilted over one eye, gave him the jaunty look of a soldier.

He sang an old military tune: 'There's something about Molasses, there's something about Molasses, there's something about Molasses that is fine, fine, fine.'

Molasses fell over sideways – an expression of approval, Barbara said.

When he returned to the barn, the Siamese greeted him with that reproachful stare that meant their bedtime snack was late.

* * *

That evening, instead of waiting for the call that never came, Qwilleran made one of his own – to Wetherby Goode. 'Joe. Great party! Great music!'

'Yeah, you can always tell when old Betsey has been tuned. I pound the ivories so hard, she has to be tuned four times a year. It has something to do with the felts and the hammers. Don't ask me what!'

'Really? Who does it?'

'Young guy in Lockmaster.'

Qwilleran asked, 'Would Dr Feltzanhammer make a good story for the Qwill Pen?'

'I don't know. He's young and kind of shy. But he's likable.'

'I'll give it a try. Before interviewing anyone on an esoteric subject, I read all about it in the encyclopedia, so I know what questions to ask and what he's talking about. What are felts and hammers? My mother was a brilliant pianist, and she never mentioned felts and hammers.'

'By the way, it was the piano tuner's girlfriend who was killed by a bee sting at the Old Manse.'

At that moment, Koko interrupted with a gut-wrenching howl.

'What was that all about?' Joe asked.

'Koko wants the lights turned out.'

Sixteen

In spite of the ups and downs of his current life, Qwilleran had the steadying influence of home and workplace: feeding the cats twice a day and writing the Qwill Pen twice a week. Filling the thousand-word hole on page two kept him alert for ideas.

The morning after Joe's party, Qwilleran was feeding the cats when he received an unexpected phone call from Rhoda Tibbitt.

'Qwill, I hope I'm not calling too early. I have exciting news. I've discovered the answer to the Brown Paper Bag Mystery! I was preparing Homer's suits to give to charity, the way he wanted, and I found some little brown paper bags in the pockets! And two of them contained tiny flasks.' She paused for breath – or effect. 'I tasted the contents: one of them still had . . . black breakfast tea! And the other had the afternoon tea that Homer liked. Lapsang souchong!'

Qwilleran said, 'Don't say a word to anyone! They're talking about a refreshment stand for the lobby of the auditorium, something with class . . . and I'm going to suggest the Homer Tibbitt Tearoom! . . . But don't explain, and neither will I. We'll keep Homer's secret.'

Qwilleran had an opportunity to use his privileged information from Rhoda Tibbitt when he called on Daisy Babcock in the refurbished auditorium. He complimented her on the metamorphosis of the building, and she praised his book review. There were daisies from Fredo on her desk – and a daisy wallpaper on the wall above a gray dado.

She said, 'We've been thinking about a refreshment stand on the main floor – not a hangout for kids but something more civilized.'

'How about a Homer Tibbitt Tearoom?'

'Qwill. You come up with the best impromptu ideas!'

A chart on the wall gave the status of local projects. The Old Manse Museum of Art and Antiques was open two days a week with trained guides – twenty dollars a ticket – and people coming from all over the country – even Europe. She then added, 'But they won't go into the garden. They've all heard about the danger of bee stings.'

'Have you had any more trouble?' he asked.

She shook her head and looked sad.

Also on the chart were the following:

> Senior Health Club – Ready next year.
> Wildlife museum – Buildings
> finished/mounted animals and art
> being moved in.

There was a photo of the Ledfields on Daisy's desk, and Qwilleran said, 'Handsome couple. I never met them, but their efforts for child welfare alone were commendable.'

Daisy said, 'That's because they were childless and regretful. Bringing busloads of kids from Pickax Schools to view the mounted animals gave Nathan great pleasure. He would be thrilled to know that we're erecting two buildings downtown and the city is renaming the Old Back Road the Ledfield Highway.'

> *Cats* musical – Now being rehearsed.

Qwilleran asked, 'How are the *Cats* rehearsals progressing? Is Frankie still the accompanist? Who's turning Frankie's pages?'

'Uncle Louie's wife. Hannah. She's a wonderful woman and does what needs to be done. She can accompany the chorus or even direct the show, and yet she'll sweep the stage if necessary, or make sandwiches for the cast. It's amazing what the McLeods have done with the orphan they adopted.'

'So is Frankie doing all right?'

'It appears so.'

He asked, 'Do you think he would make a good interview on piano tuning? I could kill a couple of birds with one stone and do chauffeur service for a rehearsal.'

'I know. This is what we've worked out. We could drop off Frankie at the barn, and you could drive him back to the theater at seven-thirty. You could give him a bite to eat; he isn't fussy, and he'd love to see the barn and meet the cats. I know the barn doesn't have a piano, but Frankie has one of those roll-up keyboards!'

Qwilleran agreed. 'You're an expert coordinator, Daisy.'

He had decided against doing a Qwill Pen column on piano tuning. It was another no-story.

When one of the Linguini brothers (Mungojerrie, not Rumpelteazer) arrived at the barn, Frankie jumped out the passenger side, gazing in rapture at the lofty barn and saying, 'Oh, wow! Oh, wow!'

Qwilleran realized high praise when he heard it.

Koko and Yum Yum were cavorting in the kitchen window as they always did when a vehicle arrived, and – as first-time visitors always did – Frankie asked, 'Are these your cats?'

Qwilleran always felt like saying, 'No, these are a pair of pet crocodiles.' But he said amiably, 'Yes, this is Koko and Yum Yum.'

Both Qwilleran and the Siamese found Frankie a likable guest. The Siamese followed him around and put on their flying-squirrel act from the top balcony to entertain him.

The Siamese were fascinated by the 'thing' strapped to his back, somewhat like a blanket roll but actually a four-octave electronic piano. (Later, when they heard it, though, they went and hid.)

'Do you come from a musical family?' Qwilleran asked.

'My dad raises horses, but my mother is a piano teacher, and I have an uncle who's a piano tuner.'

'Did he teach you about felts and hammers?' He was enjoying a private joke.

'He taught me everything,' Frankie said seriously.

That explained everything except his inability to drive,

and his friendship with Libby Simms had taken care of that.

Locals in both counties had said, 'They're a darling couple. Do you think they'll marry? It's a touching romance.' And then there was the incident of the bee sting.

Now Qwilleran was about to show Frankie the premises.

'First we must order our dinner,' Qwilleran said, handing his guest a menu card. 'Order anything you like and it'll be delivered in fifteen minutes. I'm having ham and sweet potatoes with asparagus spears . . . a cheese muffin . . . apple-and-walnut salad . . . and chocolate cake. I have my own coffee machine.'

'I'll have the same,' Frankie said.

'While we're waiting, Koko will show you their apartment on the third level. They have a twistletwig rocking chair that you might try sitting in; it's an experience.'

Apparently the three of them were 'communicating', because Frankie had to be called down for dinner. It was served in the screened gazebo, and that was another experience, since small animals came up to the screen and communed silently with the Siamese.

Frankie said, 'Libby would have loved this. Did you ever meet her?'

'Yes. Charming young woman.'

Two tears rolled down the young man's face. 'Now my

life's ruined. Libby and I . . . we were gonna get married and travel around on concert tours. But she went out to the garden without the kit the doctor gave her.'

'I hear she kept it in the pocket of her garden coat.'

'Yeah, but she wore that jacket when we went on dates, too. She must've taken the bee kit out and forgot to put it back. She ruined my life as well as her own.'

The Siamese, not used to seeing anyone cry, came forward to watch, and stroking them gave Frankie some comfort.

From then on, he was a sullen guest . . . 'I hafta get back to the theater.' He jumped up and bolted out to Qwilleran's vehicle without a word to the cats.

Qwilleran drove him back to the concert hall. He dropped him without receiving thanks, but Daisy was in the lobby.

'Thanks, Qwill! How did it go?'

'Okay, but I think he was nervous about getting back on time.'

After dropping off Frankie unceremoniously at the concert hall, Qwilleran returned to the barn to feed the cats and was greeted by two agitated Siamese. It meant the phone had been ringing but no message had been left.

He prepared their plate of food and watched them devour it, but they did so nervously, with frequent glances toward the back door. While they were bent over their plates the phone rang – and they jumped a foot.

Daisy was calling from the theater. 'Frankie got back on time but he was a wreck. Hannah had to sub for him. What happened?'

Qwilleran said, 'Bears discussing, but not over the phone. I'll see you tomorrow.'

Writing in his journal that night, he remembered overhearing conversations in the coffee shop after the girl died from a bee sting at the Old Manse. One always heard gossips sounding off. They had been saying: Sounds fishy to me! . . . They're not telling the whole ball of wax . . . My cousin works at the Old Manse, and she says they're not allowed to talk about the accident.

As the press had been led to believe, it would affect public response to the Old Manse and its gardens. And it had.

Seventeen

Late Saturday night, Qwilleran phoned Wetherby Goode at the Willows.

'Joe, I'm tired of living in the Taj Mahal of Pickax and showing it off to every visiting celebrity. We're moving back to the Willows.'

'Good! We'll have a pizza party!'

'Will you bring Connie and Barbara down here for Sunday supper and a concert? As you know, the acoustics are incredible, and I have some recordings of the Ledfields' violin-and-piano duets that I have to return to Maggie Sprenkle. Pat O'Dell will deliver the food. Then we'll all go up to the Willows and be ready for the *Cats* show next Saturday.'

On Sunday afternoon the delegation from the Willows arrived at the barn bearing gifts: Wetherby: a bottle of something; Connie: homemade cookies; Barbara: a tape recording of a jazz combo.

The two women, first-time visitors, were escorted up the ramp by the Siamese to enjoy the fabulous view.

Qwilleran said, 'Try sitting in their twistletwig rocker for a stimulating experience.'

It apparently worked, because all four were frisky when they returned to the main floor.

Qwilleran thought, Well, anyway, it's the last time I'll have to go through this charade for six months.

They consulted the caterer's menu, orders were placed, and they had aperitifs around the big square coffee table while waiting for the delivery, during which Koko returned to the top balcony and did his flying-squirrel act, landing on a sofa cushion between the two women guests. They screamed; drinks were spilled. Qwilleran said, 'Bad cat!' The two men made an effort to keep a straight face.

There was plenty of conversation about Connie's spring trip to Scotland and Barbara's annual visit to the Shakespeare Festival in Canada. Wetherby said he never went anywhere but Horseradish.

Dinners were delivered. The decision was made to serve in the gazebo, where it was cool but pleasant.

Connie said, 'The residents of Indian Village are agitating to have the open decks screened for summer, if it can be done without darkening the interiors. When are you moving back, Qwill?'

'Tomorrow!' he promised.

Then questions were asked about the barn: Who designed the remodeling? Is there a lot of upkeep? Are you handy with tools?

Qwilleran said, 'You probably know Ben Kosley. He takes care of emergencies. I wrote a poem of praise about him in my column. Would you like to hear it? It sums up life in an old apple barn.' He read it to them.

Call 911-BEN-K
The locks don't lock; the floorboards squeak;
The brand new washer has sprung a leak!
The phone needs moving; the pipes have burst!
You're beginning to think the barn is cursed!
CALL Ben!
There's a hole in the floor; the windows stick.
You need some help with the toilet – quick!
The chandelier is out of plumb.
The electric outlets are starting to HUM!

DON'T WORRY . . . CALL Ben!

The sliding door could use a new lock;

There's something wrong with the oven clock.

The garbage disposal refuses to grind.

The dryer won't dry. You're losing your mind!

NO PROBLEM . . . CALL Ben!

The TV cable is on the wrong wall.

The bedroom ceiling is threatening to fall.

There's a great big crack in a windowpane.

A wristwatch fell down the bathroom drain!

OOPS! . . . CALL Ben!

The porch roof is hanging from two or three nails!

When anyone sneezes, the power fails!

A buzzer just buzzed . . .

A bell just rang . . .

THE KITCHEN BLEW UP WITH A TERRIBLE BANG!

DON'T PANIC! . . . CALL Ben!

Then they asked about the history of the barn – if any happened to be known.

'Yes – if you're not squeamish. It's something I've never talked about.'

He had their rapt attention.

'The property dates back to the days of strip farms, two hundred feet wide and a mile long. What is now the back road was then the front yard and the location of the farmhouse. Apples were the crop, and this was the apple barn. We knew the name of the family, but we didn't know what had become of them, and we don't know why the farmer hanged himself from the barn rafters.'

Qwilleran's listeners looked around as if searching for a clue.

'The family moved away, and the property was abandoned until an enterprising realtor sold it to the Klingenschoen Foundation. I needed a place to live, and the K Fund had money to invest in the town. We hired an architectural designer from Down Below, who is responsible for the spectacular interior. And we don't know why he, too, hanged himself from the rafters.'

There was a long pause. Then Barbara jumped up and said she had to go home and feed Molasses. Connie jumped up, too, and said she had to go home and feed Bonnie Lassie.

'Wonderful party!' they both said.

'Let's do it again!' Wetherby said, and the party ended without the playing of the Ledfield recordings.

The pocket-size gift that Barbara had brought Qwilleran from Canada temporarily disappeared during the move to the Willows – but reappeared appropriately in a pocket of his coat. It was a tape recording of a jazz combo with swaggering syncopation that churned his blood and revived memories. The Siamese also reacted favorably. Their ears twitched, they sprang at each other, grappled, kicked, and otherwise had a good time.

When Qwilleran checked in at the bookstore that week, Judd Amhurst sermonized on the Literary Club problem: 'The time has come for forgetting about lecturers from Down Below who have to be paid and then cancel at the last minute. We can stage our own programs!'

'Good! Never liked Proust anyway! What do you have in mind?'

'More member participation? Remember how Homer Tibbitt liked *Lasca*? Lyle Compton likes "The Highwayman" by Alfred Noyes, early twentieth century.'

'Favorite of mine, too. He was an athlete, and there's an athletic vigor in his poetry.'

'Lyle says there's a cops-and-robbers flavor to the story.'

'And the poet has a forceful way of repeating words.'

Qwilleran quoted: ' "He rode with a jeweled twinkle . . . His pistol butts a-twinkle . . . His rapier hilt a-twinkle, under the jeweled sky." '

Dundee came running and wrapped himself around Qwilleran's ankle.

* * *

In Pickax, Qwilleran's annual move from barn to condo was as well known as the Fourth of July parade. The printers ran off a hundred announcements, and students addressed the envelopes. Mrs McBee made a winter supply of chocolate chip cookies. Friends, neighbors, fellow newsmen, and business associates were properly notified. And on moving day, the Siamese went and hid.

Nevertheless, the move was always successfully accomplished, and Qwilleran's household was relocated for another six months.

Eighteen

That night Qwilleran wrote in his private journal:

It's good to get back to the country quiet of the condo.
I had Chief Brodie in for a nightcap before leaving,
and he said he would keep an eye on the barn. I
returned the Ledfield recording to Maggie Sprenkle
and had my last nice cup of tea for a while. I've
decided 'nice' is a euphemism for 'weak', bless her
soul.

And there was a message from Daisy Babcock on the

machine: 'Qwill, sorry to bother you but I've discovered a disturbing situation at the office, and Fredo said I should ask you to look at it. I don't want to talk about it on the phone.'

Nineteen

Unanswered questions always made Qwilleran nervous, and he slept poorly after receiving Daisy's message. The Siamese slept very well. After living in the round for six months, they gladly adjusted to the straight walls and square corners of the condo. The units were open plan, with bedrooms off the balcony and a two-story wall of glass overlooking the open deck and the creek. In front of the fireplace, two cushiony sofas faced each other across a large cocktail table on a deep shag rug. It would make a good landing pad for an airborne Siamese, dropping in from the balcony railing.

Qwilleran told them to be good, and their innocent expressions convinced him that a naughty impulse never entered their sleek heads.

The distance to downtown Pickax was longer than that from the barn, and so Qwilleran drove, parking behind the auditorium. Walking around to the front of the building, he bowed and saluted to greetings and the usual question: 'How's Koko, Mr Q?'

When he arrived at Daisy's office upstairs, the hallway was piled with empty cartons waiting for the trash collection. Her door was open. There were more boxes inside. Daisy was on the phone. She waved him in and pointed to a chair. She was speaking to her husband.

'Fredo, Qwill has arrived, so I'll talk to you later.'

Qwilleran was reminded of the Box Bank at the Old Manse: cartons, clothing boxes, hatboxes, and shoe boxes.

Daisy's greeting was 'Excuse the mess. Throw something off a chair seat and sit down.' She jumped up and closed the door to the hallway.

'I see you finally moved out,' he said lamely. 'It looks as if you raided the Box Bank.'

'I had accumulated so many things – clothing for all seasons, beautiful books that the Ledfields had given me, magazines we subscribed to and couldn't bear to throw away, and desk drawers full of pens, pencils, cosmetics, all kinds of personal items. The women at the Manse brought me boxes, and I just dumped things in them. It was Alma's day off, and I wanted to get out to avoid a scene.'

'I can understand,' he murmured.

She handed him a shoe box. 'Open this and tell me what you see. Don't touch.'

He did as told, and asked, 'Is it toothpaste?' The fat tube was lying facedown, showing only fine print on the back.

'It's the missing bee kit! No one else in the Manse had ever had one. Someone must have sneaked it from Libby's jacket and tossed it into the Box Bank, perhaps expecting to retrieve it later and blame Libby for carelessness. Who knows? Fredo said you'd know what to do.'

'Hand me the phone,' Qwilleran said. 'We'll get George Barter here to look at it. Fingerprints might be the answer.'

He declined coffee and said he wanted to think for a few minutes. Daisy left him alone, and he remembered what he'd heard.

Libby suspected that Nathan's treasures, being sold for child welfare, were not reaching their intended charity. She wanted to accuse Alma to her face but had been advised not to be hasty. Libby had apparently made the mistake of impetuous youth. She was defending her Uncle Nathan's wishes, and his memory.

The law office was only a block away, and Barter arrived as Qwilleran was leaving. They saluted and shook their heads in disbelief. Arch Riker had been right: 'When there's so much money floating around, somebody's going to get greedy.'

Qwilleran went to his parked car to think. Koko was always right – no matter what! The cat had sensed something wrong at the moment of Libby's death. His gut-wrenching death howl was never mistaken. It meant that someone, somewhere, was the victim of murder. In fact, there were times when Koko sensed it was going to happen before the fact! When Alma visited the barn, Koko tried to frighten her. He tore up her black-and-gold catalog. He staged a scene over the used books that came in a box that originally held a punch bowl sold by Alma. He made a fuss over the pocket-size copy of *The Portrait of a Lady*. Was it because the author was Henry *James*? Not likely, Qwilleran thought, but who knows? And then there was Koko's reaction to Polly's accident in Paris – at the Pont de l'Alma tunnel.

Qwilleran hoped he would never be asked to state all of this on the witness stand. 'They'd put me away,' he said aloud. And yet . . .

He drove to Lois's Luncheonette with his New York paper to listen to gossip. Everywhere, there were pedestrians in twos and threes, talking about the scandal; one could tell by their grave expressions.

At Lois's, the tables were filled. He sat at the counter, ordered coffee and a roll, and buried his head in his paper. From the tables came snatches of comments like:

'Nothing like this ever happened here!'
'They bring people in from Lockmaster, that's what's wrong.'
'Nothing's been proved, but everyone knows.'
'Imagine! It happened in a city museum!'
'Nathan will be turnin' over in his grave!'
'My daughter-in-law says she has a friend . . .'

Everyone was talking about the Purple Point Scandal, preferring to associate it with the affluent suburb rather than nature's useful honeybee. Qwilleran returned home to the Willows and avoided answering the inevitable phone calls. They could be screened by the answering device.

One was from Wetherby Goode: 'Qwill, looking forward to the *Cats* show Saturday night. I'll provide the transportation. The gals will provide the supper. Barbara wants to know if cat food will be appropriate.'

Qwilleran liked Barbara's sense of humor. When invited in to meet Molasses, he liked her taste in design, too.

Replacing Polly's elderly heirlooms was a roomful of blond modern furniture, accents of chrome, and abstract art. Yet an old paisley shawl with long fringe was draped on a wall above the spinet piano.

Barbara said, 'My mother brought that home from India when she was a college student and had it draped over her grand piano all her life. I'd drape it over the spinet, but Molasses is a fringe freak.'

On Saturday night, before driving to the theater for the musical, the Willows foursome gathered at Barbara's for a light repast.

At the performance, it was the usual happy audience found at *Cats*. The stage was full of furry costumes with tails, and there was a five-piece orchestra in the pit.

Barbara said, 'I should have named Molasses Rum Tum Tugger. He will do as he do do, and there's no doing anything about it.'

Connie cried when Grizabella sang 'Memory'.

At intermission Wetherby said he identified with Bustopher Jones, and Qwilleran said Old Deuteronomy would probably write a newspaper column.

And so it went; Qwilleran was pleased with his new neighbors.

They were all exhilarated as they drove home, until they

heard the disturbing sound of sirens from speeding fire trucks.

Wetherby phoned the radio station, and the voice that came over the speaker shocked them all: 'It's the barn! Your friend's barn, Joe! Arson!'

There was a stunned silence in the vehicle.

Qwilleran was the first one who spoke. 'I'm only thankful that the cats are safe at the condo.'

There were murmurs of agreement from the women. Joe said, 'Do you think there'll be something on TV when we get home? I think we all need a stiff drink.'

Barbara voiced everyone's opinion when she said that the fire was the work of lawless gangs in Bixby. 'They torched the Old Hulk and got away with it because it was of little value, but the barn is known around the world for its architecture and beauty.'

Dr Connie said, 'My friends in Scotland had heard about the barn and asked for snapshots of it.'

Qwilleran said, 'The problem is to distinguish between pranksters and criminals. The new wildlife museum consists of two buildings filled with millions of dollars' worth of mounted animals and art. How do we protect it against these irresponsible marauders? And should we be obliged, in the twenty-first century, to protect our heritage against malicious neighbors?'

It was a solemn foursome that arrived at the Willows.

That night the Siamese sensed his feelings; they slept in his bed.

The next morning, Qwilleran walked downtown to the city hall and climbed the back stairs to the police department. Chief Brodie was at his desk, muttering over a stack of papers.

'Well, Andy,' the newsman said, 'it looks as if we've had our last friendly nightcap at the barn!'

'Ach!' was the dour reply.

'Were they the Bixby vandals again?'

'There was more to it than that! We'll talk about it later.' He gave Qwilleran a sour look and waved him away.

Qwilleran walked to the auditorium building and climbed the stairs to Daisy's office.

'Qwill! You'll never believe it!' (Daisy still had her contacts at the Old Manse.) 'A van with a Lockmaster license plate drove away from the Old Manse last night, loaded with Nathan's treasures!'

'That's stealing from a city museum!' Qwilleran said.

Daisy said, 'The good part is that Alma went with them! I hope they catch her.'

* * *

Back at the Willows, Koko was waiting with that look of catly disapproval: Where have you been? Was the trip necessary? Did you bring me something?

Koko had known from the beginning that Alma was up to no good. Qwilleran gave the cats a snack and then read to them from the bookshelf. They had finished *The Portrait of a Lady*.

In the days that followed the barn burning, there was no such thing as business as usual in Pickax. The jollity of the coffee shops was reduced to a subdued murmur, and shoppers clustered in twos and threes on street corners, putting their heads together in serious conversation. Even the bankers were more serious than usual.

At the supermarket, customers filled their shopping carts hurriedly and left the store without exchanging chitchat. Qwilleran and his friends felt the same vague uneasiness.

The *Moose County Something* printed editorials, and preachers addressed the subject from the pulpit.

At home, Qwilleran tried to write a trenchant entry for his private journal and was unsuccessful. Strangely, even Koko stalked around on stiff legs, looking nervously over his shoulder.

* * *

Reference was often made to 'The Bad Boys of Bixby'. This nebulous group of ill-doers had for years – probably generations – been blamed for anything that went wrong in Moose County. It was a joke and sounded like a showbiz act. A few years ago, one of them had sneaked across the county line and painted pictures on the Pickax city hall wall, after which he was dumb enough to sign his name.

One day while Kip MacDiarmid, editor in chief of the *Lockmaster Ledger*, was lunching with Qwilleran, he claimed to have found what was wrong with Bixby.

'Moira was trying to sell a marmalade cat to a respectable family in Bixby, when she discovered that indoor cats are prohibited by law in that county. Did you ever hear of such a thing? I think that explains their whole problem.'

'Moose County gave the country trees, gold mines, and fish. Lockmaster gave the country politicians, movie stars, and racehorses. Bixby County gave us a pain in the . . . esophagus!'

Twenty

Following the fire, the arson was the talk of the town, and Qwilleran's phone rang constantly as townsfolk called to commiserate. They meant well, but – in self-defense – Qwilleran stopped answering and let the message service take over.

He welcomed Barbara's call and phoned her back.

She said, 'Qwill, I've been meaning to ask you: could you help me start a private journal like yours? I think it would be rewarding.'

'It would be a pleasure!' he said. 'We can have supper at a new restaurant I've discovered – if you like to live dangerously!'

She accepted, and he made another convert to his favorite hobby. He took two of his filled notebooks as examples – plus a new one to get her started.

After being seated, Qwilleran told Barbara that the restaurant had been started by a member of the Senior Health Club and younger members of her family. It was named the Magic Pebble as a joke, because it was across the highway from the Boulder House Inn.

He said, 'The latter, as you know, is the grotesque pile of boulders as big as bathtubs, which has been famous since Prohibition days.'

Qwilleran handed Barbara a flat stone. 'Do you know what this is?' Without waiting for a reply, he said, 'There's a creek that comes rushing out of the hills into the lake near the Boulder House. The creek bed is filled with pebbles as big as baseballs, but at one point the water swirls them around and flattens them out mysteriously. The natives call them magic pebbles. If you hold one of the flat stones between your palms – and think – you get answers to problems. Even Koko reacts to a magic pebble. He sniffs it, and his nose twitches. Who knows what ideas are forming in his little head?'

During their conference he told her, 'I don't recommend typed pages in a loose-leaf binder. There is something inspiring about the primitive challenge of handwriting in an old-fashioned notebook.'

Barbara said, 'I'm going to dedicate my journal to Molasses on the front page. Whenever I'm sitting in a chair and thinking, he jumps onto the back of the chair and tickles my neck with his whiskers. I sign my entries BH. I have a middle name, but it begins with A and BAH doesn't make a good monogram. When I was in school, the kids called me Bah Humbug.'

Barbara complimented Qwilleran on his Friday column, in which he had urged parents to be more careful in naming their offspring. He often thought parents naming their newborns should consider what the baby's monogram would be. He had gone to school with a nice girl named Catherine Williams, but her parents gave her the middle name of her aunt Olive, and she grew up being kidded about her initials. Also, he knew a Pete Greene whose middle name was Ivan, a fact his friends never let him forget.

Qwilleran liked Barbara's conversation, and they discussed numerous topics.

Barbara asked, 'Are you writing another book, Qwill?'

'Yes, as a matter of fact. On the subject of rhyme and rhythm. I've been writing humorous verse since the age of nine. We had a fourth-grade teacher that no one liked. I wrote a two-line jingle about her that got me in trouble.'

He recited: ' "Old Miss Grumpy is flat as a pie. Never had a boyfriend, and we know why." '

'That was precocious for a fourth-grader,' Barbara said.

'I had heard grown-ups talking about her, but I got all the blame. Actually, it solved a problem. The kids went to her class smiling, and Miss Grumpy was less grumpy. Yours truly got reprimanded at school and at home, but I discovered the value of humorous verse. Now I specialize in limericks. There's something about the "aa-bb-a" rhyme scheme and the long and short lines that can only be described as saucy. Its appeal is universal. I know a newspaper editor who carries one around in his pocket. He says he reads it whenever he needs a boost. And cats love limericks. I tested my theory on them. They don't even speak the language, but they respond to the lilt of the rhythm and to the repetition in rhymed words.'

Barbara nodded approval.

Qwilleran said, 'I'm working on the subject of limericks and how humorous verse often solves a problem by making people smile. The guests at the Hotel Brrr were always disgruntled about having to swim in the hotel pool when the temperature was too low in the lake. Now, each arriving guest receives a card with a limerick, and they walk around smiling.

He referred to:

There was a young lady in Brrr
Who always went swimming in fur.
One day on a dare
She swam in the bare,
And that was the end of her.

When they returned to the Willows, Barbara invited Qwilleran in to say good night to Molasses, and he accepted. He liked her range of interests, her forthright advice, her sense of humor. They were met by Molasses, very much in charge of the premises.

'You two have met,' she said as the two males stared at each other. Throwing back his shoulders and taking an authoritative stance, Qwilleran recited:

'Molasses, an elegant cat,
Would not think of catching a rat.
His manners are fine,
He drinks the best wine,
And on Sunday he wears a hat.'

Molasses flopped over on his side, stiffened his four legs, and kicked.

Then Qwilleran broached a subject he was not prone to discuss: Koko's whiskers.

'Dr Connie has volunteered to count them when he's sedated for his dental prophylaxis, but somehow I feel guilty because I know he won't approve. He's a very private cat.'

'Then don't do it!' Barbara said. 'What purpose will it serve? Some humans are smarter than others. And some cats are smarter than others!' Qwilleran was impressed by her clearly stated opinion.

'You're right!' he said. 'We won't do it!'

Now you can buy any of these other bestselling books by **Lilian Jackson Braun** from your bookshop or *direct from her publisher*.

The Cat Who Wasn't There	£6.99
The Cat Who Went Into The Closet	£6.99
The Cat Who Came To Breakfast	£6.99
The Cat Who Blew The Whistle	£6.99
The Cat Who Said Cheese	£6.99
The Cat Who Tailed A Thief	£6.99
The Cat Who Sang For The Birds	£6.99
The Cat Who Saw Stars	£6.99
The Cat Who Robbed A Bank	£6.99
The Cat Who Smelled A Rat	£6.99
The Cat Who Went Up The Creek	£6.99
The Cat Who Brought Down The House	£6.99
The Cat Who Talked Turkey	£6.99
The Cat Who Went Bananas	£6.99
The Cat Who Dropped a Bombshell	£6.99